Ritual and Identity

the Tufnell Press,

London,
United Kingdom

www.tufnellpress.co.uk

email contact@tufnellpress.co.uk

British Library Cataloguing-in-Publication Data
A catalogue record for this book is
available from the British Library

paperback ISBN   *1872767133*
ISBN-13   *978-1-872767130*

Printed in England and U.S.A. by Lightning Source

Ritual and Identity;
The staging and performing of rituals in the lives of young people

Christoph Wulf, Birgit Althans, Kathrin Audehm, Constanze Bausch, Michael Göhlich, Stephan Sting, Anja Tervooren, Monika Wagner-Willi, and Jörg Zirfas

Translated by Alice Lagaay and Elizabeth Hamilton

Contents

Acknowledgments

We would like to thank the German Research Foundation (Deutsche Forschungsgemeinschaft) whose support allowed us to carry out the work presented in this book as well as subsequent research of the Berlin Study on Rituals over a ten year period. For the numerous suggestions received throughout many plenary meetings and theory groups, at the summer university, in several conferences and countless individual discussions, our deepest thanks are due to all our colleagues in the Collaborate Research Centre (Sfb) 'Cultures of the Performative' at the Freie Universität, Berlin. Without their active support this research would not have been possible. We are grateful to Prof. Dr. Ralf Bohnsack for showing great interest and generously sharing his extensive experience in matters pertaining to qualitative research, and to Frau Weber, Frau Greif-Gross and the other teachers involved in the research, whose kindness and commitment made this study possible. Sincere thanks also to the families who participated in the project by allowing us an insight into their lives, and to the many children at the school who accommodated us so openly and joyfully. Finally, many thanks to Elizabeth Hamilton and Alice Lagaay for showing such commitment in translating this volume and to Dr. Michael Sonntag for his help with abridging the German version of the book and preparing the English translation for publication.

Christoph Wulf

Introduction

With the exception of social anthropology there has never been much interest in the study of rituals in the social sciences and the humanities. This is now beginning to change, as we have come to realise that rituals play a far more important role in creating, maintaining and transforming the worlds of human beings than has generally been assumed. The purpose of this study is to contribute to a better understanding of the significance of rituals in the lives of young people finding their way in the world. We will demonstrate that many interactions are staged and performed as rituals. These ritual actions are complex social processes that can vary widely in their intention, content and context. Therefore our study of ritual situations requires multi-dimensional concepts of ritual action. Rituals have a tendency to force people to comply with their rules or to fit in and are sometimes quite oppressive, but over and above this they have a creative quality, an aspect that has often been overlooked. Rituals create social cohesion and help groups or communities to overcome problems and conflicts that arise within them.

In this book we aim to show that rituals are necessary for the development of young people. They are among the most effective forms of human communication and interaction. We may think of rituals as actions in which staging and performing play a central role (cf. Tambiah, 1979). Insofar as rituals in the worlds of children growing up at home, at school and in social situations are performances and enactments of the body, they tend to have greater social weight than mere discourses. For with their bodily presence, the ritual actors invest the social situation with 'something extra' in addition to the spoken word. This 'something extra' is rooted in the material nature of the body and in the physical existence of the individual.

Through the staging and performing of rituals, differences are constructively dealt with and cultural communalities are produced. Young people stage themselves and their relations, and in so doing produce social life. Rituals produce systems of order, often hierarchical ones expressing power relations: between social classes, generations and between the sexes. By virtue of being performed and expressed by people using their bodies in a certain way, rituals take on the appearance of being 'natural' and universally accepted. By inviting people to 'join in and play along', ritual performances facilitate the unquestioning acceptance of the cultural *status quo* or system that they embody. Children and adolescents who decline the invitation to 'join in and play along' put themselves beyond the pale, are excluded and can become scapegoats upon whom the hidden negativity and violence inherent in the community is projected (Girard, 1989; cf. Dieckmann et al., 1997).

Young people learn to learn, to behave and to live together through rituals (Delors, 1997). These are important ways of learning those skills that will eventually be needed in the fields of work, the family and in the wider community. The study of the rituals of childhood and adolescence cannot therefore be divorced from research into rituals in other areas of our society.

In contrast to purely linguistic forms of communication, rituals are social constellations, in which individual and communal social actions and the way they are interpreted produce structures and hierarchies (McLaren, 1993; Alexander, Anderson and Galegos, 2004). The spectrum of ritual actions comprises liturgies, ceremonies, celebrations, ritualisations and conventions, from religious rituals, transitional passage rites on occasions such as birth, marriage and death all the way to everyday rituals of interaction (Grimes, 1995; cf. Bell, 1992, 1997). Areas in which everyday rituals are particularly important are child rearing, education and social development. In today's society where there is much discussion about the disintegration of social cohesion, the loss of values and the search for cultural identity, rituals and ritualisations are growing in importance. Alongside this we find a more complex view of rituals. For a long time it was the aspects of rigidity, stereotypes and violence of rituals that were the prime areas of research. Now, there is an expectation that they will bridge the gap between individuals, communities and cultures. They tend to appear today to create cultural cohesion mainly by virtue of presenting forms which, through their ethical and aesthetic content, offer security in times where the bigger picture is easily lost sight of. Rituals hold out the promise of compensating for the experiences of loss associated with modernity: loss of a sense of community, loss of identity and authenticity, of order and stability, furthermore, of compensating for the tendencies towards individualism, abstraction and virtualisation which flow from the erosion of social and cultural systems (Soeffner, 1992; Gebauer and Wulf 1998, 2003; Wulf and Zirfas, 2004; Hermès, 2005).

Being complex social phenomena, rituals are the subject of many different academic disciplines. As a consequence, international research lacks a universally accepted theory of rituals, since the positions in the various disciplines are simply too variegated. Depending on the field of inquiry, the discipline and the methodological approach, different aspects are emphasised. There is, however, today a far-reaching consensus that it makes little sense to restrict the richness and variety of perspectives in favour of one particular theory. Instead we need to put the rich variety of points of view on the agenda in order to reveal the complexity both of rituals themselves and also the different lines of research.

Interaction and ritual

Social communities are formed through verbal and non-verbal forms of interaction and communication. Ritual tableaux are, as it were, performed on 'stages'; by means of staging and performing, bonding and intimacy, communal solidarity and inclusion are engendered. Communities are distinguished not only by a collectively shared symbolic knowledge, but to an even greater degree by cultural action, in which they stage and perform such knowledge in rituals in which the particular social system is expressed, projected and reproduced (Wulf, 2006b). Communities are dramatised fields of action, which come into being through symbolic performances in different areas of life through rituals.

Human beings communicate and interact in ritual practices and tableaux. Rituals, such as Christmas parties, children's birthday parties or ceremonies marking the first day at school and summer festivals at school, use body language and are performative, expressive, symbolic, rule-based and efficient. They are repetitive, homogenous, liminal, playful, public, demonstrative and operational (Wulf et al., 2001, 2004, 2007, 2010). Rituals are institutionalised templates in which collectively shared knowledge and collectively shared practices are staged and performed and the way in which the social or cultural system projects and interprets itself is reaffirmed (Wulf, 2002, 2005, 2009).

Rituals have a beginning and an end and therefore put communication and interaction into a time frame. They take place in social situations which they in turn help to shape; ritual processes embody and display institutions and organisations. They have a pronounced character, they are conspicuous and they are determined by the way they are framed (Goffman, 1974). In rituals transitions between one social situation or institution and another are shaped and differences between human beings and the situations they are thrust into are negotiated and worked out (Wulf and Zirfas, 2004, 2005).

Rituals as performance

Central to our study is the performative nature of rituals (Wulf, Göhlich and Zirfas, 2001; Wulf and Zirfas, 2007; Alexander, Anderson and Gallegos, 2004). We look at how ritual practice in the worlds of children growing up and finding their place in the world comes about, how it connects to language and imagination, how its particular character is made possible by social and cultural patterns, and how its event-like character relates to its repetitive quality.

We aim to show that the effects of rituals that are rooted in institutions are determined above all by the fact that ritual activity is based on habitual actions that have been acquired by the body and through mimetic processes involved in staging a scene. Here boundaries are drawn, attitudes created and skills defined. This enables processes of social acceptance to take place, the performative quality of which contributes significantly to the creation of social cohesion or communities. If social life is structured through actions of 'instituting people' in social positions and creating institutional structures which build social life by labelling, categorising, and structuring it, then we may speak of ritual 'acts of instituting' (Bourdieu). These practices clearly play an important role in the fields of education and socialisation.

Here group identities are created through verbal and non-verbal ritualised forms of interaction and communication which are constantly being acted out on a 'stage'. It is precisely this 'performance' that determines the identity of the members of the group and the way they bond together and become a cohesive, intimate, integrated whole. This means that groups or 'communities' are characterised by symbolic knowledge that is collectively shared (Douglas, 1986; Wulf, 2005) and also that they *enact* this knowledge through rituals that confirm the cohesion and reproduction of the *status quo* (Liebau, Schumacher-Chilla and Wulf, 2001) Communities are dramatic arenas of action created through rituals and their symbolic enactments (Mannheim, 1982). They create a system of interaction that acquires unity by means of all forms of interaction, including divergences.

We will demonstrate that for the production of social cohesion in rituals, their properties and characteristics as theatrical productions, as stagings and performances are of special significance. The performativity of rituals has three central dimensions (Fischer-Lichte and Wulf, 2001, 2004).

Rituals may firstly be grasped as communicative *cultural performances* (Singer, 1959), i.e. they are the result of enactments and processes of performances by the human body. They involve a number of ritual scenes, in which participants in the ritual fulfil different functions. These ritual arrangements may be construed as the outcome of cultural actions, in the course of which divergent, conflicting social forces are integrated into an accepted social and cultural order (Wulf, 1997, 2002, 2009).

Secondly, the *performative character of speech* is of crucial significance in ritual action (Austin, 1979). In rituals of baptism and confirmation, of transition and investiture, for example, the words spoken during the performance of the ritual practices contribute substantially to the creation of a new reality. The same is true for cultural practices in which the relation of the sexes to one another is clearly defined and in which repeatedly addressing a child as 'boy' or 'girl' contributes to the development of gender identity (Butler, 1997).

Finally, the performative also comprises an aesthetic dimension, an important ingredient in artistic *performances*. This aesthetic perspective points to the limitations of a purely functionalist view of the performativity of ritual acts. Just as the aesthetic dimension of artistic *performances* prevents them being reduced to acts that are determined merely by the aim of attaining functional goals, so it reminds us that rituals are 'more' than displays of concrete intention (Wulf and Zirfas, 2004; Huppauf and Wulf, 2009).

Even when the intentions of rituals are identical, the staging of bodily performances of rituals often exhibits important differences. Among the reasons for this are general historical conditions, cultural and social conditions and, finally, conditions associated with the uniqueness of the protagonists. The interplay of these factors produces the performative character of linguistic, social and aesthetic action in ritual stagings and performances. When we consider the aesthetic dimension and the fact that rituals are staged like events and also processes, the limits of their predictability and manageability become apparent; we also become aware of the significance of the style of cultural practices. The difference between what is consciously intended and the multiple layers of meaning implicit in the way bodies are used to stage scenes is obvious. The performative character of ritual action invites many different interpretations and readings, without this difference in interpretation diminishing the effect of the ritual arrangements as such. On the contrary: part of the effects of rituals derives precisely from the fact that the same rituals can be read in different ways, without detrimental consequences for the social magic of their practice.

Social communication crucially depends on *how* people make use of their body in their behaviour and action, which is culturally determined. This involves how much space people leave between them, what body postures they adopt, what gestures they develop. By these means, people communicate much about themselves and their approach to life, about their way of seeing, feeling and experiencing the world. Despite their central importance for the effects and consequences of social action, these aspects of bodily performativity are missing from many traditional theories of ritual, in which the actors are reduced to their cognitive side, while the sensual and contextual conditions within which they act are ignored. In order to avoid such reductionism, we have to bear in mind how ritual action comes about, how it is linked to language and imagination, how the uniqueness of rituals is made possible through social and cultural patterns and how they are both one-off events and repetitions at the same time.

The creation of social cohesion in young people's lives through rituals

Our study on rituals constitutes a thematic case study in which we investigate how social cohesion and community life are created through rituals and ritualisations in the four major fields of socialisation, i.e. 'family', 'school', 'peer group' and 'media'.

The focus of our study is on everyday rituals in the world, or worlds, of 300 children aged between six and thirteen with twenty different ethnic backgrounds at a primary school in an inner-city district of Berlin. Within the same inner-city environment of this school, three families were chosen, each with a different family structure: one family with two children, one family with three children and a single mother with one child. Of all the family micro-rituals, the ritual of eating is at the centre of our study. At the primary school our particular interest is in the micro rituals of transitional situations in school. Threshold rituals and ritualisations are studied in three classes of nine to thirteen year-olds, including children from various ethnic origins and social strata. In the realm of child culture, our study focuses on the ritual games that children play during break-time in the playground and corridors. The significance of television media for everyday ritual community-building processes in child culture is investigated through the use of video staging—a method developed especially for this purpose. Finally, an example is used to show how practical ritual knowledge is acquired through mimetic learning in the performance of ritual processes (cf. Willis, 1999; Woods, 1986, 1996; Woods, Jeffrey, Troman and Boyle, 1997; Zinnecker, 2000; Wulf et al., 2001, 2004, 2007, 2010).

Our research pursues several aims. To begin with, our aim is to reconstruct the educative and socialising effects of rituals in four main areas of children's life. The result is an ethnographic case study of the inner-city life of children at the turn of the millennium. We then develop a multi-dimensional performative concept of the ritual based on the analysis of this material. Furthermore, we will show how ritual action creates a sense of community as well as what is understood by this word 'community' (*Gemeinschaft* in German) in the various contexts. Finally, we will attempt to reconstruct how rituals and ritualisations are learnt mimetically, or by imitation, and how the inner-city environment finds expression in these performances.

The family as a performative unit

In order to understand the ritual dynamic of family life, we placed the ritual of family mealtimes at the centre of our study. During the breakfast ritual, generational differences, for instance, are dealt with and the family performs as a 'normative community', establishing its own norms and standards. The family creates and confirms itself as a socially cohesive group through ritual processes. The family members' specific interaction is constantly portrayed on the 'family stage'. Different roles are incorporated and learnt; family intimacy, solidarity and inclusion are staged and portrayed in performative arrangements. We use detailed ethnographic material to reconstruct the way families are formed, upheld and transformed through ritual acts and symbolic performances, in recognition of the fact that families are both heterogeneous and homogeneous at the same time. If family cohesion is endangered, the family members will stage ritualised ways of restoring it. By enacting and displaying collective knowledge which is shared by the family, the family group becomes a dramatic arena where, through the habitual, typical patterns of behaviour that are displayed in them, rituals bring about a normative order by means of controlling or sanctioning mechanisms. Three forms of family mealtime rituals emerge: rituals in which differences surface, are observed, dealt with and resolved; rituals of passage or transition in terms of space or time or even socially; bonding rituals in which family crises are overcome.

Rituals in daily school life

Micro-rituals are also of central interest when it comes to reconstructing ethnographically the world of school. The child has two roles in school—that of the child with his or her friends and that of the pupil in the classroom—and constantly moves backwards and forwards between the two. Our analysis focuses on these transitions from being the child in the playground who identifies with the peer group to being the 'pupil' again and vice-versa. Our objective is to reconstruct the rituals that emerge during phases of transition, and to establish how they contribute to creating social cohesion between the children. Here again, we understand ritual activity to be recurring interactive patterns of behaviour that create, confirm and transform the boundaries, structures, values and norms of a group or community. This ritual activity is to be seen in body language, stylised gestures and the way scenes are staged. It is through these rituals and the practical knowledge required for their staging and performance that collective identity and differences are generated and dealt with. The game-like elements of rituals open the way for spontaneity and creativity. Our study concentrates on the particular transition from break-time to lessons.

GoGo performance in the playground
During playtime children develop their peer group culture with great intensity. In the playground and the school corridors a whole range of games are staged that allow an insight into inner-city child-culture. These areas are characterised by a high social density and heterogeneity of children from various ethnic origins and different family backgrounds. The focus of our investigation is how boys and girls behave during the ritual playtime games in which there is a constant turnover in groups of players and on-lookers. We focus on the GoGo game, which happened to be a favourite among the children at the time of our study. It involves players gathering in a particular place, the swapping of game figures, an approved order in the game, the pragmatics of establishing common rules, and a style of movement and play that is characteristic of the group. The practices of giving, swapping and winning figures used in the game, as ritual forms of social exchange, result in there being a continuous change in group composition. We are particularly interested in the relation between gender and the way groups are formed in this game, which is primarily, though not exclusively, initiated by boys.

The creation of peer-group identity through TV adverts and popular shows
The new media, and television in particular, are another part of life in which rituals are important. Ritual activities and processes are portrayed on television and our everyday life as viewers becomes ritualised, as do our perceptions of reality. Media-related ritualisation processes are a central aspect of living in the media-dominated world. The social reality that the media stages in its ritualised portrayals becomes absorbed into children's practical knowledge through mimetic learning processes. They then draw upon this knowledge when it comes to their own social relationships. In order to show how we resort to media models in everyday life our research group developed an experimental method to reconstruct these practices. Video workshops were set up in which

children were asked to think up, perform and record scenes for a video. During this process, they clearly drew on rituals and ritual actions that they were familiar with from television and used these as a model upon which to base their own productions. Among the types of programme that shaped their conceptual world, commercials and chat shows were found to be particularly prominent. During the staging of the video films, intense community-building processes were at work between the children. Regardless of ethnic origin, they drew on a collective world of concepts communicated by television to fulfil their task. The young people adapted the ritual activities that they had acquired mimetically through television and combined them with scenes arising from their own imaginative world, to produce an original performance dealing with issues that are of concern to young people at this stage of their development.

The role that mimesis plays in rituals

Since in our view rituals are forms of practical action here we examine how this action and knowledge are acquired. When we reconstruct ritual acts in the social world, we notice that ritual knowledge and the ability to apply it in practice are assimilated through mimetic processes. So the main question we attempt to answer is how practical knowledge is acquired through reference to models. The theatrical nature of ritual action, and the fact that it is performed by the body, plays an important role in it becoming firmly rooted as a habitual action. Ritual competence comes about above all through the mimetic acquisition of particular movements and gestures. Furthermore, the performative character of ritual knowledge allows us, through an act of mimetic re-creation, to gain access to its inherently symbolic and bodily elements. Mimetic assimilation of ritual knowledge is a question of using the senses in a practical way. A group identity is thus established, confirmed and modified through a shared taste or liking for something (Wulf, 2005; Gebauer and Wulf, 1995, 1998, 2003; Wimmer, 2006).

The creation of social cohesion in rituals

At the heart of our study is the performative nature of rituals and ritualisations. This raises a number of issues that are deserving of further investigations. The following are central elements of our research and may be considered as our contribution to the theory of rituals (Kreinath, Snoek, and Stausberg, 2006). Among these elements are: the complexity of ritual arrangements; the performative character of ritual actions; the aesthetic and playful nature of ritual performances; the corporeality and sensuousness of ritual actions; the role of mimetic processes in the staging of rituals; the inbuilt power structure in ritual performances; the implicit rules in ritual arrangements; the iconology of the performance in rituals; the staging of macro-rituals; and the sacred in ritual arrangements.

The city as a performative space

In this final section we show how the city, as the area where the children live their lives, can be seen as a performative space. This is important for understanding their lives in school, their families, their peer groups and also their attitude to the media. The city's architecture, class structure and variety of cultures, its history and particular traditions all contribute to moulding the lives of the members of the school and the families in our study. People's lives are shaped by their environment and the atmosphere peculiar to it; this particular space is constantly reshaped and re-created by its population. Authors like Georg Simmel (1995) were quick to recognise the social significance of a particular space. Contemporary observations confirm this view and inspire us to give the performative character of this environment and its atmosphere its due. Life in the neighbourhood and the immediate surroundings of the school are important factors in the children's world.

Ethnographic methods

We use ethnographic methods, which allow us to find answers to the questions that have guided our study while remaining very close to the structure of the field and the perceptions of the ritual actors (cf. Troman, Jeffrey and Beach, 2006). Moreover, reconstructing and evaluating the empirical material allows us to expand these key questions further. Grounded Theory, with its propositions regarding 'theory as practice', remains an important source of inspiration (Glaser and Strauss, 1969; cf. Strauss and Corbin, 1990, 1994). Our assumptions regarding the relation between rituals and the way in which group identities are formed through performance can only be formulated adequately through reconstructing and interpreting the ethnographic material (Wulf, Göhlich and Zirfas, 2001; Wulf and Zirfas, 2004, 2007; Borneman and Hammoudi, 2009).

Throughout this process methodological reflections have often been challenged by situations that have led us to change our assumptions. It has been important to constantly check how we reconstruct the material, how we interpret it and relate it to the theoretical questions of the investigation (cf. Woods, 1986, 1996; Woods, Jeffrey, Troman and Boyle, 1997; Wulf, 2003). In our efforts to understand the dynamics of ritual behaviour, we have also considered sequence analysis (Oevermann, 2000), which has helped us to understand the sequential nature of human action, the significance of latent structures of meaning for ritual behaviour, and the important role of crises within normal case scenarios. In addition, consideration of narration analysis (Schütze, 1983), ethno-methodological conversation analysis (Eberle, 1997), biographical research (Krüger and Marotzki, 1998; Délory-Momberger, 2000) and ethnography (Geertz, 1973; Spindler and Spindler, 1987; Schechner, 1977; Beach, 1993; SEE, 2004 ff.; Walford, 2008; Borneman and Hammoudi, 2009) has also contributed significantly to our methodological approach. The constructive elements of our own research play a particularly important role throughout the study, so that we are led to confirm the conclusion that the notion of 'one' social reality (the thing itself) is replaced by various realities as versions of the world by its participants. Natural protocols are revealed as methodically constructed texts. The idea of latent structures of meaning as objective, given reality which can be objectively proven, becomes therefore highly questionable (Flick, 2000, 2006). This epistemological view has also evolved, in our context, from insights into the historical and cultural nature of knowledge, which is currently of great interest in historical cultural anthropology and historical cultural anthropology of education (Wulf, 2009, 2002).

Ethnographic methods of research are best suited to our purpose. Since the staging and performance of social life in rituals is our focus, participatory observation and video-supported observation and also our own method of video enactment will play a central role. The methodological problems inherent to participatory observation are well known; those that accompany video-supported observation, however, less so. The very fact that one is recording the ritual transforms the ritual process significantly. This must be taken into account. Further research is needed in order to acquire a more precise understanding of these processes that are, in part, unintended results of the iconic nature of the recording (Denzin, 2000; Krüger 2000; Zinnecker, 2000). The ever-increasing importance of images and the iconic turn in cultural studies and the social sciences suggest that we need to develop an iconology of the performative in the context of visual anthropology (Mollenhauer and Wulf, 1996; Schäfer and Wulf, 1999; Knoblauch, Schnettler, Raab and Soeffner, 2006; Pink, 2007; Bohnsack, 2009; Huppauf and Wulf, 2009).

Considering the limitations inherent in any method of research and the well-known advantages and disadvantages of the various approaches to participatory observation, the most appropriate procedure is clearly to analyse a particular ritual process using overlapping methods, that is, through triangulation (Flick, 2000). Thus, we have used recordings of conversations, group discussions, and interviews too (Bohnsack, 1997; Weigand and Hess, 2007). In the various areas of our investigation, these methods are exploited in different ways, according to the different kinds of questions in each area and the varying conditions of study. As a result, the multiplicity of methodological approaches to the reconstruction of rituals opens up new ways of comparing different forms of the performative creation of social cohesion.

Chapter 1

A space for rituals: the family as a performative unit

This chapter focuses on performative practices within family life. Certain performative criteria, which play an essential role in the forming of group identities, will be related to rituals and ritualised practices within families. By performative criteria we mean how space is used, how the scene is staged, atmospheres, physical forms of (inter)action, power relations and mimetic processes of adapting to and staging situations. By using a micro-analytical method of reconstructing and deconstructing, we propose to apply these criteria to show the extent to which families re-enact and reconfirm their 'community' or group identity on a daily basis through ritualised patterns of action. Our objective is, therefore, to develop the notion of *family as a space where ritual life takes place*.

How the family reinforces its identity through ritual performance

Our focus here is on families as performative units. Central to this is the idea that family ritualisations or rituals constitute the particular 'location' in which social life is created. We would like to put forward the view that families become socially cohesive units through verbal and non-verbal forms of ritualised interaction, which are constantly enacted on a 'family stage'. Moreover, it is only through these enactments that individual roles, feelings of intimacy and solidarity and the sense of family cohesion are at all possible. Our starting point is the hypothesis that we must first engage in a reconstruction and deconstruction of rituals in order to reveal these particular aspects.

   The idea that groups and communities are created, sustained and transformed in and through rituals has been widely accepted in ethnological, sociological, political and educational discourses ever since Emile Durkheim's *Elementary Forms of Religious Life* (1912). Yet studies have tended to overlook the performative nature of rituals by concentrating on their symbolic content. Our performative analysis of rituals will emphasise the performative processes at work in ritual interaction in families, and their power to generate meaning. Only then will it become clear that groups and communities are defined through ritualised patterns of meaning and action. Our purpose is to transform Victor

Turner's thesis that the smallest unit of a ritual is the symbol, into the idea that *the smallest units of a ritual are symbolic enactments.*

This performative analysis involves a qualitative study of mealtime rituals in four Berlin inner-city families—a Polish family with a son, a German family with a son and a daughter, a German family with two daughters and a son, and a German single mother with a daughter. These families, whose children all go to the same primary school, are all of the same generation and have the same educational and social background.

This project on family rituals will help us make a performative analysis of rituals as formal events, and here we will focus on how social cohesion comes about. So far, research on rituals in families has often focused on describing intergenerational and individual rituals in families, rites of passage in families with adolescents, and on establishing a typology of rituals. Most of these studies have tended to emphasise the intentional and functional significance of rituals for families. Thus, they have often focused on the therapeutic context of rituals (ritual as therapy and therapy as ritual), and consequently the performative character of rituals has been overlooked. However, we by no means wish to decry the valuable insights into ritual differentiations and rules that these studies have contributed.

From a performative perspective, our criticism is directed towards two aspects in particular. As already mentioned, we are opposed to reducing rituals to symbolic processes, preferring to see them as a *staging of the symbolic.* We are also wary of clear-cut, causal, linear and generalising explanations of ritual practices, which tend to emerge from the perspectives of functionalism. Instead, we prefer to acknowledge *the heterogeneity and difference at work in rituals, their significance as processes and pieces of theatre, the ways in which people's bodies are presented in them, how power and the staging of a scene are displayed in them, as well as their ludic (or playful) and mimetic elements.*

Conceiving the family as a performative social group underlines the ritual patterns of difference management that regulate conflict situations in a family, thus establishing the existence of implicit models of integration and solidarity. We see the 'family as a cohesive social group' as a ritualised space for action and experience that is characterised by elements of staged, mimetic and playful action and power structures. Here the family is referred to as a system of interaction:

> This study of the patterns of personal relationships in the family led directly to the conception of the family as a unity of interacting persons.

By unity of interacting personalities is meant a living, changing, growing thing. … At any rate the actual unity of family life has its existence in the interaction of its members. For, the family does not depend for its survival on the harmonious relations of its members, nor does it necessarily disintegrate as a result of conflicts between its members. The family lives as long as interaction is taking place and only dies when this ceases.

(Burgess 1926, 3-9).

A few words about methodology

The general aim of this investigation is to reconstruct a family's individual ritual and performative style. This family style will then be analysed using methods of qualitative ethnography based on 'Grounded Theory (GT)' (Glaser and Strauss, 1969). Highly relevant to this research is the notion of 'theory as a process', suggesting a qualitative method that takes into account the connection between collecting, coding and analysis (ibid., 43, 71). Thus, we have recorded family processes that reveal clear patterns and regular recurrences of interaction, and the dynamics of action involved in family rules and relations. Since a wide range of methods can be applied in this field of research, it is necessary to explain our choice. First of all we have chosen two methodological approaches which each allow different performative aspects to be empirically observed: the recording of conversations and participatory observation.

In analysing recordings of *family conversations*, we propose to focus on the theatrical aspects and the organisation of discourse involved in a sequence. We will also look at the indexical dimension of utterances, concepts and elements, and at role assignment and the forms of speech that are used. In our *participatory observation*, we will concentrate on fleeting actions; on the indexical value of actions, repetitions and physical effects; on gestures, mimicry and body presentations; on the aesthetic dimension; and on atmosphere, time and space. Yet observation reaches its limits when faced with moments of fleetingness and performative complexity which result in researchers 'drowning' in a superabundance of events which they are unable to present simultaneously. In order to avoid this, as far as possible we have chosen total observation as our preferred mode of examination. Apart from a few unavoidable exceptions, we, therefore, do not actively take part in the rituals ourselves. This mode of observation is essential because it permits synaesthetic moments and contextualisation to be perceived, such as, for instance, the atmosphere in a room, smells and music (elements that pictures lack), as well as the aesthetic

combination of a ritual set-up—disregarding small discreet actions that escape
the angle of the camera.

Family rituals as a way of managing differences

Our considerations so far can be summarised as follows: the family as a cohesive
social group 'occurs' (Buber) where ritualised forms of cohesion are created. In
cases where family cohesion is at stake, a ritualised, normative and binding
ordering structure is brought into play, either verbally or non-verbally, in an
attempt to solve the problem of interaction. This attempt at interaction is
supported by symbolic knowledge as well as by dramatic staging. Not only does
a family 'think' as a cohesive group (Douglas, 1986)—i.e. confirm and reflect
shared collective knowledge—it also acts, by staging this shared knowledge
in rituals that attempt to confirm the way the family sees and presents itself.
Communities or groups are, thus, dramatic arenas where action takes place.
Seen in this way, rituals can be described as habitualised, reciprocally typified,
cohesive patterns of action, whose purpose is to secure the group's normatively
binding social structure through historicity, control and legitimation.

Our study is based on the theory that rituals constitute a system for dealing
with differences, by which we mean how they are *generated*, what *characterises*
them and also how they are perceived, as well as the *attempt to resolve or
dismantle differences*. This theory follows from the case studies presented below.
Rituals are events that define the daily procedures of family life. When rituals
mark a transition in terms of space or time, identity or social concerns, we use
van Gennep's classical concept of the *rites of passage*. When, on the other hand,
rituals emphasise the overcoming of a crisis within an already established social
group, or when their purpose is to reinforce the group's cohesion, we use the
term *connective rituals*.

Ritual and educative forms of interaction during family mealtimes are at the
centre of our investigation. Mealtime rituals constitute a ritual type that embraces,
on the one hand, everyday habits and forms of learning that are more or less
without symbolism, and on the other hand, highly symbolic family celebrations,
such as Christmas or wedding festivities, which contain moral, political and
metaphysical dimensions. Our analytical interest is directed first of all towards
ritual scenes or sequences, which are all parts of the 'larger' ritual. In the analyses
that follow, ritual scenes or sequences are taken to be:

1. verbal and non-verbal arrangements and presentations of interactions (procedures, conventions, etc.) that
2. represent a normative claim,
3. are limited in time and space,
4. suggest a scenic-mimetic performance, in which
5. attempts to transform are carried out by a community and in which
6. the community can be described as both a medium and a result of this process.

Ritual sequences reveal how families as communities that have a shared experience manage to carry out interactions which help them to deal with their central problem, which is to maintain unity despite differences and to combine continuity and change.

Thus, ritualised sequences are a part of the overall family ritual. Their complexity is in every way equal to this 'larger' ritual. Their *functional* dimension contributes to confirming and consolidating the sense of community, their *coordinating* aspect offers opportunities for social integration within the community, from a *socialising* point of view, they are the medium through which identities and roles are worked out, and from a *symbolic* perspective, they refer to the family's history and its social embedding. From the *performative* perspective all these aspects combine to become dimensions of enactment and staging that are important elements in the shared experience of rules and structures within a community. Rituals are performed above all whenever the manifest appearance, or the latent threat, of differences comes to somehow question or put the family unit at risk. Differences may occur in relation to generations, taste or preferences, gender, communication, morality, and education, or to cases of damage or tragedy within a family. In what follows, we propose to reveal the ritual patterns which families use to solve difficult issues. We will present ways of dealing with these differences by introducing various types of ritualised scenes, in which the families' style of management, or what we call their *performative style*, is clearly visible. In order to do this, a particular family (the Zobels) and their ritual activities will be placed at the centre of our investigation. In the analysis of recorded conversations, observation protocols and group discussions, this family's rituals will then be compared with similar activities in other families. Our central purpose throughout this analysis is to identify the Zobel family's *performative style*.[1]

1   In the interest of anonymity, all the names in this book have been changed.

The bread of life and the daughter's salt: the symbolism of eating and the importance of taste

In a first step towards clarifying the relation between symbolism and performativity, this section reconsiders the definition of ritual as a symbolic enactment aimed at processing differences in families. Central to our thought here is the idea that it is mainly through performative (i.e. staged and ritualised) sequences of action that symbolic statements are made. Performativity is thus the metasymbolic context through which the symbolic effects of processes that help to establish social bonding during mealtimes can be explained. Mealtimes, and breakfast time in particular, are to be seen here as formal social occasions which are performative vehicles for symbolic characteristics, and which guarantee cohesion and differentiation at one and the same time. Not only is a whole social order represented here, but it is also embodied. In a nutshell, mealtimes can be seen to represent *the* fundamental model of culture.

Having breakfast together

What is symbolised in a particular family's breakfast? And how is this symbolism staged? But let us first introduce the Zobel family. There are five members: the mother, who works two half-days a week in education, the father, who holds a managerial position in church-based social work (both are in their early forties), the twelve-year-old twins, Anna and Bjorn, and their nine-year-old sister Carolyn. Breakfast in the Zobel family consists of toast, crackers, rye bread, wholemeal bread, butter and margarine, mortadella, salami, camembert, cheese spread, various jams, marmalades and organic spreads, fruit and vegetables (apples, cucumber). There is coffee to drink (for the parents) and (skimmed) milk for the children. The food is placed in a particular order on the table. Moving from the wall outwards there is the breadbasket, the cheese platter, the coffee (on a coaster), butter and cold meats. The jams are in various positions around the table, and the coffee is always in the middle. Main topics of conversation at breakfast are school, activities of the previous day and of days to come, the food, family and cultural activities (music, television, books, etc.).

At first sight, the array of food seems balanced and deliberately nutritious classical, traditional, staple food that is rather over the top: bread, cold meats and cheese. Within this trio the choice of bread alone is excessive. The selection seems not only to reveal an awareness of nutritious properties, but also a conscious concern for health. From a performative perspective the difference between the bread at breakfast and the bread the children take to school is relevant. The children often make their school sandwiches themselves and, together with some fresh fruit (apples which they wash themselves, grapefruit which they cut themselves), put them into their special lunch boxes—which they sometimes rinse first. The fact that children generally feel responsible for their school packed lunches marks a culinary transition from the institution of family to that of school. This does not mean that they are not supported by the mother in preparing their packed lunches. But it does clearly reveal not only a culinary transition to school but also a process of gradual detachment between the generations. Indeed, by gradually learning to provide for themselves in the institution that is most relevant to them, the children are making a significant step towards adulthood. The partially shared activity of sandwich-making defines the transition from a temporal perspective. It is above all the mother who helps the children in this process by calling them to get on with making their sandwiches or by actually helping them do it.

Thus, from a performative perspective, the symbolic significance of bread, which is often used as a metaphor for life, takes on a double generational dimension. It draws together the parents (or at least the mother) and the children in the transition process from family to school, and it formalises the passage from child to adult. The bread here not only symbolises family life in the face of work—a life that can only be earned through effort, restriction, progress and self-control. The shared, and at the same time individual, activity of preparing sandwiches reveals that a full and complete life can be achieved on a shared basis in such transition processes. It is no coincidence that there is a close connection etymologically between bread (in Latin *panem*) and the idea of community expressed in the Latin word *companium*, which can be translated as 'bread-community'. Rituals such as breakfast can serve to shape such transition or separation processes, without the individual participants being consciously aware that they are taking part in 'more' than sandwich making.

The intergenerational processes involved in sandwich making that reinforce the sense of community contrast sharply with the drinking of coffee and milk, for these constitute a difference within the family. The father is primarily in charge of the coffee. He is the one who makes it and takes the coffee pot from the machine that is kept in the kitchen to the left of the table on a work surface. He is the one who pours the coffee and, if necessary, refills the cups (also for the observers). But for the children coffee is taboo. When Anna asks if she can have some coffee too, the father's answer is friendly but categorical. 'No', he says, with a firm shake of his head. The parents drink their coffee black, without sugar. Sugar can be seen as a taste enhancer and also as both a symbol of unhealthy food and a status symbol of enjoyment, waste and luxury. In a word, breakfast in the Zobel family is not about sugary indulgence (note also the skimmed milk!). However, Anna's resolution to give up sweets and sugar for Lent suggests that sugar is available in the family, although dietary or religious considerations may require them to avoid using it periodically.

Milk is drunk only by the children. Both the parents and the children perform the task of fetching the milk from the refrigerator, pouring it out, refilling the glasses, etc. Coffee and milk can be seen to function as constituting a generational difference. Parents drink coffee; children drink milk. The children will continue to drink milk at school, as is revealed by the milk money the mother provides. Thus, the milk, like the bread, constitutes a kind of bridge between home and school life, whereas contrast and differentiation are expressed in the family through whether or not one is allowed to drink coffee. The children are not allowed to drink it, because the parents consider it to be unhealthy for children. This shows the parents' performative power. They create a difference between the children and themselves by means of the coffee.

The significance of the kind of food available at breakfast in the Zobel family must not be underestimated: cold meats, cheese, jam. This constitutes the 'backdrop' of food, to which all the family members mutually refer, whether by getting it out of the refrigerator, by cutting and preparing it, or by consuming and enjoying it. This food is available all the time for everyone and therefore constitutes an intergenerational culinary background that is commonly accessible and unquestionably shared by all.

From a performative perspective we are also interested in the fact that the meal takes place at a table. We will focus here on the relevance of the table as an element that creates performative rules. Erving Goffman refers to clearly restricted areas, to which individuals have temporary claim, as 'stalls' which structure and stabilise the spatial claims. In Western societies, the most common 'multi-person stall' is the 'multi-person table' (Goffman, 1971: 32 ff.). In these societies, the table is a symbol for community, for, people who gather around a table together clearly indicate that they do not intend anyone around the table to be excluded: a table, especially a round table, stands for integration, which may, nevertheless, allow for differentiation. In most Western societies, people usually gather around a table and not, or not yet at least, next to each other at a counter in the kitchen or living room, and not on a carpet on the floor.

Considered as the scene of a multi-person stall, the table thus inaugurates *performative* processes of physically being together, and in the Zobel family one may only leave it briefly, usually to carry out an action that is directly connected to the organisation of breakfast. The table thus creates a kind of physical co-presence, offering the participants a system of reference. The fact that everyone sits at the table situates the bodies in relation to other bodies which define certain territorial boundary lines: both distance and relationship are made possible through the table as a territorial arrangement. Sitting together constitutes a performative community to the extent that through the spatial and physical relations between up/down, in front/behind, outside/inside, close/far etc. particular values and taboos are expressed, experiences pre-figured, attitudes stabilised and perceptions channelled. On the horizontal level, not only is it significant to see who sits at the 'head' and who sits at the 'side' of the table, but also to see who sits in relation to whom, where the table is, and whether there is an order of seating, etc. From a vertical perspective, the table allows a separation between up and down, between head and hands, and legs and feet, whereby the table's 'meridian' is at the level of the stomach. Through the table's double axial system, individual bodies are related and coordinated to each other, and stabilised and fixed in a reciprocal physical connection. The table thus allows normalised behaviour to be controlled by representing, through its co-ordinate system, its own normative set of values, which are then charged with social and civil significance: 'table manners'. Seen in this way, the table presents a model for the staged production, shaping, testing and practising of physical *and* linguistic behaviour. At the table certain forms of behaviour are forbidden, and important elementary norms of behaviour and social competence are acquired. Mealtime at the table represents—both symbolically and performatively—the social situation *par excellence*. Put in a nutshell, 'the meal puts its frame on the gathering' (Douglas, 1966).

From the point of view of *time*, breakfast is a critical period, since it gathers together the individuals who have been separated by sleep, and draws them into a place where they reaffirm their social cohesion as a group, so as to avoid falling into the anarchy of unregulated togetherness. In other words, breakfast can be described as a ritual in which the 'tense relation between the solitary existence of the individual eaters and the fact that they are also part of a collective whole' (Mattenklott, 1984: 184) is brought to a state of relaxation by means of the particular place and time, the actions carried out, the seating arrangement, the food chosen and the aesthetic moments that arise, so that the isolation brought about by sleep gives way to the shared world. Thus, breakfast can be interpreted as a directly effective, positive, dynamic and pleasant ritual, which results immediately in the reinforcement of the sense of community and is therefore able to prevent the threatening crisis of family dissolution.

Seen in this way, the main significance of breakfast is that it structures a particular time of day that is valid for all the participants. It constitutes a fixed temporary point in the group structure, one that implies a certain binding nature for all the participants and at the same time defines a frame in which the life of the family, which is united by shared memories and projects, can be planned and designed. The shared meal acquires enormous ritual significance, because not only does it constitute a set time within the daily routine, but it also defines the length of the meal and its rhythm. The word 'meal' is etymologically connected to the notion of measure, mark, or appointed time, time for eating. And what power could be greater than the power over human time? The breakfast ritual thus signifies that a community can only exist when clear boundaries of time and space are defined. The fact that these boundaries cannot always be made available to group members in order to reveal the significance of a community (from a moral, social or communicative point of view) is understandable to the extent that a member must always have already 'estranged' him or herself from that community in order to be able to reflect upon—not within—it. According to this thesis, communities are formed when their origins and borders are forgotten, and forgetting is achieved by means of ritual behaviour. Thus, rituals express the paradox that establishes the demarcation lines of a family in a symbolic (and performative) manner. Reflection upon what makes one's own community possible actually dissolves community insofar as theoretical recognition always raises the problem of what might happen and also of otherness, that tends to endanger communities. It is therefore forbidden to constantly reflect upon what created the common bonds of one's own community and what their limitations are.

If eating can be seen as a shared, group activity, it is striking that eating (and drinking) is in fact both the most ordinary and commonplace activity of all, a *conditio humana* so to speak, and the most individual, a totally atomistic event. Everyone eats on their own, yet at the same time together. The creation of social ties is explained here in terms of the frequency of opportunities for social interaction which draw the individuals into a community through the shared act of eating. On the other hand, the establishing of a social side to eating also draws attention to the ambivalence that is related to food. For there is surely a sense in which the physiological individualism of eating must constitute a threat to the community to the extent that if something has been eaten it can no longer be eaten by the group. It would seem that precisely where, from a physiological point of view, the individual has no need for the community, a form of cultural behaviour that is universal endeavours to incorporate the individual into the community. From the point of view of the physiological digestion of food, the shared meal ought perhaps not to be interpreted as the natural expression of the human social constitution so much as the community or group's ritualised attempt to define and maintain its own boundaries. This suggests that eating together is a symbolic gesture par excellence, because, on a symbolic level, it underlines the relevance of the community precisely where the individual is in fact most distanced from it. During a shared meal, individuals reciprocally signal to each other that they belong together precisely because eating radically individualises and blocks out the *Other* from the individual horizon. In this context people can learn and experience the fact that what is most individual can converge with the general. Thus, eating together deals, among other things, with the paradox involved in communicating the incommunicable: the primordial importance of that which is physiologically individual is cancelled out by, or encompassed within, the general. And for this very reason, a shared meal is always presented in a symbolic way. Since it follows the conventions of people joining together, its object is the community rather than the food itself.

'How do you like the food?'

In order for food and eating to signify the community, the symbolic level is dependent on *performative* acts as in the above examples—dealing with food, the table, time, the common activity of eating, etc. In the process of making individual eating and enjoying the food a shared or group activity, the link between symbolism and performativity is perhaps nowhere as condensed and pertinent as in the answers to the simple questions 'How is it?' or 'How do you like the food?' For in contrast to hearing, seeing (and touching), the sense perceptions connected with the food are not really social because the feelings and emotions to which they relate remain locked inside the individual eater. Thus, the saying *De gustibus non est disputandum*, or 'There is no arguing about tastes', is also valid in the context of family community. Seen in this way, the question 'How is it' carries a certain risk, involving the danger that the family may be split according to their different tastes. Nevertheless, there is perhaps no more common topic of table conversation than food itself and the taste that it evokes. And on the other hand, there seems to be no greater bond of community than that created through common taste. Thus, the ritual question 'How is the food?' in fact aims to bring about a physical sense of community, one of common smells, tastes, feelings, and therefore of natural closeness and unity. Seen in this light, it is in fact the dictum *De gustibus est disputandum*, matters of taste *must* be discussed, that is most valid for communities.

A small example can be used to demonstrate this. It is taken from a conversation recorded in another family, the Mayers, a mother and a twelve-year-old girl, whom we have called Dorothea. The mother is a divorced teacher and Dorothea has just finished primary school. The Mayer family usually eat lunch and dinner together. Lunch is usually at around 2.30 p.m., and dinner between 6 p.m. and 7 p.m. Mother and daughter are sitting at the dining table in the living room (they have breakfast in the kitchen).

The 'lemonade (vitamin C) tablet and salt' sequence
It is Wednesday; lunch time begins at 2.30 p.m.; German pop music can be heard in the background (*Die Phantastischen Vier*); after about a minute this passage occurs:

1	*Dorothea:*	I'm starting.
2	*Mother:*	Enjoy!
3	*Dorothea:*	Enjoy!
4	*Mother:*	There's freshly grated cheese.
5	*Dorothea:*	Spaghetti.
6	*Mother:*	That's my lemonade tablet.
7	*Dorothea:*	So?
8	*Mother:*	Well, I'm just saying.
9	*Dorothea:*	How much salt did you put in?
10	*Mother:*	Salt and pepper.
11	*Dorothea:*	(getting up) I'll get some salt.
12	*Mother:*	Why don't you at least taste it first.
13	*Dorothea:*	(from a distance) I always need salt.
14	*Mother:*	Mmm, but it's not good for you. O.K. then.

Two different contrasts of taste are apparent in this scene—first, in lines 6-8, when the mother refers to her lemonade tablet, and second, in lines 11-13, when the daughter requires more salt. In both cases family unity is affected by the different food items, calling into play (ritualised) patterns of difference management. For both cases reveal that a particular substance distinguishes one person's food from the other's. Moreover, the fizzy drink tablet may suggest either that the mother is unwell, or that through reference to the tablet, she is expressing a state of physical and mental exhaustion, or else that she is stressing to her daughter the importance of healthy food. Either way, the mother is drawing attention to a problem that the daughter does not have herself and is thus underlining a difference. At the same time, she moves away from what she as an individual is drinking to articulating the problem through communicative discourse and works towards relieving the tension. For a start she is 'just saying' (line 8) about the tablet, and, although she is aware of the health problems associated with too much salt, she consents grudgingly with a resigned 'O.K.' In both cases the mother manages to 'save' the situation, firstly by playing down the difference between her and her daughter with regard to the vitamin C drink, and then by acknowledging and confirming her daughter's eating habits by giving her consent. However, although the mother tries to overcome differences between them *discursively* she does not overcome them through any helpful *action*. She could, for instance, have put the salt out for the daughter.

In this scene, the mother's efforts seem inconsequential if one considers that the taste of the food has primarily to do with seasoning. Seen in this way, seasoning not only contributes to creating the taste identity of the food, but also of the eater, for it can both create a sense of community (think for instance of ketchup) as well as negatively affect someone's body odour (like garlic). To the extent that taste contributes to the whole atmosphere, in order to avoid 'spoiling the atmosphere', the mother must consider the daughter's taste. Thus, the mother in this situation can be interpreted as entering into the daughter's taste world, albeit discursively. Whereas the daughter 'justifies' herself using set phrases and clichéd expressions (lines 7, 13) and therefore shows a certain desire to distance herself from her mother, the mother's utterances, on the other hand, suggest something of a discursive mimetic approach. Precisely because taste represents an approach to the world which inevitably implies something quite individual, relating only to oneself, in order to maintain a sense of community, the mother cannot possibly react in an aesthetic-mimetic manner, and is forced to resort to a discursive form of consent. Although salt is not healthy (line 14), it is a necessary addition to food for the daughter (line 13); and therefore, in order to sustain the family's sense of community, despite differences, the mother is obliged to accept her daughter's taste. In terms of the process of creating a sense of community the different sense perceptions of individuals can only be approached discursively.

Seen in this way, the mother's discursive mimesis of consent may be regarded as compensating for the aesthetic mimesis of taste.

Indeed, the *connectivity of taste* as an agreed taste judgment is a social operator which relates individual oneness with food to social oneness of aesthetic judgement. Thus, in line with Hegel, we may say that food negates and transforms individuals in relation to what they eat, and taste agreement negates and transcends individuals in relation to the community. Taste thus emerges as the operator, instrument and result of community forming processes. It represents a performative expression that outlines the symbolic borders of the community.

How shared rituals create a sense of community

To summarise our thoughts so far, we may say that, as conventionalised and obligatory forms of expression, rituals express common values in a symbolic manner. In other words, they stage symbolism. Rituals require shared group action and this is what gives them the character of rituals. The community or group is thus the cause, process and effect of ritual action. A dissolution of rituals would therefore amount to dissolution of the community. Rituals order human co-existence through repeated interactions so that contingent events or coincidental proceedings are disregarded as insignificant social interactions or experienced as contradictory patterns of action. Thus, rituals take on an eminently normative character—they call for a community spirit through shared actions, they demand transparent communication between all participants, and they constitute a certain a priori moral knowledge, which claims unquestioned social validity.

In a word, rituals create the rules that are subsequently considered social conventions and that enable the community to decipher symbolic meaning. In rituals it is therefore not a question of truth. Rather than truth, it makes more sense to speak of the correctness of collective action, which also means the ability to decode the rules constituted by a ritual. Rituals aim to be performed correctly, that is, in accordance with the rules of action to which all participants are collectively bound. It is precisely for this reason that this kind of action—like truth itself—has always been described as being independent of time or place.

The effect of the location on performative
processes within the family

Although characterised by other elements as well, rituals stand out by the fact that they take place at particular times and in particular places and follow repeated patterns of interaction. In this way specific spatial constellations open up and mark out particular possibilities for ritual behaviour. We will now take a closer look at environments and the performative processes that relate to them in our main family.

On weekdays the Zobel family have breakfast in the kitchen of their six-room rented apartment. On average, breakfast takes about three quarters of an hour, from about 7.15 a.m. to 8.00 a.m. However, they are not all at the table at the same time, either because they 'are late' or because they have to leave for work early. The rectangular kitchen, used here as a breakfast room, is about 12m². It has a fitted kitchen with, on the long wall on the right, a kitchen unit with all the usual household appliances (refrigerator, cooker, dishwasher and washing machine). Half of the opposite wall is taken up by cupboards, whilst the remaining part of that long wall contains a table, which is pushed against the wall. The table comes out into the room perpendicular to the kitchen units. The door is at one end of the kitchen, and there is a window at the other end, close to the table. There are four chairs around the table and a light above it. Above the table there is a picture on the wall and at the end of the kitchen, next to the window, there is a clock. All the crockery, the food and groceries required for breakfast and the cutlery and other utensils (napkins, breakfast jars) are all kept in the kitchen. Since the room is quite small, this makes for a feeling of closeness, physicality and intimacy, which contrasts visibly with the room's otherwise functional quality.

What follows is a reconstruction of a typical breakfast in the Zobel family. Whilst the father generally lays the table, it is later cleared by different people according to work and school times and also according to age. Carolyn is exempt. The first four family members to arrive for breakfast sit on the four chairs around the table, whilst the fifth brings in a chair from the living room and places it at the end of the table. Usual seating positions may vary but two remain constant—the father always sits with his back to the door on the side of the table facing the window, and the mother always sits opposite him on the window side. Two of the children sit opposite each other on the wall side, and one child sits at the head of the table on the chair brought in from the other room.

On Saturdays and Sundays, the Zobel family have breakfast in the living room. On these days breakfast begins later, on Saturday at about 9.00 a.m. and on Sunday at around 8.30 a.m., and lasts on average fifteen minutes longer, i.e. about an hour. The living room is a rectangular room of about 35m² and is separated into two different sized sections, a 'dining area' and a 'living area'. In the dining area, apart from the large oval table with six chairs that dominates that part of the room, there is a small cupboard for crockery and a sewing machine table (used to keep things on). A music centre placed on the floor marks a threshold to the living area, as well as a plant (*ficus benjamini*) and a few vases and pots on the windowsill. Above the dining table there is a hanging light. The fact that this section of the room is sparsely furnished is emphasised by the fact that there are no pictures on the white wood-chip walls. The large oval table with its six chairs thus occupies a central position in the dining area. In contrast to the rather sparse room arrangement, the table is pleasantly decorated with a tablecloth, a sacramental (white) candle, a bread basket covered with a cloth, brightly coloured crockery and cutlery (the same as during the week), and linen napkins with embroidered monograms. The seating order is dominated by the mother. She sits at the head of the table close to the window. The father sits to her left, and Bjorn and Anna to her right, whilst Carolyn sits to the left of her father. The sixth place opposite the window and facing the door remains empty.

There are several points of interest here.

a) The fact that the family have breakfast in the dining room at weekends suggests that the Zobel family assign breakfast at the weekend a higher importance than during the week. Indeed, the increased work involved in bringing all the crockery and food out from the kitchen into the dining room corresponds to the fact that breakfast at the weekend is allowed to take more time, and also more space. The table is more elaborately laid than during the week. Instead of the coffee, a candle is placed in the middle of the table, indicating an atmosphere of transformation and celebration. Relocation into the dining room signalises therefore a move away from everyday profane 'dullness', away from a period of mundane normality, into a time of celebration which the family consciously stages and lives out. The move into the dining room area constitutes a fixed ritual in itself, one which, from a topographic perspective, takes on a temporal quality. A conscious attempt is made to contrast familiar everyday normality, which is pre-structured, normalised, and 'tainted' to a certain extent by school and work, with the different, more autonomous quality time of breakfast at the weekend—family time *for* the family. The ritual repetition of a particular place at a particular time emphasises the family's special status at weekends. They find themselves in a liminal state which is defined by a particular collective mode. By means of the move into a different spatial environment, the family disconnects itself from the (kitchen) world that is associated with work, and reconstitutes itself in the *living* room. The family thus transforms itself from a formal and functional community of separate individuals, who are all doing what they have to do, into a homogenous community where personal relationships count.

b) This is further emphasised by where the family sit at table. Whereas during the week the members of each generation sit opposite each other with the parents forming the family frame, the fact that members of the same generation sit next to each other at the weekends makes way for a more intergenerational constellation. The very fact that the parents have moved to sit next to each other makes it possible for this intergenerational community to be seen in terms of pairs, which also serves as a model for the children. At the same time, the new seating arrangement emphasises the 'porous' structure of the family as a community. Not only do the family consciously treat themselves to a 'time of celebration', but also to a larger space for freedom of movement. Moreover, to the extent that the functional weekday frame is now replaced by a frame of solidarity which pre-supposes a higher level of commitment on the part of the participants, this freedom calls for more intensive individual initiative.

During the week, gathering around the rectangular table in the kitchen produces a different kind of community. Here, every seating position is clearly identified, and the right-angled constellation creates clear demarcation lines. Although the oval table used at weekends also allows for certain demarcations to be identified, it tends more towards a circle. As the traditional location of repetition, this presents a complete and closed world that is separated from the rest of the world and in which time can almost come to a standstill because it is constantly beginning anew. Seen in this way, the family's move into the dining area for breakfast constitutes a move not only into a new time mode but also into a new spatial and social mode. For, not only do rituals that take place in a circle or what is almost a circle integrate the difference between past and present, old and new, they also bring about a paradoxical spatial concept, insofar as they hold an entirety within a small section, integrate a totality *en miniature*, carry out an escape from the world within the world, and represent the province as an enclave. Moreover, circular rituals also relate to a new social concept, insofar as a certain equality reigns in them since all the participants are at (almost) the same distance from the centre. The circle can thus be seen to secure the centripetal forces of social life. If we interpret the dining area's larger spatial openness in the light of these considerations, then the way in which members of each generation move to sit together can be seen as indicating a departure from the structured connection of physical normativity within the family. The weekend seating arrangement breaks the mimetic normativity of bodily closeness in favour of a more indirect form of physically sitting next to each other, which therefore—in the oval—allows for more flexibility.

c) This increased flexibility is suggested once more when one considers the difference between, on the one hand, the way the family circle is closed in the kitchen by the bringing in of an additional chair, and on the other hand the complementary opening of the circle at the dining table in the living room through the 'missing' sixth person. Structured closedness and liminally structured openness have been distinguished from one another (by Turner) as paradigms of social ways of life. This does not mean that switching to the living/dining room necessarily results in an unstructured breakfast. Rather, the more strictly defined roles, normative constraints and physical limitations that apply in the kitchen are compensated for by the greater latitude that exists in the living/dining room. Indeed, the dining area allows more scope for individual behaviour, spontaneity and expression. Being more generous and flexible, it encourages the family to free themselves from differences. As a result, at weekends the community also tends to dissolve less formally than during the week. The end of the breakfast ritual is not signalled by the fact that everyone stands up and the extra chair is taken away. Instead, the children usually leave the table of their own accord and the communal breakfast 'ends' without a formal closure. Inversely, bringing in the extra chair marks the beginning of breakfast for the whole family, whereas the empty chair at the dining table suggests at least the possibility that someone might change seats and contains therefore the possibility for structural change.

d) If one relates the contrast between a functional spatial arrangement and the intimate atmosphere of the group sharing a meal to the ways in which the family presents itself as a community or unit, what stands out is the fact that the kitchen and dining room areas always remain structurally the same. This isotropic environment represents stability for the individual. Whichever room one is in, one is surrounded by the same structural conditions, which, therefore, do not call into question the family's identity. For indeed, if a community's identity is fed not only by common traditions, memories, values and experiences but above all by the experience of a constant spatial environment, the family's switch from the kitchen into the dining room can be interpreted as a repetition of spatial sameness, which expresses the way the family focuses on itself. However, there is also room for significant contrasts within this common ground. For this 'focus' is suggested by the fact that the family members, and, in this case, above all the children, are more actively involved in preparing breakfast than during the week. The dining table, which more or less everyone helps to lay, thus represents a state of order that has been jointly achieved from the starting point of a structurally constant spatial frame that both supports and places limits on this achievement. This frame supports the sense of community in the ritual of laying the table through the way the family share the act of turning the *tabula rasa* into a *tabula composita*. The individuals experience their significance for the family within this frame. However, because this frame only allows certain specific forms of community to be created, at the same time it also limits the extent to which social bonds are established. Because of the way the space is arranged, a certain performative style suggests itself. In the case of the Zobels this seems to reside within their habit of playful or teasing asceticism (*ascesis* meaning self-discipline), in a context with which they are all familiar.

e) The kitchen and the dining area, as places in which breakfast takes place, are places of transition—from night into day, from family into work, from individuality into life as a member of the group, from hunger into satisfaction, and, at weekends, from everyday life into the day off. Time and space are shared; all the family members come together and sit together, thus creating a space for communicative action. Changes of place (like social or temporal changes as well) have always been accompanied, i.e. opened and closed, by shared meals, sometimes including party celebrations and processions. As a secular ritual, breakfast carries on this tradition by preparing the group members' transition from one world to another by means of a ceremonial period in between.

Dealing with generational differences through ritual

Joint family mealtimes reveal themselves as a platform for overcoming family conflicts, a ritual in which boundary lines are established and dealt with. The drawing of boundaries allows the individual members of a family to apply different conflict resolution strategies and to be recognised as individuals in the staging of the community. The fact that a conflict can be resolved does not mean that it will not recur, but simply that in its ritual enactment, the family unit will not fall apart. In this process, time and again, the members of a family are assigned identities, their roles and duties are distributed, negotiated and changed, and generational differences worked out. In what follows, we propose to reveal the various conflict management strategies that mother and father employ in a situation in the Zobel family in which the father's fault is negotiated in a discussion at Sunday breakfast. The situation clearly highlights a pattern in which boundary lines are drawn within a family. Breakfast on this particular day started at 8.25 a.m. and the following passage began about ten minutes later.

1	*Mother*	Guess what your father managed to break?
2	Anna	(incomprehensible)
3	*Mother*	Much worse, ah—the glass spoon.
4	Anna	Ha?
5	*Mother*	From the gravy jug—the one that belongs to the glass jug.
6	Carolyn	Oh no, not that one. When?
7	*Mother*	Last week, after we'd used it for the custard cream.
8	Carolyn	For that...
9	*Mother*	Yes. (short)
10	Carolyn	THAT SPOON?
11	*Mother*	Hm.
12	Bjorn	Well it doesn't really matter.
13	Carolyn	YES IT DOES! It was...
14	Bjorn	Not really.
15	Carolyn	It was a really *nice* one.
16	Bjorn	Yes, it was nice, but...
17	Anna	It was a really deep one.
18	Carolyn	Oh no.
19	Anna	OH Daddy!
20	*Mother*	Oh Daddy! Well you can get us a new one. And go round the
21		shops for once yourself.
22	Anna	And somebody has also...
23	Carolyn	And bring home a new sofa too.
24	*Mother*	Phhfff (laughing).
25	Anna	And daddy also broke the fish, the fish (?)
26	*Mother*	That's right.
27	A	(incomprehensible)
28	*Mother*	Oh, all our lovely old things.
29	Carolyn	And Bjorn a cow glass, and a, and a...

30	*Bjorn*	But you can get new ones everywhere.
31	*Anna*	But not the bowl.
32	*Carolyn*	Yeah the bowl. The flower bowl.
33	*Carolyn*	What a shame!
34	*Mother*	I got that for one Deutschmark from the junk-dealer.
35	*Anna*	Ts! He always used to lose it in the same place, and afterwards
36		he didn't have any flowers for weeks…
37	Father	But the junk shop has re-opened. You can go there
38		straight away and buy something new.
39	*Mother*	Ha ha.
40	Father	Well it's there.

To begin with the mother calmly brings up a problem regarding the father. It has to do with something the father has broken (a glass spoon). The eldest daughter, Anna, is the first to react. Her mother's reply shows that the object was one she valued and treasured. It was used by the family at the weekend. By asking about when the spoon was broken, the youngest daughter, Carolyn, turns the problem of the lost possession into a serious offence. Both daughters make sure the problem is dealt with by the children. The 'we' in the mother's reply suggests that the broken spoon is a topic that is relevant for all (lines 1-9).

After Carolyn's loud exclamation emphasises the problem, Bjorn intervenes in the conversation (this is his first utterance at breakfast) in an attempt to get the matter back into proportion. But Carolyn insists on its importance and Anna supports her. From the daughters' statements the value of the spoon, which consists in its beauty, can be inferred. Anna makes a first attempt to resolve the conflict by addressing her father in an ironic tone. It is not the father, however, but the mother who reacts to this by repeating what her daughter has just said and by giving it a more serious touch with the request that the father replace what he has broken. The damage would be repaired if the glass gravy jug were made intact and complete again. As it is he who caused the problem in the first place, the father is called upon to make an effort to acquire a replacement. This serious request, which is meant to solve the problem, aims to prompt the guilty person, who has already been identified and recognised by all, into taking pains to restore the order and attractiveness of the Sunday breakfast table. An effort is needed to right the situation. Carolyn counters her mother's suggestion by complementing this demand with her own (a couch). The mother laughs. This takes the edge off her seriousness and the importance of her request that the wrong is righted by an effort on the part of the guilty person (lines 10-24).

This is followed by the listing of other damaged objects whose value has to do with their age and beauty rather than their financial worth. Bjorn, who had previously spoken out in defence of his father, is now named by Carolyn as a culprit himself for having broken something. Bjorn defends himself by claiming that it did not matter because the object in question can easily be replaced. Anna counters this argument by referring to yet another broken object. In this sequence, the issue of attractive and practical objects being broken is recognised by the children as a problem that concerns the whole family and they thus give positive sanction to the fact that the mother has raised the topic. They deal with the issue amongst themselves so that the mother is not obliged to emphasise it as her own or to justify bringing up the contentious issue (that of damage and compensation). At the same time, in dealing with the matter amongst themselves, they let their father off the hook. However, the one who speaks up in defence of his father (Bjorn) comes under fire by his sisters. This suggests that a differentiation according to gender is taking place (lines 25-33).

Although like his father the son is responsible for breaking something, his mother does not demand that he should compensate for it in the same way as she does her husband. Instead she reacts by recalling how she had acquired the object in the first place. This is not associated with much effort on her behalf, but with an experience. Anna brings up a story about the junk-dealer, which underlines the experience factor and at the same time moves the conversation away from the problem. Only now does the father get involved, referring to the experience value (in other words dismissing the effort argument) and the ease of acquiring new things to replace those broken (i.e. supporting the son's argument). He suggests that those who brought up and underlined the issue (i.e. mother and Anna) should acquire the new things needed. As far as he is concerned the problem is thus resolved—and so it is for the whole family (lines 34-40).

In this sequence, the mother again seems to be the one who brings up issues relating to responsibility within the family. The father is presented as the person who has broken something. The solution put forward by the mother is that the person to break something should also be the one to put it right. With the help of the children she turns her problem into a problem for the whole family. She begins by pointing out the importance of what has been broken and brings the others in to confirm it. The breakage thus becomes an issue to be brought up at Sunday breakfast. However, she cannot simply mention the fact that something has been broken, she also has to go into it in detail. When the son breaks something, the mother does not turn it into a problem for everyone—it is something between just the two of them. The conflict that arises from beauty and order having been spoilt and the mother's need to have her own commitment to the family recognised is to do solely with the father. Care for the family, keeping it safe and unbroken ought, in her mind, to come from the parents. The children are called upon to legitimise and recognise a conflict as being a family issue. They are brought into managing the problem, but the demand for a resolution stems from the mother. This shows that a boundary line is drawn between parents and children as well as between mother and father. A noticeable fact in this sequence is that whenever the mother speaks of 'we' or 'us' she means the family without the father (the same is signified in the 'you' and 'your' at the beginning). When the mother speaks to the father, either directly or indirectly, she places herself in a communal grouping with the children, which has been defined by the damage caused. By means of the broken object a form of part-loyalty is created in the family. The mother speaks in the first person when she claims to represent the whole family, for instance when she acquires something 'for all', in line with the motto 'one for all'. The father, on the other hand, represents the inverse principle 'all for one', when he encourages the family to rectify the damage together ('You can go there straight away and buy something new'). Two totally different models for resolving crises in the family are put forward. In the mother's model a 'scapegoat' is called upon to repair the damage he is blamed for, damage which, in this case, is defined primarily in material terms. And in the father's model, damage can only be made up for by all, or rather, by the mother and the daughters as well as perhaps the son, in inter-generational teamwork. In the first case, problems relating to the group are individualised, whereas in the second they involve all the participants together and can thus only be resolved by all. Everyone carries responsibility for the success of the whole community. Community is thus presented as a living organism, whereas in the first case it is directed towards a system of individual issues.

The eldest daughter takes over managing the problem discussed. By using irony, she puts the importance of the issue back into proportion somewhat. At the same time she follows the boundary lines drawn by the mother as well as later by the youngest daughter and strengthens their arguments in her indirect conversation with Bjorn. Her calm and matter of fact attitude prevent any escalation of excitement or emotion. Although Anna follows her mother in telling an anecdote which underlines the experience-value involved in buying a bowl at the junk shop, she also moves the conversation away from the actual issue and thus makes it possible for her father to find another resolution to the conflict.

By referring to the exact time at which the spoon was broken, the youngest daughter brings up the actual act in question. Her excited tone and the way in which she emphasises the importance of the issue (by which she positions herself on the side of the one making the complaint) show that she clearly does not wish to be made responsible for the deed. She seems to know about all the other similar cases of things having been broken and by whom. She recognises the issue raised; she is able to participate in the discussion and does so often and loudly. She follows the boundary lines drawn by the mother without ever referring to the mother's utterances directly, and she speaks out in support of her mother by placing Bjorn, who does not follow, on the side of the perpetrator. Before this, she also takes the opportunity to draw attention to her own request. Although her exaggerated demand (that her dad buy a sofa) considerably de-escalates the conflict by stepping way out of the contextual frame, at the same time it strengthens the boundary line that is drawn around the father, for whether it is a question of making amends for breaking things or something completely different, it is the father who is considered responsible for fulfilling the family's needs and requests.

Bjorn tries to prevent the issue of the broken spoon turning into a problem. In so doing he contradicts the mother's need and interrupts her legitimation strategy. This is negatively sanctioned by his sisters. After siding with the mother, the sisters point to Bjorn as a further culprit. This suggests that a boundary line is drawn between the siblings. It also corresponds to a clear boundary between the two genders. The male members of the family are the accused, even though the difference between the generations remains significant. For indeed, only the father is called upon to make up for his deed. The twins' behaviour also reveals how gender roles are incorporated mimetically. Whilst Anna clears and straightens things out in a similar way to her mother, by directing the discussion towards clearly naming facts and finding a resolution, Bjorn, on the other hand, more like his father, attempts to calm the situation down. The twins can also be seen to be repeating their parents' role distribution.

In the father's eyes, the damage does not consist in the broken objects but in the fact that the problem is brought up and demarcation lines drawn within the family. His resolution strategy, like the mother's, follows a perpetrator principle, but his proposal re-establishes the family as a community without internal boundaries. From a performative perspective this shows that here accusations are staged in such a way as to prevent the implications of an accusation (that would be usual within the family) from occurring. The question that arises on a performative level in the family, through the mother, has to do with how to put things right without the perpetrator of the fault being 'harmed' in the process, for the fact of negatively judging a member of the community may threaten solidarity within the community. By bringing up the topic, by referring to 'your' father, the mother at the same time draws the children's attention to the father's role in setting them a good example, to his responsibility in moral and social matters and to the fact that the issue in question represents a loss for all the members of the family. But with the words 'managed to break' she also signals that the following context is not that of a trial in court which is meant to pass a final judgement on an (already clearly recognised) victim, but rather, to undermine it ironically. Reference to the father's evil doing, which in court is usually used to undermine the character of the accused, is here, in a performative form of alienation, transformed into the opposite. The information contained in the accusation, i.e. your father is to blame, which is not unproblematic for the family, can only be dealt with in a particular way, i.e. in banter that the children are invited to take part in. The fact that the father is meant to be 'put on the rack', that the mother is pushing for a solution to the issue and the father is being ultimately summoned to compensate, becomes clear in line 20 'Oh Daddy, well you can get us a new one'— but here again, the fact that the mother uses the childish term 'Daddy' allows for a humorous caricaturing of the situation. The father is generally expected to acquire replacements and to buy things for the family—this is what the mother (energetically) demands, and in so doing expresses her dissatisfaction whilst at the same time placing herself on the side of those affected by his lack of action.

What is demonstrated here is that the performative 'framing' of an accusation in the form of banter and caricature makes it possible for an issue to be dealt with without intra and intergenerational boundary lines turning into irresolvable differences. In families, roles are not defined legally and institutionally in the same way that the roles of the accused, the prosecutor, judge and defendants are defined in court. Yet, nevertheless, a procedure is always required to settle conflicts and to arrive at working conclusions. The question remains as to how formal, set procedures, rules and demands are to be brought into harmony with the solidarity and cohesion of a family.

Discussions at the table: How family performances are used to establish norms and standards

In the following, two examples will be used to analyse how the family establishes its rules through performative rituals. In the first, a recorded conversation at breakfast in the Zobel family is used to illustrate how, despite the fact that in this case maternal authority fails, family rules for communicating with each other continue to be recognised even though further rules are violated. The second case study is an observation of evening dinner in the Hauser family which reveals how the parents clear directives to their five-year-old son Eric to eat are eventually successful as he gradually begins to turn to his food, albeit in a playful way.

'Everyone keeps interrupting me'
How maternal authority in the Zobel family is undermined
    The Zobel family is having breakfast in the kitchen, which takes over forty minutes.
    As soon as the father has left the breakfast table and gone out of the kitchen to go
    to work, and just before breakfast comes to a close, which is usually signalled by
    the preparation of school sandwiches, the following conflict escalates.

1	*Anna:*	Guess what. At school now we have to write a weekly task sheet.
2		We have to write in what we've done and then assess ourselves,
3		and then write a plan for the next day either to try and work…
4	*Mother:*	CAROLYN!
5	*Anna:*	… faster or to continue at the same pace.
6	*Mother:*	I see.
7	*Mother:*	And how are you doing? Are you, are you within your time-
8		limit?
9	*Carolyn:*	Mummy, have you made … (incomprehensible)
10	*Mother:*	Are you faster than your plan?
11	*Bjorn:*	(incomprehensible) sandwich, because this is quite thick.
12	*Mother:*	I'M STILL BUSY TALKING TO YOUR SISTER.
13		EVERYONE KEEPS INTERRUPTING ME. IT'S A
14		REALLY BAD HABIT OF OURS. IT REALLY IS AWFUL.
15	*Anna:*	Of ours??
16	*Mother:*	Yes, we all do it. And yes, I include myself. But it's still
17		a terrible habit. We really (.) must (.) try to get out of it. We
18		must all try and think about it a little. So tell me now *Anna:*,

19		how are you doing with the planning, are you working faster or
20		slower?
21	*Bjorn:*	Butter, please.
22	*Anna:*	I think I'll make myself another sandwich.
23	*Mother:*	O.K.
24	*Mother:*	Are you doing well?
25	*Bjorn:*	Mummy...
26	*Mother:*	Bjorn, I just said something about butting in,
27	*Anna:*	Has hardly started and he starts up
28		again with bread and butter.
29		Silence (1)
30	*Bjorn:*	Mum, I'm the only one at school who hasn't ever forgotten to do
31		their homework yet.
32	*Mother:*	Do you mean in the term or in the whole year?
33	*Bjorn:*	In the whole year.
34	*Carolyn:*	Mummy ...
35	*Mother:*	Wow, Bjorn, that's really great. I'm so glad to hear it.
36	*Carolyn:*	Mummy...
37	*Mother:*	Look it's really not funny ... are you all making a hobby out of
38		interrupting?
39	*Bjorn:*	Ha ha ha! Why are you making such a fuss, mum? Stop nagging.
40	*Anna:*	(Will still get a letter)
41	*Carolyn:*	(Sings)
42	*Mother:*	My dear boy, I am allowed to voice my own opinion, aren't I?
43	*Bjorn:*	Yes.
44	*Mother:*	Well, that's all I'm doing.
45	*Anna:*	I had a bad dream. I dreamt I had to give V. my hand (.), it was a
46		nightmare.
47	*Mother:*	Anna:, you can save that for now, you know.
48	*Anna:*	But why?
49	*Mother:*	I don't want to talk to you anymore right now.
50	*Anna:*	Well, you don't have to.
51	*Mother:*	Right, so you're making your own sandwiches now are you?

The atmosphere remains tense even though Bjorn conciliates once more and at the end shows appreciation for the bread his mother has bought.

Throughout breakfast, it is mainly Carolyn who disturbs the conversation by singing, interrupting and playing tricks. The mother becomes increasingly irritated. Towards the end of breakfast, when the children usually prepare their sandwiches for school lunch, she allows the conflict to escalate. Right until the end, however, she maintains the conciliatory gesture of taking over the children's task of preparing sandwiches. The mother finally 'explodes' when Carolyn interrupts her conversation with Anna about school (lines 1-10). But she avoids criticising Carolyn personally. Instead she makes use of the interruption to bring up a problem which in her view involves the whole family. In so doing she attempts to preserve the family as a unit or community by including herself in the criticism by using the pronoun 'we' even though it is in fact illogical for it to be a 'habit of ours' that we keep interrupting *her* (lines 12-14). At this point we must consider whether by using the plural 'we' the mother may here be reacting to the fact that the family is recording their conversation. This would suggest that 'we' or 'ours' is intended as a performance in front of others, which shows that the mother is viewing it from the perspective of an outsider. The mother then reacts in a way that is typical for her in this situation, repeating a pattern which she often reiterates in similar situations involving different problems, and which gives the impression that the others are familiar with it. She often begins to define a problem within the family by calling on all of them collectively, and here too she attempts to turn something that she herself sees as a problem into something that concerns everybody.

Anna's subsequent question shows that she sees through this attempt. Her critical comment (line 15) could open up a space for a discussion about the rules and about how they should be acknowledged. But instead, in her reply, by including herself in the criticism, the mother again attempts to present a personal wish as a behavioural norm for the whole family. In so doing, she presumes and reaffirms her authority to set rules. She reasserts her opinion that it is bad manners to interrupt others when they are talking. Her suggestion of a way to solve the problem is that everyone should get out of the habit and think about it (line 18). And although she maintains, as a conversational norm, that one should not interrupt, we may wonder, why this should be so. Without pausing, the mother attempts to pursue her conversation with Anna, leaving no room for the problem and her suggested solution to be discussed. Instead it is assumed that she must simply be obeyed without discussion. The mother's appeal to the whole family group in fact implies an implicit request that the children recognise her authority. The way in which she justifies her appeal would seem to imply that the children ought to be able to voice their views and answer her. Otherwise, appealing to their community spirit makes no sense, for although the others are explicitly asked to recognise the norms of the community, they have no actual say in establishing them.

It is here that the mother's authority can be seen to fail. The children do not argue with the rule, but they do not respect it either. Bjorn undermines the mother's authority by breaking the rule once more, but at the same time he shifts the discussion on to a level that the whole family considers important (lines 30 and 31). Indeed, one of the functions of breakfast is to organise and control the children's school behaviour. It is a particular characteristic of the Zobel family that the parents support and encourage the norms of the primary school that all three children attend. While the conflict is going on, this is clear in the mother's reaction to the task plan at school that Anna has told her about and which is obviously designed to teach the pupils self-control and discipline. In repeatedly asking the daughter how she is getting on with the task plan at school, the mother implicitly supports the strategy (lines 7-8, 10). By picking up on the topic of school Bjorn shifts the conversation from a (pseudo) 'discussion' about rules of communication to a conversation about school. In presenting a positive image of himself with regard to the school norm of doing homework, Bjorn relies on the positive acknowledgment of this norm by the whole family, thus reaffirming the family as a community after the mother's ineffectual explosion. Although Bjorn implicitly rejects the mother's claim to authority, in attempting to pursue as a family the conversation that he interrupted between mother and daughter, he actually confers meaning to the rule of letting others speak, even though he breaks it. There is implicit acknowledgement of a communal norm here despite its explicit violation. Moreover, Bjorn recognises the mother's authority when it comes to supervising and controlling achievements at school. In shifting the conversation in terms of its participants and in recognising the mother's authority, Bjorn is in a sense offering her a compromise. The mother yields to this even though at first she reacted negatively to being interrupted (line 35). In the family conversations about school, there is often a certain competition in the air between Anna and Bjorn. Here, through his interruption, Bjorn picks up the mother's praise instead of Anna. Yet Anna seems to support *this* compromise because she does not protest against his breach of the rule (line 32). A possible explanation for this may be that perhaps Anna's intention was to de-escalate the developing conflict in the first place by drawing her mother's attention away from the disruption caused by Carolyn and bringing the conversation round to school. Thus, later, despite her critical reaction to her mother's explosion she does not insist on discussing the problem. This would explain why Anna and Bjorn seem united in their reaction to the mother, and their usual rivalry disappears behind this united front.

However, if Anna and Bjorn manage to re-establish a fragile union within the family, it is immediately disrupted again by Carolyn (lines 36-38). This results in the mother criticising all the children and claiming that they are enjoying being disruptive and annoying. In so doing, she erects a barrier between herself and the children, thus showing that she is not prepared to have her authority undermined. Thus, she gives up her own legitimation strategy, for now it is clear that the children alone are accountable for the disruption. As a consequence, even Bjorn is no longer prepared to compromise with his mother. He changes the conversation again to criticise the general way the mother imposes her authority when it comes to the legitimation and acknowledgement of family rules. He says she is making too much of a fuss and should stop 'nagging' them (line 39). This results in the mother becoming defensive. Bjorn's short 'yes' shows recognition of the mother's right to voice her opinion. This rule applies to them all and the mother is not asserting her rights here as a higher authority than the children. Yet she has to have the last word. This is the mother's final attempt to assert her authority (lines 42, 44).

Anna, who has been interrupted first by Bjorn then by Carolyn, tries once more to calm down the conflict by changing the subject yet again, but the offended mother rejects this attempt (line 49). Now that her strategy has failed, she feels unable to welcome another shift. The mood remains dampened until the end, yet the mother does not step out of the breakfast circle. She refuses to continue making Anna's sandwiches and instead turns to Bjorn who crowns her efforts by showing appreciation for the bread, that is for her ability to care for the family.

Rules for communicating in the family and the recognition of school norms are the topics brought up in this scene in which the mother's strategy to assert her rights fails. Nevertheless, by caring for her children's well-being she manages not to let the unity of the family collapse altogether. Bjorn and Anna show proof of their ability to make room for compromise by shifting the levels and topics of conversation. The mother's authority is partially recognised, a) through the *implicit* recognition of her care for the children's well being, and b) through the *implicit* communal recognition of school norms in the family, which the mother enforces and controls. On the other hand, the children see through the mother's strategy and reject her claims to authority. Anna attempts this first directly, but otherwise the children achieve it by changing the levels of conversation. It is not the communication rule as such that the children refuse to acknowledge; they merely refuse to follow the rule when their mother attempts to turn what amounts to a personal problem into the breaching of a *supposedly* communal rule. The children do not legitimise this authority, and at this point the mother becomes the one to threaten the unity of the family because she fails to follow her children's strategy for resolving conflicts.

The Hauser family consists of four people: the two forty year-old parents, their thirteen year-old daughter Frederica and five year-old son Eric. The family try to have at least one meal together every day, and this, for reasons of work and organisation, usually takes place in the evening. Friends often join the family for dinner, whilst the father's job sometimes prevents him from being there. A calm and clear-cut arrangement of family daily life that is also open to spontaneous change is characteristic of this family. Indeed, the relaxed manner in which rules and acts of disobedience are usually managed in this family contrasts rather with the sequence we recorded and observed in which Eric is disciplined to eat properly.

'Eat properly!' How Eric mimetically learns table manners in the Hauser family

After everyone has picked up their knives and forks there follow a couple of minutes of silence. Everyone is busy eating. The mother opens the table conversation by asking Frederica a question which turns into a discussion on the reasons for her being late. Later on, the main topic of conversation remains Frederica's recent change of school. … Throughout all this Eric keeps grumbling and fidgeting. At one point he gets up and leaves the room to go to the bathroom provoking his mother to exclaim "Ohh Eric!" in a drawn out manner. Eric goes to the toilet, leaving the bathroom door open, sings, and comes back with his braces down. He asks his mother to help him do them up, but she says he can leave them down. Eric gets back on his chair at the table...

Frederica begins a conversation with her mother. During the long opening phase of this sequence, the mother turns to Eric in a solicitous and calming manner. Eric is still grumbling and fidgeting. His mother says "Come on now, sit still and be good". Whilst the mother is dealing with Eric, the father asks Frederica some questions. The mother then turns back to Frederica and ignores Eric's continued whining for a while; she answers Frederica's questions and asks some questions herself. …

The doorbell rings. The father gets up and goes to the back door of the apartment but there's no one there. When the bell rings again, this time the mother gets up and goes to the other door. It is the next-door neighbour bringing back some plates. Just as the door closes and the mother comes back down the long corridor, Eric gets up to see who is there. When he sees it is too late, he quickly sits down again. The mother walks past the sitting room area, puts the plates back in a cupboard and a conversation about the neighbour develops between her and Frederica. … When the mother has sat back down at the dining table, Frederica continues the conversation about the difficulties of changing schools. … Throughout this sequence, the mother reprimands Eric who is fishing bits of vegetable out of his soup with his fingers. His mother tells him to eat it all up otherwise he will not be allowed to go to his friend's house later …

Frederica begins to talk about and describe her (new) school-friend's big apartment. Her mother is especially attentive. She nods her head and shrugs her shoulders but does not ask any further questions. Whilst this is happening, the father devotes himself to Eric. He inclines his upper body towards Eric, bends his right arm and supports himself with his lower arm and wrist on Eric's chair. He looks down on Eric from an angle and talks to him quietly but firmly, underlining his sentences by nodding his head at the same time. Twice Eric reacts to his father's reprimand with the stereotypical reply "So what!?" His father's position and voice do not change. The second time his mother responds with a quiet, short and dry laugh … In the meantime, Frederica has finished her description and after the second "So what?!" the mother turns her head towards the father and says that Eric has a new girlfriend at nursery school. Frederica asks if it is true and Eric confirms that it is true and begins to talk about it. Whilst talking, Eric confuses the words 'tomorrow' and 'yesterday'. His sister corrects him, but he does it again. This time his father corrects him cheerfully, and then his mother tells him which one is right. This is not done in a condescending or teaching tone, but rather humorously.

Again the mother calls Eric to "Eat up now". Her voice is more energetic; she moves her left arm briefly in his direction, bending her upper body towards him too. The father reacts by turning towards Eric in a similar way (without leaning his arm on his chair this time). This is just a quick gesture; he then turns back to his food. He bends his upper body slightly towards Eric and says in a firm, short and still quiet manner, "I don't want to sit at table with you!" He underlines this utterance by waving the spoon in his right hand. Eric now turns towards his mother and says "Can I have a drink?" The mother replies "When you have finished!" Eric complains with a whine to which his mother says firmly "No" and repeats her request.

Frederica and the parents have now finished eating. They are now talking about some things that the father is supposed get the next day... Eric says to his mother "Mum, I'm full up", to which she replies "Eat it all up!" this time more loudly and energetically. She also repeats the condition: "If you don't eat it all up...." The father, Frederica and her mother are waiting for Eric to finish. The mother says "I don't want to sit at the table for so long". Frederica agrees, "Nor do I". The mother now asks Frederica if she has done all her homework; Frederica says yes. The father begins to clear away his and Frederica's plate. Frederica asks her mother if she can leave the table. Her mother says yes. The father does not sit down again but looks down at Eric's plate. Eric shouts out "Finished!" which his mother then confirms with a relieved "Thank heavens for that", and says to Eric: "You can clear up your plate now."

Even before the meal began, Eric had made it clear that he was not interested in eating. He especially did not want to eat with the others. His mother reacted quite calmly at first, stating simply and clearly that Eric was not allowed to eat on his own and that there would not be anything to eat later on either. Her response suggests that this is a recurrent issue at the moment and not a performance Eric is putting on especially for the benefit of the still unfamiliar observers on this occasion, in order, perhaps, to draw particular attention to himself. To begin with Eric refuses to eat anything at all and right up until the end, verbally, and for a long time non-verbally, he resists the family eating rules which consist in eating together, properly and not too slowly, not drinking with your mouth full and eating up what's on your plate.

When Eric answers his father's rebuke with 'So what?' for the second time, his mother avoids an open conflict by bringing up the topic of his new friend at nursery school. At this point she seems to contradict the role she had taken up earlier of supervising Eric's eating behaviour. The fact that the father has now taken on this role means that she is able to ease the conflict by changing the topic of conversation (after Eric has spoken she takes on the role of supervisor again). Frederica shows interest and reacts positively by asking her brother a direct question. The father nods emphatically too, showing his recognition (he purses his lips in a gesture of deliberation that shows the importance of what is being said). Eric looks at his sister and immediately begins to tell the family about his new friend. It is above all the mother who explains to him the correct temporal forms of 'yesterday' and 'tomorrow'. The tone of conversation both in Eric's telling and in his family's questioning remains friendly and pleasant. Eric's world is taken just as seriously as that of the other family members. His confusion of time words, a common phenomenon amongst children of his age (Piaget, 1968), is corrected, but in fact both his mother and sister have given him the space to prove his cognitive (the capacity to tell), social (establishing contacts, making friends) and aesthetic (painting) competence. He is corrected, but not in a condescending manner, and thus his potential competence turns to real competence in the eyes of all the members of his family.

In stark contrast to this are the constant reprimands (and orders) that come from both sides—both spatially, as Eric sits in between his parents, and socially, for both his mother and father intervene. The father, who, like his wife, did not express any emotions with regard to Frederica's transgression of being late, now makes his indignation at his son's behaviour clear: he does not wish to sit at table with someone who eats like Eric. Whilst the content of these words may seem to imply inconsistency, the clear delivery of what he says does not. Before the mother's admonition takes the form of explicit commands she makes the rules and the consequences of not obeying them, absolutely clear to Eric. Eric is not at risk of being explicitly excluded from the family group. Such a punishment is impossible because the mother clearly states that Eric will not be allowed to eat alone. The clear normativity of this statement stresses the importance that both parents confer to the shared meal.

Since all the reprimands and orders and the emotional and explicit sanctions seem to cut no ice with Eric, we may wonder why, in the end, Eric finishes his food after all, even though he does not give up his oppositional stance. He makes progressive steps towards eating up the food on his plate. At first he refuses to eat altogether and disappears off to the toilet. Then he protests against eating, saying that he's not hungry and does not like it. Then he begins to play with his food. And finally he more or less eats it up. This progressive move towards the food and eating has nothing to do with the parents' constant intervention which reaches a climax in the mother telling him to eat up and then in his father's emotional statements, after Eric had played around with his food and then told a story which distracted him from his food for a while. It is only when Eric begins to eat seriously and properly that his parents stop telling him off. His parents' attention seems to be focused on Eric's verbal protest, which never quite ceases until the end of the meal. Yet Eric's resistant behaviour is not criticised as such.

The normative pressure to eat properly, finish up what is on one's plate and not drink whilst eating is neither discussed nor explained. Difficulties with Eric seem to be a common feature of family mealtimes, for both his opposition and his mother's stereotypical exhortations are ritualised. Eric's indignation is suppressed by the three people around him. In this the family seems to follow the mother's example. The mother here becomes the vehicle for traditions that are handed down. In this role she is also the only one who does not bring topics of her own into the conversation at table. Eric's protest attracts everyone else's attention. Their attention finds its climax not in the admonition, which, despite increasing in intensity, does not turn into aggression, but remains, rather, a subtle strategic threat of withdrawn love. The mother's ritualised strictness results in a ritualised protest on the part of Eric who manages to force both his father and his sister to pay him more attention. Only after he has held their total attention and everyone else has finished eating does Eric finally agree to settle down to his meal. The calm and generally relatively relaxed atmosphere, the fact that attention is diverted away from Eric's misbehaviour and a conflict avoided, stand in stark contrast to the discipline, repression and power struggle that takes place during the meal. It is hard to say who 'wins' in the end. Eric finally eats up his food, but only after the others have finished. In other words, he does not eat with them which is what he announced that he didn't want to do before the meal. On the other hand, he does finally follow the normative pressure to eat properly. And because the others respect this norm by not getting up from the table but waiting for him to finish, they allow Eric to assimilate the norm they have established of eating together by imitating the others, in other words, mimetically. The parents do not explicitly insist on Eric giving in to their wishes, indeed here too they justify their complaints about him on the level of feelings of like and dislike; and they do not expect Eric to explicitly (verbally) subordinate himself to their rules. They do not therefore present the normativity of the meal as meeting their own expectations. The parents' behaviour and the implicit normativity of parental authority create a frame in which Eric can assimilate mimetically the norms that govern social behaviour. He is thus able to satisfy his hunger as well as partially assert his resistance without breaking any rules. The special attention he receives and the fact that the others wait for him show that he is recognised as a member of the family with equal rights. And in Eric's mimetic behaviour, the norms of the community win through in the end.

Performative style

In the daily mealtime ritual the family is symbolised and staged as a community. Performative style might be defined as the interrelation between the elements of content and form that are performed and acquired as patterns in the family's ritual enactments, and that control *what* a family works out as a community and *how*. A family's performative style shows how it arranges its shared realm of experience and how the family presents itself as a united whole of interacting subjects. The following are the essential requirements of content: *ritual scenery* (i.e. how time, place and requisites are used) which determines the exterior frame for processes of creating the family community; *power relations* and the *sense of order* in ritual sequences, which determine the assignment of roles, duties and identities; and the *handling of difference and unity* in the ritual by creating the reality of the community. In terms of their form, what characterises rituals most fundamentally is the *playful, mimetic and physical character* of the interactions and performances they involve.

Typical for the Zobel family are the patterns of strictness and play that shape both the content and the form of ritual enactment. That which is rational, regulated and normative, on the one hand, and that which is humorous, playful and 'chaotic', on the other, combine to determine the boundaries within the family, which, precisely because of the clear division of duties between the parents, are flexible enough to ensure that everybody's various interests and priorities can be given due recognition, different as they are, so that the unity of the family only threatens to disintegrate when all the members are not physically present.

The family's move into the dining room for breakfast on Sundays shows how, despite the prevailing strictness in this room, there is still space for relaxed and playful interaction between and among the generations. The fact that the kitchen is basic and rather cramped makes it a space for closeness, caring and intimacy between parents and siblings. Despite the apparent predominance of verbal interaction, this intimacy is communicated essentially through physical relations. Whether in the kitchen or in the dining room area, there is nothing that might detract from the family's coming together. Indeed, the way the rooms are arranged implies that attention is focused on collective interaction, which is not disturbed even, for instance, when the children leave the immediate surrounding of the table to prepare their packed lunches for school. The mother's strictness, and her role in regulating the family's everyday life, imposing family norms and checking how the children are behaving at school, finds a contextual framework here that makes it possible for her not to be an outsider. Instead, despite her role, it gives her space to be amusing and imaginative, to be close to the children and care for them even during moments of conflict.

What is striking is the explicit normativity that goes along with the family's assignment of duties. This explicit normativity calls for legitimating strategies which, in this particular family, rely on reason, practical sense and rationality. It is clearly the parents who have the power to make the rules, and this is neither questioned nor discussed, although it is somewhat undermined by the critical evaluation of the adolescent twins, who make use of the contradictions of normative performance to limit their mother's assertions, e.g. when a norm that is supposed to be communal and valid for all is contradicted by the mother's authority. They do not undermine the normativity of a rule, however, but discuss the logic of it even if they do not follow it. In this way, parental authority can be questioned, but the authority of the community or family unit is constantly reconfirmed by all. This also happens when, in the case of a conflict, the issue of blame or responsibility is negotiated and, although the group may succeed in naming the person responsible, a teasing approach avoids condemning the person as 'guilty' (Garfinkel, 1982). The conflict situation in the Zobel family is not so much about identifying someone as being to blame, but, rather, about confirming the family identity as a community. Whereas the staging of the family is regulated above all by the explicit naming and imposition of certain rules (mother), the family organises its cohesion by means of closeness, intimacy and care (another part of the performance) through physical acts (father). That the mother sets norms explicitly and the father implicitly is by no means clear-cut. This behaviour is the result of a clear division of duties resulting in a division of roles that has nothing to do with set identities. This assignment of roles and duties is best seen as a scale between two poles, which stand in reciprocal relation to one another in the family's ritual enactments and are in constant communication. Thus, the mother is able to identify with her own role as well as with the role assumed by the father within the family group. Assigned identities can therefore be shaped more flexibly, precisely because the roles are relatively inflexible. The flexible frame to the set norms allows boundaries and difference management in which the family's shared experience of reality is developed, to be treated in a light hearted way.

Mimetic relations take place on the level of language as well as on the level of role behaviour, even although the children are already at an age in which learning increasingly has to do with processes of reflection. The mimetic acquisition of behaviour comes to the fore when, in conflict situations, the children follow their parents' example, e.g. when in dealing with her younger sister, Anna copies her mother's way of showing her younger sister how to behave, reducing the emotionalism of the situation and organising matters. Bjorn on the other hand assumes his father's way of defending himself, though playing the situation down and using humour.

The Zobel family's performative style turns assignment of roles, mimetic acquisition and learning into ways of working on and disciplining themselves. However, the strict frame permits them, in a teasing and light-hearted way, to relate to each other and at the same time to come to terms with the prerequisites and conditions of the group or community. Our term for this style is *ludic asceticism*.

Chapter 2

Rituals in daily school life

In this chapter we will address the question of how social life is constructed through rituals within the context of school. We will show how, in a particular school, 'communities' (peer groups, tutor group and teaching group identities) are established, negotiated and confirmed performatively. In accordance with the assumption in ritual theory that such processes are most clearly visible in transitional phases, we will concentrate on transitions as an essential process in school life. Of primary interest are the micro-rituals in which everyday transitions between various school contexts occur.

Since our particular interest is in the nature of rituals as processes, we will also look at forms of interaction and behaviour that have not yet been shaped by conventional or standardised forms. Those who engage in such modes of behaviour are often unaware of its ritual content. These forms of interaction are therefore more appropriately characterised by the concept of 'ritualisation'. The main questions we propose to tackle are *what themes and forms of ritualisation can be found in school transitional phases and how these contribute to the emergence of social cohesion among those participating in the activities of the school.*

Rituals and forms of ritualisation are recurring interactive patterns of action which, by means of physical expression, stylised gestures and scenic arrangements, constitute and confirm the boundaries, the customs and practices, values and norms that apply within a given community. Rituals are characterised by the form that their repetition takes, their sacred dimension and the fact that they generate and transform collective identity and difference. Ritualisations are characterised by collective practical execution and reflection, repetitions and mimetic processes (cf. Gebauer and Wulf, 1995, 1998).

The focus of our study can be outlined with reference to the works of Victor Turner (1969), who was particularly interested in liminal phenomena, i.e. threshold phases of transition from one social group to another. According to Turner, a ludic dimension is central to the liminal phase of a ritual, ludic being the dimension of play that is at work in symbolic expression. The scenes discussed below show the extent to which children play with these possibilities in liminal phases of school activities.

Investigating the *performativity* of ritualisations, we focus on what ethnologists such as Turner and Clifford Geertz call 'cultural performance', i.e. community-related and community-forming physical performances (cf. Göhlich, 2001; Wagner-Willi, 2001). What we are most interested in is the scenic arrangement—dramatic composition, stylised gestures, the use of 'props' or requisites in ritualisations (Goffman, 1971; Rittelmeyer, 1999).

By using the concept of performativity, also based on the works of Gregory Bateson and Erving Goffman, we will consider the symbolic aspect of actions and interactions. While Austin's notion of performativity aims to understand statements as actions, our work aims to understand bodily performances as statements and in some cases as frames (Bateson, 1972; Goffman, 1974). The symbolic content of a cultural performance, in other words what it signifies and what effects it has as a process, is of particular interest here.

When we speak of communities we refer not to a fixed, established community but to the shared ritual patterns that govern the creation and management of difference, ritual patterns that give form to the otherwise rather vague threshold phases. Turner's concept of *communitas* is a helpful term to denote the unstructured form of 'community' that typically emerges in these phases. Since in a school, a structure of sorts is always present, at least in terms of spatial layout, we prefer to speak here of a 'weak structure', referring to the fact that in transitional phases we find a mixture of structural elements from different contexts rather than a single social structure being dominant. Since social behaviour needs to find a direction or framework forces from this mixture there emerges a dominant structure. Traditional structures are re-established and transformed and new structures created. It is through the transformation and creation of structures and structural elements or differences that the 'weak structure' comes to be strong and productive, in that transitions open the way for new possibilities.

In the daily routine of school there are a number of transitional situations that can be considered liminal phases, such as the transition into the school week on Monday mornings, the inverse transition at the end of the week, transition phases within lessons, transitions during break-time in the school playground, transitions from lessons to break-time, and from break-time to lessons. Of all our empirical material, that which relates to the *transition from playtime to lesson* is by far the richest. The liminal phase here is particularly open to influences from all sides and shows the children's different positions within and attitudes towards their peer groups as well as the school institution. This threshold phase, which recurs every day, opens the way for the clash between child-culture and institutional rules and regulations which is a feature of the reality of school, and it also contains a range of situations that are key parts of school life.

Thus, our focus here is on these threshold phases of transition between playtime and lesson. We hope to shed further light on how, within this significant threshold realm, a ritual production of social life occurs in which boundaries and differences are embedded. In particular, our purpose is to understand how transitions become productive, how a sense of community is constituted within them and how the community becomes, of necessity, flexible in the ritualisation of these transitions.

The study involves three tutor groups of nine to thirteen year-olds in a Berlin primary school: firstly *Tutor Group 4y* and *Tutor Group 5x*, and then, as *Tutor Group 4y* became 5y, we study the same group one year later.

Whilst the teachers are German, the tutor groups contain girls and boys of different ethnic backgrounds, with a variety of mother tongues. We will thus also take gender and ethnic groupings into consideration. On closer examination a further sub-group stands out—whether the pupils have a positive or negative attitude towards school.

The school in question has embraced certain educational reforms that explain a few details. The children eat their breakfast snack, for instance, *before* break; food is not generally taken into the playground at all. The school provides plastic cups for drinks, and milk can be purchased in small bottles. When it is time for the longer break, this is not announced by a bell but by each teacher individually. Playtime is over when one of the teachers rings the bell in the playground. Teachers usually have an individual bell on their desk that they use mostly when the class is too noisy. The first few minutes after the long break are usually spent on individual activities such as reading or painting. This is meant to 'calm the children down'. This practice is common to all three tutor groups.

In *Tutor Group 4y* there are twenty-six children (twelve boys and fourteen girls) aged between ten and twelve and of Bosnian (1), German (13), Yugoslavian (2), Lithuanian (1), Russian (1) and Turkish (8) origin. In terms of numbers, Germans and Turks dominate, but there is a balance between pupils of German and non-German origin. A year later 5y is made up of twenty-seven children between the ages of eleven and thirteen, again more or less half girls (13) and half boys (14). Their nationalities are German (14), Yugoslavian (1), Lithuanian (1), Russian (1) and Turkish (10). The numerical dominance of German and Turkish children has slightly increased, whilst the balance between Germans and non-Germans has remained almost the same. *Tutor Group 5x* is made up of only twenty children—nine girls and eleven boys—who are between the ages of eleven and thirteen and of German (7), Lebanese (1), Portuguese (1), Russian (1), Turkish (9) and Tunisian (1) origin. There is a majority of German and Turkish pupils, but there are more non-Germans than Germans in this tutor group.

We have employed a variety of methods to record our empirical data: participatory observation, video-based observation as well as interviews and group discussions. The recording and interpretation of material focuses on video-based observation. Using a digital video recorder, the transitions from break-time to lesson periods were recorded in the classroom. These video recordings were then expanded by participatory observation.

Whilst there are tried and tested methods for analysing interviews and group discussion (cf. Hitzler and Honer, 1997), no such method has been developed for video-based observation. Our evaluation of empirical material largely follows the documentary method (Bohnsack, 1999). This multi-level interpretational approach is based on Karl Mannheim's methodological explanation of the observer's attitude in terms of a switch from *what* to *how* (Mannheim, 1964). This 'genetic attitude' (Mannheim) tallies particularly well with our interest in the performative, in the question of *how* rituals and ritualisations are developed, and *how* they contribute to creating social reality. Comparative analysis is central to the documentary method and is also important when it comes to selecting the material to be recorded (cf. Glaser and Strauss, 1969). This involves tracing similarities (Mannheim, 1964) or patterns (Bateson, 1972) that are documented in the activities and interactions recorded on video. We then carry out a systematic comparison on the basis of the empirical material.

The first phase in interpreting our findings involves translating the audio-visual material into a written text. We use micro-analysis and replay the observations as many times as necessary to obtain a detailed view of the different layers of interaction, by observing both body language and spoken language. It also shows the way territories are established and used, the positioning of pupils and teachers and their movements in the room, stylised gestures, facial expressions, aesthetic aspects, the forms that interactions take, the way the scene is set, and also the timings of the scenes.

Then the meaning, context and the way the interactions emerge as processes and social performances are examined. This involves analysing the interactions in terms of their form, i.e. their sequencing and symmetry, how one action complements another and how the interactions develop almost as a piece of theatre. We have systematically compared interactions, firstly in a video scene, then in the various scenes of a whole video recording, then in the recordings of a particular class or tutor group, and finally in various classes. By doing this we have sought to reveal similarities and differences in the most prominent rituals and ritualisations of everyday school life.

We look first at different performance areas or requisites and their function in rituals. These are the door and entrance, the aisles and blackboard area, classroom desks, chairs and seating arrangement, clothing, and other objects relevant to playtime and lessons. Our purpose is to describe and interpret the ritualised use that is made of them. The question is to what extent and how the ritual use of requisites facilitates the establishing and working through of differences, thus making the group a flexible unit. Since our focus is on how social life is constructed, we will first investigate the repetitions and mimetic processes that form an important part of ritualisations and will then turn to an examination of the sacred nature of the territories and the requisites involved.[2]

The chapter closes with an attempt, within the various ritualised scenes, to identify and sum up forms of daily school micro-rituals.

The door as threshold and frontier

Whilst the classroom doors in this school are not attractive to look at, their security technique is elaborate: they can be shut *and* locked. It is clear from the age of the school building that they were put in and fitted with security locks at a later stage. Each particular door we focus on here is the only connection between the classroom and the corridor, leading both to the outside (out of the classroom) as well as inside (into the school building). The classroom door thus contains a certain ambivalence because, while it leads exclusively into the classroom as an area of highly structured school organisation, as an exit it leads into the corridor as a comparatively weakly structured school area, which can be used as a transition into other lesson rooms or into the playground or else onto the street and into the world outside school. These various possibilities contribute to the signification of the corridor and relate to the way the classroom door and its surrounding area are used.

The doors in question are larger than ordinary doors. Several children can enter simultaneously. Furthermore, the wall between the classroom and the

2 The significance for communities of ordering the world into profane and sacred elements has already been pointed out by Durkheim (1995). His studies gave rise to the recognition that any object can become a sacred being—things that everybody knows and recognises and yet which, in certain situations, take on a significance that goes beyond their merely instrumental use.

corridor is about 40 cm thick. The width and thickness of the door opening in the wall confers upon this area a spatial dimension of its own. The threshold area and its undefined quality are thus extended in space.

At first sight the classroom door appears to be a place through which the children come in and out, pushing and getting stuck, like in a traffic jam. Closer observation reveals certain recurring patterns. Some children come into the classroom and promptly move away from the doorway, towards the coat hooks and their desks, without stopping. Others do the same, yet then gravitate back towards the door and remain in the threshold area for a while, playing around with the door. Some leave the classroom again, while others seem to hang around in the doorway area, crossing over the threshold time and again.

The first pattern can be interpreted as an element of school affirming ritualisation. By walking into the classroom without hesitation, hanging up their outdoor clothing, sitting down at their desks and taking out their school things, the children actively contribute to defining the class territory as a place of learning and signal that they have taken on the status or identity of pupils. This pattern will be further highlighted when we consider the function of the doorway as a threshold.

The following recurrent actions observed in the doorway can be interpreted as ritualisations: confirmation of the tutor group boundary on the one hand and granting pupils from other tutor groups permission to enter, on the other.

How the tutor group reconfirm their identity by defending their territory

Closing the door marks a boundary excluding those who do not belong in the tutor group. This boundary is re-established every day, drawing a clear demarcation line between the tutor group (independently of lessons and without teacher involvement) and the other interaction systems of the school, as shown in the following scene.

Tutor group 4y, 10:25

The pupils return to the form room after break in the playground. The door is wide open. Martin, Birgiel and Hanna are sitting on their chairs. Paul is sitting on his desk. Binol, Cennet and André are standing at the desks of Andrea, Lore, Sybille and Hanna and chatting to them. André turns round on the spot, takes off his coat, which he had previously begun to undo, and walks towards the coat hooks in the classroom.

A boy of about the same age but from a different tutor group shows up in the doorway. André sees him, shouts "Hey! Get lost, man!" and continues walking towards him. Paul turns his head and upper body towards the boy in the doorway. When André is about two metres away from the door the boy moves away slowly into the corridor. André walks past him towards the cloakroom area. He keeps his eyes on the boy the whole time.

At the same time, Cennet moves away from Lore and Andrea's desk and goes towards the door too. She glances at the scene at the door but does not appear to react to it. She looks towards the front of the classroom area from which Lisa and Birgiel are approaching.

Paul gets up from his table and walks towards the door, pushing past André who is hanging up his coat. The boy from another class disappears from the doorway. Paul stands at the doorway from inside, holding on to the left side of the door frame; he leans out of the door, looks out to the left and yells something at the boy.

These children defend their tutor group boundary without needing to plan or discuss how. The tutor group members' reactions to the 'intruder' overlap with apparent natural ease to make sure the doorway remains clear of anyone who does not have legitimate access. It is through this natural, mimetically interwoven action of demarcation and exclusion that the tutor group sense of solidarity is demonstrated and reconfirmed.

At first, André only notices the intruder by chance as he is on his way to the coat hooks. But this prompts an immediate reaction, which can be described as a ritual sequence or a ritualisation because of its daily repetition and the symbolic significance of the door as the boundary of the territory belonging to a particular group. André's tone of voice is aggressive. The word 'man' following the firm imperative 'Get lost!' is an element of peer group language and underlines the fact that it is not merely the boundary of the tutor group as part of the school institution that is being defended here, but the boundary of the tutor group as a 'community'. The exclamation 'man!' underlines the opponent's sex as well as emphasising the seriousness of the message 'from man to man' and the risk of physical retribution if the order is not obeyed. Yet, at first, the command only results in another member of the tutor group (Paul) being alerted to the problem; it is not enough to make the 'intruder' move away. He only begins to move away when André actually moves towards him. André seems to be satisfied with this gradual or half retreat. But Paul is not. He steps in as the executor of the aggression suggested by André's 'Get lost!' The boy is able to recognise André's approach towards the door as being part of his progression towards the coat hooks by the fact that André is taking off his coat and holding it in front of him at the time. André's threat can therefore be understood as merely safeguarding against any further intrusion. However, the speed, direction and urgency of Paul's movement towards the door are clearly intended solely for the purpose of putting on a show of hostility towards the intruder. Only now does the threat become effective and the boy retreat from the threshold.

Cennet's passive participation is not insignificant. The fact that she glances at the scene without intervening in defence of the boy outside, encourages and reinforces the hostile action. The sequence of interaction as a whole can be regarded as a ritual co-ordinated and performed by the members of the tutor group as a whole, excluding a non-member and thus reconfirming the tutor group boundary.

This relies on the fact that someone who can be considered as *Other* appears. From an ethno-psychoanalytical perspective, Erdheim (1988) has drawn attention to the important role the figure of the outsider plays in the dynamic between family and culture, either as a temptation that brings about change within family and subsequently within cultural relations, or as a threat or danger that calls for a confirmation and reinforcement of existing relations. In order to relate Erdheim's theory to school reality, two more of his arguments must be taken into account: that institutions tend to recreate family structure and that during the latent period of adolescence and puberty children turn towards culture in the form of school and peer or friendship groups. Seen in this way, school and peer groups are cultural institutions which allow children to enter into a new, unfamiliar world and at the same time create and offer structures that are similar to those of the children's own families.

Allowing pupils from other tutor groups to enter

The concept of framing (Bateson, 1972; Goffman, 1974) serves here to outline the question of how the door becomes framed not as a boundary but as an opening, a gateway and connection. There are essentially two ways in which this change occurs. The first is when a pupil from outside the class expresses, through words or body language, the wish to approach a teacher in the classroom for a particular reason. The second is when the pupil expresses the wish to approach a pupil in the tutor group for a particular purpose, and this is accepted by the members of the group.

Tutor group 4y, 10:27-10:28

> Yussif from 5x enters the room. He is carrying in both hands two large brooms crossed over each other in front of him, about a metre above the ground. He steers them directly towards the teacher, Mrs. Kasek, who is standing in the blackboard area. He walks down the middle aisle to the front, past Sören, André, Canel and Martin, who is standing in the middle aisle at the overhead projector and moves to let Yussif past. Mrs. Kasek turns to Yussif, takes one of the brooms off him and says 'lovely' … Martin watches Yussif hand over the broom. Samuel walks up (from the front) to the table next to the teacher's desk and picks up a tin from a box. He holds it up briefly, looks at Yussif and the broom and stands still for a moment. Sybille stands in front of him and watches the broom being handed over … Yussif picks up the broom that belongs to 5x, presses the pen into Mrs. Kasek's open hand and leaves. He carries the broom about half a metre above the ground, rapidly walks back down the middle aisle, turns left towards the door and leaves the room. Birgiel turns his head to watch Yussif walk through and out of the room.

Yussif is carrying in front of him his legitimation to enter: the brooms. This manner of visibly carrying something that is institutionally recognised as having to do with school organisation can be read as a silent message. Holding something out in this manner means holding it up for all to see. The object thus becomes a particular prop for ritualised interaction, with which the carrier performs a kind of procession. The broom is transformed from a functional object into a symbol of the way the school as an institution is run and thus assigns to its carrier the power that goes with it. The fact that this transformation occurs by means of a performance using body language (carrying the brooms) reveals how effective performance is in social life. This dimension of social performance, i.e. the use of body language, has tended to be overlooked by the focus on linguistic performativity.

The door seems to have undergone a transformation from being a threshold or a crossing to being a gateway or passage. The example shows that the way in which pupils from a different tutor group enter and leave the room follows a clear pattern of interaction, which is uncomplicated and easily readable. Entering the room without hesitation, carrying a signal, walking in a straight line, not staying any longer than necessary, walking straight back to the door and leaving the room without hesitation, these swift actions constitute a ritualised whole.

Tutor Group 5x, 10:23

Ömer enters the room and goes towards the middle aisle; when he reaches the
level of the blackboard he is called back by a boy from another tutor group who
is now standing in the doorway. The boy at the door is wearing a woolly hat and
looks somewhat older. Directly after him, Ayla, Hatice and Medine come rushing
in all at once. After entering the room, the boy from another tutor group comes
to stand against the cupboard, leaning on it casually. Ayla, Hatice, Medine, Ömer
and Uzman, who has joined the others from the back of the room, are all standing
close to the door between the cupboard and the first row of desks, and for a
moment they form an oval shape with the three girls standing opposite the three
boys. When Ömer leaves the oval, Medine pushes Hatice onto the boy from the
other tutor group. For a moment, Hatice and the boy look at each other and then
they turn away. The boy shouts something at Ömer. Ömer, who is now already in
the middle aisle again, turns around, answers him, and turns back again towards
the cloakroom area. Still in the area close to the door are Hatice, Medine, Ayla,
Uzman and the boy from the other tutor group, who is still standing with his
back to the cupboard. Hatice pushes Medine away from her and moves further
into the room, followed closely by Medine who pushes her from behind. When
Hatice goes past Uzman, she pushes Medine back, walks around Uzman from
behind and comes to stand between Uzman and the boy who does not belong
to this tutor group. Ayla steps closer to the three who are standing in a tightly
knit group (boy from outside, Hatice, Uzman), forming a circle of four with two
boys and two girls. Medine returns to the group again too, placing herself slightly
outside the circle, next to Hatice.

Uzman leaves the group and goes to the door. The three girls are now standing
next to the boy from outside, who is still leaning on the cupboard. The girls are
talking to the boy and laughing. Uzman stands in the doorway and peers out into
the corridor. From the back of the classroom, Tacim comes quickly up to the group
in front and pushes past Hatice and Ayla; he stands in front of the door. Talking
and gesticulating, he turns towards the boy from outside, pointing up towards
the camera or observers. The boy looks in that direction. Ayla leaves the group
and walks towards the teacher's desk/middle aisle. The boy from outside waves at
the camera/observers and goes out of the door. Hatice follows him, opening the
door again (which the boy had slammed shut when he left). She peers out into the
corridor and goes out. Medine follows her. Just before passing the first row of desks,
Ayla, who is walking slowly towards the middle aisle, bumps into Ömer, who is on
his way to the front of the room from the back. She exchanges a few words with

him briefly and then turns back towards the door again. Ömer goes past her and behind Medine and walks out of the door. Ayla follows him quickly.

A boy from a different tutor group enters the room after having called out to a tutor group member within the room. This calling out (cf. Butler, 1997) associates him with the power of the peer group which exists beyond the institutional organisation of children into tutor groups. His action obviously relies on a certain position of authority that he must hold within this peer group and which allows him to call Ömer back. His entrance is approved by the tutor group member in question and other tutor group members, some of whom actively welcome his presence. His presence is especially encouraged by two girls who stand around him in a circle, which can be read as a kind of ritual dance. The boy from outside is clearly considered an outsider in this dance, however not in the sense of not belonging to the tutor group or peer group, but rather in the sense of not being female. Indeed, he clearly represents the attraction of the opposite sex.

Despite this multi-level justification for his entrance, the boy remains next to the doorway the whole time, leaning on the cupboard, thus protected against potential hostile approaches from behind and able to keep an eye on the whole tutor group. When a tutor group member draws his attention to the camera this suffices to reinstate the primacy of the form room boundary, but it does not immediately restore the sense of tutor group cohesion and its closed boundaries. The boy leaves the room promptly, but all those who welcomed his presence follow him out too. At this point the door becomes part of a game in which a peer grouping that transcends the different tutor groups is confirmed.

Tutor group territorial spaces: aisles and the blackboard area

The aisle as a place in which group identities are confirmed
By *aisle* we mean the space within a classroom that is used as a way of getting to a particular place, like the route from the door to the teacher's desk or from the coat hooks to the pupils' chairs. The following scene begins when almost all pupils and the teacher have returned to the form room after the second long break. The lesson officially begins at 12:15 p.m.

Tutor Group 5x, 12:16:40-12:17:15
  The teacher, Mr. Maier, walks slowly from his desk into the area in front of the board facing the class. He holds up some pieces of work and calls "Sabah?". A boy

calls back, "She's not here! (.) Shall I take it down to her? She's downstairs." ... Mr. Maier looks down at the work he is returning for a moment, takes the top piece and places it in the middle of the pile. He leans forward, shrugs his shoulders, shakes his head and lets his hands drop by his thighs. ... With an ambiguous smile he turns back towards his desk.

At the same time, Yussif enters the classroom followed by Stefan who shuts the door. They walk down the middle aisle towards the coat hooks and look back at the teacher as he passes. The boys take off their coats as they go. Walking down the middle passageway, they go past Mehmet's desk. Mehmet, who is sitting on his chair, turns his upper body towards them as they approach. When Stefan goes past him, Mehmet lifts up his right hand and points his middle finger up whilst keeping the other fingers bent. At the same time, laughing, he covers his mouth with his left hand. Stefan looks into Mehmet's face and then onto his right hand and walks on while looking back. Mehmet looks back at Stefan and calls out "Come here you", but Stefan shouts back "No way!" Mehmet leans to one side and pulls his chair slightly away from his desk.

Mehmet follows Stefan with his eyes. Just as Stefan is coming back from the coat hooks, trying to keep out of Mehmet's way by walking round him, Mehmet quickly gets out of his seat, goes up to Stefan and punches him twice in the shoulder. Laughing, he then strokes Stefan's upper arm with his hand. Stefan defends himself, goes past Mehmet's desk, frowns at Mehmet and shouts "Stop it, you just stop it" and sits down at his desk nearby. Mehmet's eyes follow Stefan's movements. Yussif comes back from the coat hooks, barges into Mehmet from the side, moves up behind him, grabs him around the neck lightly with both hands, lets go, strokes his back with his hand and sits down next to him. He then turns his head towards Mehmet, who has also sat down again now, and whispers something into his ear.

Yussif and Stefan are a bit late. The teacher is engaged in a lesson-related activity—giving back a piece of written work to a pupil. The fact that he is standing facing the class in the blackboard area, with a pile of papers in his hands, can be seen as a symbol for school activity. Moreover, his moving into this central place, his upright, standing position, and the fact that he calls out the name of a pupil can be read as a possible opening phase of the lesson.

The two boys walk straight to the coat area, undoing their jackets as they go. In constantly looking back they are keeping an eye on their 'observer', for they may yet be reprimanded for being late. They stand out clearly in the open space between the door and the coat hooks, especially since most of the other pupils are already sitting at their desks on the other side of the room. However, the teacher does not show any negative reaction.

On their way to the coat hooks the boys walk past some of their classmates, including Mehmet. He has already carried out the sequence of institutionally ordered steps: entering the form room, walking over to the coat hooks, hanging up his outdoor clothing, going to his place and sitting down, getting out his lesson equipment. Mehmet leaves this position by provoking Stefan. The aisle now serves as a place for interactive involvement induced by Mehmet. Stefan is thus drawn away for a moment from the pattern of action expected of him. The aggressivity of Mehmet's stylised vulgar hand gesture is underlined by the challenge to a fight, 'come here you!' Stefan rejects this invitation and continues towards the coat hooks, thus maintaining his conscientious attitude to the lesson. The dramatics of interaction begin to escalate. Returning from the coat hooks to his desk, Stefan tries to avoid Mehmet, but he fails. It does not take much for Mehmet, who is sitting at the edge of the aisle, to move close enough to be able to get at Stefan physically as he goes by. He concludes his attack with a soothing gesture accompanied by laughter, which is intended to mark the playful character of his activity, even though Stefan does not seem to accept this. He remains serious and calls upon Mehmet through his body language and verbally to stop attacking him.

This scene shows the aisle as a forum that allows interactions to occur beyond the course of lesson-related patterns of action. Interaction of this kind takes place above all in the school playground and originates in the frame of reference of the peer group. The institution's territorial arrangement, its temporal and organisational structure, is the background for the interaction between Mehmet and Stefan. This arrangement includes the gathering of a large number of school children in a relatively small space and routes to particular areas in the classroom.

The structurally weak liminal phase of transition from break-time to lesson is of particular relevance here. Although the teacher has taken the first steps towards beginning the lesson, the organisational system of 'school' has not yet taken control. At the same time, the peer group system is not unbrokenly maintained. When the teacher is present, the pupils cannot avoid observing, registering, and to a certain extent even performing, the territorial and symbolic gestures that acknowledge the lesson to come. Yet this happens in various intensities, with moments of rupture or suspension, and with a certain reluctance being shown to shedding one's playground identity and taking on the social identity of 'pupil'.

Mehmet's behaviour can be seen as an example of distancing himself from the role of conscientious pupil. He has already taken his seat and then begins to provoke his classmate. Stefan, in the process of fulfilling the institutionalised norm, manages to maintain his conscientious attitude. Yussif, on the other hand, does not stick as closely to the mode of preparing for the class as Stefan. After the scuffle between Mehmet and Stefan, he attacks Mehmet himself. This attack also remains playful in spirit and Yussif repeats the soothing gesture with which Mehmet had concluded his attack on Stefan. This time the 'victim' recognises the playful character of the attack. Mehmet allows Yussif to whisper something confidentially in his ear. In contrast to Stefan, both Mehmet and Yussif's behaviour implies a certain disdain towards the performance of actions which imply being ready for the lesson. This difference between the pupils and their mutual awareness of it might explain why Mehmet chooses to tease and provoke Stefan as opposed to Yussif, and why both Yussif and Mehmet understand the physical attack as a game.

At the same time as this interactive struggle between them occurs, a very different kind of interaction system develops in the classroom.

Tutor Group 5x, 12:16:54-12:17:38

Holding a piece of paper in his hand, Mr. Maier goes towards Jeanette who is already sitting at her desk writing. He says, "Here we are, Jeanette". He pulls a chair up, puts the paper on the desk, sits down on the chair opposite Jeanette and explains, "This is very good. (But) you must try and write a bit more accurately if you can." Nina gets up from her chair (close to the blackboard), comes over the middle aisle to where Mr. Maier and Jeanette are, and remains standing in the aisle at Jeanette's desk. She leans her arms on the desk and looks down at what is happening.

Ayla comes in, followed by Ömer. Ayla walks quickly to the middle aisle towards the cloakroom area. She meets David who is just taking his jacket off and comes to a halt briefly at Jeanette's desk. Ayla goes past him, and then turns around again and comes up to Jeanette's desk where Mr. Maier is still explaining things to Jeanette. He keeps nodding his head.

Meanwhile Ömer walks down the narrow gap between the desks and the right-hand wall (on the door side of the classroom). Dursum is sitting at his desk. As Ömer walks past he holds a thin black object in front of Dursum's eyes from behind. Dursum wards him off with his right hand. Ömer moves on, does a little turn around Dursum's desk and sits down at his place. Ömer bends down to his school bag and fumbles around in it, whilst Dursum half leans over the table and, looking at Ömer and saying something to him, grabs something from Ömer's desktop with his left hand and pulls it away. Ömer grabs both Dursum's hands which are holding the object.

Jana goes to Jeanette's desk with an exercise book in her hand. Mr. Maier is still sitting at Jeanette's desk talking to her and Nina is standing by listening. Jana stands half a metre away, following what's going on.

Medine gets up from her place and goes down the middle aisle to the group gathered around Jeanette's desk. She bumps into Ayla there, who is just turning around to go to the coat area. Medine remains standing next to Jana with her hands on her hips, looking at Jeanette and Mr. Maier. A moment later she too turns around and goes towards the coat area to approach Ayla who is now engaged in a conversation with Hatice near the coats. A lively and funny conversation develops between Yussif, Mehmet, Hatice, Ayla and Medine about a pupil from a class below.

A bit later David joins the groups standing around Jeanette. He comes to stand next to Jana and looks over Jeanette's shoulder onto her desk. For a moment, Jana lifts her exercise book up to her chest with both hands, and then she lets it drop again. Keeping her eyes constantly on the desk or on Mr. Maier, she moves a step forward when David approaches. David bends down to Jeanette and says something to her. Mr. Maier sits up. Jana says something to him and holds out her exercise book to him. He looks at the book, then shakes his head, gets up suddenly and walks swiftly to his desk, followed by Nina. The circle dissipates.

For the rest of the tutor group, the teacher's conversation with Jeanette means an extension of the threshold phase between break-time and lesson. Thus the rules that usually govern the children's behaviour at the beginning of a lesson are temporarily postponed, allowing scope for a continuation of non-lesson-related activities. But the fact that the teacher talks to Jeanette in quite a loud voice and that he faces the class (looking towards the centre of the room) gives his personal conversation something of the feel of a public lecture. Indeed, some pupils gather around in passive participation. They suspend what they were doing to follow the teacher's conversation. Jana seems eager to have her exercise book inspected too. The aisle has become a kind of auditorium for those who identify with such a teacher pupil relationship. What seems to have emerged here is a lesson scene directed towards a gradually growing sub-group of the tutor group. By communicating with his pupils in this low-key way the teacher asserts his authority to make his pupils follow the rules that govern the lesson. The effectiveness of his authority can be measured by the behaviour of those who stand around, in silence, waiting.

Ayla and Medine, on the other hand, quickly lose interest in what is going on around the teacher. They then move towards the coat hooks where they come to stand close to Hatice and engage in an interactive situation of their own with Hatice, Yussif and Mehmet. This seemingly amusing conversation takes place partly at one of the desks and partly in the bordering aisle. Again the aisle becomes a place to engage in conversation. This animated conversation is peer group oriented and involves making fun of a pupil they all know from another tutor group.

This distancing of certain pupils from the institutionalised procedure that directs the tutor group to get ready for the lesson is to be observed not only in the interactive event as a whole, but above all on a micro-level, in the short incidental interactive moments, such as when Ömer, walking down the narrow gap past Dursum to get to his chair, suddenly provokes Dursum, who is already seated. In so doing, not only does Ömer distance himself from the activity of sitting down for the lesson, but he also distracts Dursum from the lesson that is beginning. Provocations of this sort are a part of the shared field of experience (cf. Mannheim, 1982). What can be noted here is that as well as temporal coordinates spatial considerations (as in the narrowness of the gap) act as external factors which bring their influence to bear on all the various modes of interaction. Exactly how this happens depends on the particular social context.

When David and Andy join the group surrounding the teacher at Jeanette's desk the 'German circle' is completed. Despite the above average proportion of children of non-German origin in this class (65%), only children of German origin take part in this unofficial 'lesson'. In contrast, a lively peer group conversation develops a few feet away involving a group of children none of whom are of German origin. We may wonder to what extent this difference according to ethnic origin is due to the teacher's chosen mode of instruction as well as indirectly by his own ethnic origin. It is certainly interesting that the topic of the teacher's conversation is German spelling. Moreover, the addressee is a pupil who has a positive attitude towards the lesson all along. The fact that a school-affirming subgroup of the tutor group show respect for the lesson also reinforces the tendency in the other children to move away from the lesson and towards the frame of reference of break-time and the peer group.

How the school uses the blackboard area as a stage upon which to perform and demonstrate its authority

The area around the board is used predominantly by the teacher. It is generally situated at the front of the room and is a focal point which determines the position of other objects, such as tables and chairs. In most cases that we observed, this part of the tutor group territory was where the teacher's desk was placed. The board, its immediate surroundings and the teacher's desk still generally form the central part of the lesson. It is here that lessons are started and ended, oral and written information is conveyed, classwork and reports distributed; and it is to this place that pupils are summoned, even on occasion by the highest authority of the institution—as demonstrated in the following example.

It starts shortly after the teacher, Mr. Maier, announces the beginning of the English lesson and asks the pupils to get out the books and equipment they will need. All the children are sitting in their places.

Tutor Group 5x, 10:31:35-10:32:28

Mr. Maier walks from the blackboard area down the aisle through the class. "Right. English (...) Exercise books." He slowly backs down the aisle to Ömer. "Your book!" The headmistress enters. She has a pair of glasses on her head, is carrying a pile of papers in her left hand and walks slowly to the area in front of the blackboard. The teacher is moving backwards towards the desk. Suddenly he turns his head towards the door and sees the approaching headmistress. He nods at her. She says "Excuse me" and stands next to him in the middle of the blackboard area in front of the class with her right hand on her hip. She points briefly with her right hand at the front desk, which stands adjacent to the teacher's desk, and at which Tacim is sitting ... Ömer, who has lifted up an exercise book, calls out to ask "Mr. Maier, do you mean this one?" and lowers the book. Mr. Maier turns towards the headmistress and does not react to Ömer. The class is quiet. Mr. Maier asks, "What's the matter?" Nina, who is standing at her desk, moves a step closer to the headmistress and looks up at her face. The headmistress looks straight at Tacim. There is a moment of silence. "Where were you yesterday?" she asks in a firm tone. (...) "And where's your book?" The teacher moves a step to the side towards his desk. Nina turns to her table. After a short time, Tacim walks quickly to the headmistress with his book. He leafs through its pages, holding the book up to her so that she can read it. With his finger he points to two lines of writing. The headmistress takes her glasses from her head, lets the hand which is holding the glasses fall to her side, looks briefly at the exercise book and then at Tacim. "But what you have forgotten is that you are to report to my office every morning, (…) every day at midday!" Tacim looks at her and nods several times. The teacher, his hands resting on the desk, looks up at the headmistress. Nina is still standing at her table and, like most of the other pupils, appears spellbound by the headmistress and by what is going on in the blackboard area. The headmistress walks back two steps, reaches out with her right hand and puts her glasses back on her head. Tacim holds up the exercise book for another moment, closes it, and then returns to his seat. The teacher nods several times and says to the headmistress, "So I'm not supposed to remind him!?" The headmistress dismisses Mr. Maier's suggestion with her right hand stretched out flat. "You don't have to." "He's supposed to remind himself?" says Mr. Maier. "It's up to him!" says the headmistress at the same time, making a flat hand gesture towards Tacim. Mr. Maier, still leaning on the desk, nods, looks down and calls out "Tacim!" The headmistress turns round and leaves the room. The teacher (as do many of the children) gazes in the direction of the headmistress.

The presence of the headmistress has the non-negotiable effect of the English lesson being provisionally suspended. Priority is granted to the institutional matters that she represents. In accordance with the existing hierarchy, the interaction takes place via the teacher, who is informed of the matter through a gesture, by the summoning of a pupil from his seat. It then moves directly to the headmistress's actual addressee in the classroom, Tacim. The position she assumes in the classroom, and the fact that she is equipped with the corresponding requisites (pile of papers, reading glasses on her head), relate to this 'official duty'. She remains in a position of authority in the board area, near the desk, close to the somewhat surprised teacher. This area becomes transformed into the stage for the scene, the remaining space thus becoming the spectator's arena. As at the start of a theatrical performance, the play's opening silences the spectators. The teacher's question ('What's the matter?') is left unanswered by the headmistress, who focuses on Tacim, questioning him as in an inquisition. Mr. Maier moves silently to the back of the stage. The space becomes free for Tacim, who hurries up to the headmistress. He shows her the exercise book she is enquiring about and points to a written entry which legitimises his absence the previous day. Without paying attention to this evidence, she reasserts a behavioural rule already explained to Tacim which he has disregarded. This rule is designed to ensure control over Tacim's conduct, which has obviously been unsatisfactory so far. Tacim is to report to the headmistress twice a day, in what amounts to a face-to-face confrontation with the highest authority within the school. It is not only the sanction but the performance itself that clearly documents the oblique way in which the school management communicates with pupils. This humiliating ceremony is exaggerated to the extreme insofar as it is obviously staged by the headmistress to acquire maximum effect by drawing in the others as public spectators. Indeed, not only do the silent pupils play a role in heightening the dramatic effect of the scene but it is also significant that the class teacher is silenced and retreats into the background. The public admonishing of the individual pupil demonstrates the nature of institutional power to which Tacim publicly conforms, indeed is forced to conform. He remains silent and nods obediently.

What follows is the staging of institutional power through bodily movements and gestures by the departure of the school management from the stage, which coincides with the teacher's resumption of an acting role in front of the tutor group. Initially, he validates the headmistress's measures by nodding his head in acquiescence and inquiring as to whether he ought to enforce the imposed behavioural rule by reminding Tacim of what he is expected to do. However, the headmistress rejects this suggestion gesturally and verbally, indicating that part of the behaviour now required of Tacim is self-control. He ought not to need reminding of what he is to do. 'It's up to *him*.' The teacher's subsequent calling out of the pupil's name is linked precisely to this call for self-control. The interaction between Tacim and the headmistress as well as between the headmistress and the teacher, shows that behaviour management is a matter for the school as a whole and is under the control of the headmistress. This partially includes the control over *teacher* behaviour too, apparent in the headmistress's rejection of the teacher's participation in this disciplinary measure. We may also recognise the unequal balance of power in communication between headmistress and class teacher, whose authority is obviously undermined. By summoning Tacim as the headmistress leaves, he partially wins back his suspended role of actor in the class.

This scene documents in a particular way the effectiveness of performative elements in a context in which all involved are included, whether as spectators or actors. Alongside gestures, accessories, body language and the performative dimensions of speaking and being silent, the actors' spatial positioning in the classroom is particularly significant for the unfolding drama. The blackboard area functions as a stage for this scene and becomes the spatial centre of the institutional power personified in the headmistress. Silence, humility and heightened attention on the part of all those present characterise this ritual staging of the institutionally sacred.

How desks take on a function over and above that for which they were intended

Compared to the door and aisles, the desks are individual territories. However, this individual territory is also arranged and assigned a function as part of the school organisation. The ethos of the institution is expressed in the assigning of desks to particular pupils, as well as to certain positions in the form room. What the desk represents, however, is clearer than its function, which leaves room for individual and communal creativity.

Tutor Group 4y, 10:25

All the pupils from 4y are back in the classroom. Binol, Cennet and André are standing opposite Andrea, Lore, Sybille and Hanna at the latters' desks. They are talking.

Tutor Group 4y, 10:29

Binol comes from the back of the room to his desk with a book full of pictures (a comic, possibly). He sits down and looks at the book. Martin looks over from his seat, stands up, goes over to him and looks at the book over his shoulder. Binol and Martin talk.

In both situations the teacher is absent, the lesson has not yet officially started and the desk is used as a focal point. In the first example it is used as a meeting point and for creating the right amount of distance between the pupils for them to chat comfortably. In the second example, it is used as a surface upon which objects are displayed which are then viewed communally and which promote a sense of group identity.

Whilst in the second example a pairing of two children of the same gender but of different ethnic and cultural origins can be seen, the first example shows a whole group of children of both genders as well as of different ethnic and cultural origins. Both kinds of interaction contribute to constituting the sense of tutor group community. The classroom is used as a space where children choose who to interact with or befriend. Children's assignment to tutor groups has been sanctioned by the institution, and the children then accept this particular tutor group composition and adopt it as a 'community'.

This is particularly true for the first scene. The seven children are not part of a long-term stable friendship group. From our observations, friendship groups in this tutor group are mostly mono-gender and frequently also ethnically shaped. This interaction is thus all the more remarkable. Seven children, more than a quarter of the tutor group, (5) girls and (2) boys, (5) Germans and (2) migrant children meet in the form room, find common ground and remain together, at least for a period of time. It is in this way that the cohesion of the tutor group comes about. This cohesion is not based on ethnic or gender considerations, but instead on the way the school as an institution creates tutor groups made up of children of different genders and ethnic origins as part of the school policy of inclusion.

The desk in these interactions serves as a requisite that brings the participants close to each other, in a spatial sense, thus assisting communication between them. It is not clear whether such interaction, in view of its everyday repetition, can be described as ritualisation.

Tutor Group 5x, 12:15-12:16

Carlos grabs Andy by his clothes and pulls him from the corridor into the area between the blackboard and Nina's table. He flings him onto the floor, kneels on him and looks up. Nina, sitting alongside him, turns her head towards him. Carlos looks up at her and stands up, holding Andy with both hands by the collar and pulling him up too. At the same time, Nina stands up and moves around to the other side of the table. Carlos turns around and looks at Nina who is now standing opposite him behind the table. Carlos presses Andy's head and upper body on Nina's table. Nina looks on.

Tutor Group 4y, 10:26

Sabine enters the room immediately behind Sören. Sören goes to his table near the door, waving his hands in circular movements. From behind, Sabine pushes his upper body and head down onto the table with her right hand. She laughs at the same time. He lays his right arm on the table, bends it and supports his right cheek with his hand so that his upward movement ends just above the table top without his head touching it. During the upward movement Sören calls, "Oh, oh, oh, oh!"

Sabine walks on, stretches, radiates joy, holds her head up triumphantly and flicks her hair back. She puts her hands on either side of her coat which is already open, walks to her table, then turns to Sören (who after looking at her has now stood up), opens her coat wide and takes it off. Sören lowers his gaze, looks down at his table, picks up something there (a notepad?) and then puts it back down. Sabine continues to watch Sören while she is taking off her coat. In the meantime, Cennet, who was looking at Sabine while she was taking off her coat now comes into the desk-free space near Sabine. André and Canel follow. André trips up when he is walking between Cennet and Sabine, turns to Cennet and speaks to her. Sabine turns slightly towards Cennet. Canel, following André, pushes through André and Sabine and Sabine turns closer to Cennet.

Sören jumps onto his chair, stretches out, shouts out loudly "Eh, oh, … (unclear) …." and makes circling movements with his hands (the same as when he entered the room). Sabine turns towards him again, goes in his direction (or in the direction of the coat hooks behind him, holding her coat in her hand) and looks up at him. When she is with him, Sören jumps onto his chair, over Ece's chair, then onto Sabine's chair and eventually back onto the floor. Sabine watches all his movements and shouts "Maaaaaan!" Then she turns to the wall, hangs up her coat on the peg, turns round again and goes behind the teacher (who has just entered the room), towards her seat. Sören, on the other hand, walks towards his seat, holds onto Sabine's unoccupied chair while passing, and hops once on his left leg while the teacher is going around him. Whilst walking on, Sören pushes Sabine, who is walking behind the teacher coming towards him, and almost loses balance. Sabine turns round completely, comes to a halt at her chair, sits down, looks back at Sören and flicks her hair back with her left hand. Sören goes to his desk and sits on it—looking in Sabine's direction—next to his neighbour Paul, who is already sitting on his desk.

What we see here are ritualised games of power (topdogs/underdogs, taking possession of the territory of others) and gender. They generate and use those differences which give the threshold phase social structure. In the daily transitions from playtime to lessons they can always be detected, even if not always so clearly shaped.

The desk is used as a stage. This may not occur in the sense of conscious staging, like with a director, yet it does at least denote performances in which scenery, requisites and spectators all have necessary parts to play. The desk is used in a way that conflicts with its use as part of the school organisation. Through the fact that they take place in the space that belongs to the tutor group, and actors and spectators are all tutor group members, these 'anti-school' performances contribute to livening up what was at first merely a tutor group that was just a part of the organisational set-up of the school. Thus they help to create the sense of a world that belongs to the tutor group and ultimately to construct a sense of tutor group cohesion.

Let us take a closer look at the role of the desk. At the beginning of the first scene, the conflict between Carlos and Andy, which has started outside the classroom, is brought into it. What was initially a boxing fight between members of the tutor group in a context where different tutor groups were present has now become a closed performance within the tutor group. The exchange of glances between Carlos and Nina constitutes the decisive change here. The boxing fight becomes a performance in front of at least one spectator. Now another desk in the room gains significance: the female spectator's desk. On the one hand, it has a distancing function. Nina goes to the other side of the desk, placing it between herself and the fighters. It thus becomes the place from which she watches the boys' performance and defines herself as a spectator. On the other hand, the desk takes on the function of a stage or, in this case, of a sacrificial altar. Carlos pushes Andy's head and upper body onto Nina's desk, thus presenting himself as powerful and at the same time offering Nina Andy as a victim on her desk.

Although this kind of sacrificial offering is only rarely observed, the rituals of power that can be recognised in these examples are frequently performed in both classes. The second situation shows that such rituals take place also between the sexes. What we have here, however, is no longer a question of power but a ritual of love. The interaction takes on a lighter, more playful character at this point.

As Carlos does with Andy, Sabine pushes Sören's head and upper body down on to the desk. Sabine, however, is smiling and in view of the fact that Sören's head is lying comfortably on his arms, his groaning seems to be more in ecstasy than in pain. There is a similarly playful moment in the dance on the chair which draws Sabine's attention back to Sören. It becomes more serious, however, when Sören, perceiving Sabine's advance, flees across her desk and chair. This constitutes an infringement of her territory, which results in her gender-evoking protest ('Man!') as well as in a physical tussle between them. If Sabine's flick of her hair is to be interpreted as an expression of triumph, then the way Sören sits on his desk (mimetically copying neighbour Paul's pose) can be understood as an attempt to end the scene in a 'cool' and composed manner. The classmates follow all this, either directly or out of the corner of their eye. This is all in all a ritualised event which takes place inside the tutor group, the rules and meaning of which are accepted by those present and which strengthen their sense of community.

What sitting on a particular chair says about a pupil's attitude to school

Pupils' chairs form a significant part of every classroom. A chair places one in a fixed structure, specifies distances, and enlarges the space between those seated (Eickhoff, 1997: 493). Its use is meant to minimise physical movement, which is far less easily harnessed in children than in adults. Sitting, a position which every child is taught to adopt from the very first hour of school, is generally viewed as the best position in which to convey writing-related skills to a large number of children simultaneously. It is linked to a particular seating arrangement that is usually imposed for an extended period of time and often for several years, assigning each person to a particular chair. Quietening down and sitting in one's place is part of the attitude required of pupils for a lesson to begin. It is in this position that a child takes on the social identity of a pupil.

Where pupils sit is important

The process of carrying out the institutionalised practice of ensuring pupils are in their correct places at the beginning of every lesson often gives rise to certain conflicts, as is shown in the following example. All pupils are present in the classroom. The teacher is standing in the blackboard area.

Tutor Group 5x, 10:26:37-10:26:59

> Almost all the children are seated. Yussif wriggles his way through the narrow space between the overhead projector and David's chair in the middle of the classroom, putting his right hand temporarily on the overhead projector and his left hand on Ayla's desk. Yussif looks at the free chair in front of him and then looks in the direction of the coat hooks. All of a sudden he turns around completely and sits on Ayla's empty chair, to the left of Ömer, and at the same time says something in Turkish. Ayla comes out of the cloakroom area, goes directly over to Yussif, places her right hand on his right shoulder and says in an ironic, questioning tone, 'Hello Yussif'. Yussif stands up at once, Ayla takes her hand off his shoulder, makes a waving away gesture while taking a step back. Yussif takes a pen from the desk, and still standing, turns around, looks at Ayla and shows her the pen. Their faces meet a few inches apart. Ayla says "Stop it!" and stretches out her left hand for the pen. Yussif holds the pen in his hand and grinning returns to his chair at the

other table. "Hey, man, give it back!" shouts Ayla. Wrinkling her brow, she follows Yussif to his chair, stretching out her hand for the pen. She looks at Mr. Maier who is standing in front of his desk and then back at Yussif, who after a moment of waiting, holds out a long object. Ayla reaches out for it quickly and turns away. Whilst walking away she looks at the object, stands still for a moment, puts it in her other hand, turns back to Yussif and goes back to him, holding out her left hand again and gets the pen. Someone in the background laughs briefly. Ayla goes back to her place and sits down.

Yussif occupies Ayla's empty seat at a time when the teacher's position in the room and the fact that everyone has taken their places and is quiet suggest that lesson is about to begin. Only Ayla is still on the way back to her seat from the coat area. However, Yussif has taken her seat, thus playfully and subtly flouting the seating plan. At the same time, he starts a playful fight with Ayla which is part of the ritual peer group practice of provocative territorial infringement. By exchanging a few words in Turkish with the boy now next to him, Yussif draws Ömer into the game to back him as a spectator. And indeed, Ömer does nothing to drive away his new desk partner. Ayla defends her territorial claim with a few quiet words, the indexical content of which is immediately understood. Yet Yussif continues his ambiguous action by transferring the territorial fight onto Ayla's property, which he does by taking with him one of her possessions. It is significant that what he takes is a utensil for writing, an object of particular symbolic value in the context of *being ready for the lesson*. Demanding it back thus eventually becomes all the more urgent as the start of the lesson is imminent. Ayla now demands back her territorial right with increased vehemence, both in words and action, but to no avail. She then goes up to Yussif's desk herself to claim back her pen. Her glance at the teacher underlines her precarious situation, for she is in danger of potentially breaking one of the class rules, and being told off. The game is repeated again. This time Yussif appears performatively to comply with Ayla's request, but he deceives her by handing her a *different* object. Ayla turns to Yussif again and with resolute gestures insists that he return the object. Finally he does and she returns to her seat.

Yussif's complicated manoeuvre of deception repeatedly prevents Ayla from taking up the role of a pupil ready to start the lesson. This scene can be described as a form of playing around with assuming the social identity of the 'pupil', by means of which Yussif temporarily undermines the individual and territorial foundations of this identity. At the same time it can be considered a peer group ritualisation: a brief form of physical and expressive interaction between a boy and a girl, in the sense of a territorial transgression of boundaries which initiates a provocation, if not a successful public flirtation. The transition phase from playtime to lesson is particularly well suited to such activity. It offers a space for initiating new relationships, even if it also includes the danger of their failure. The liminality of this phase is shaped not least by ludic and performative elements.

Having to stay in one's own seat

The following example shows how a pupil attempts to negotiate with the teacher some leeway in the seating plan. It is taken from the transition phase from the first long morning break to the lesson. Mrs. Kasek is already present and most of the pupils have sat down and are supposed to be occupying themselves with reading, painting or such like. The children are partly talking among themselves so that there is a rather high noise level in the room. Some boys come into the room in dribs and drabs.

Tutor Group 5y, 10:27:34-10:28:14

> The teacher walks quickly from the back window area down the central aisle to the board area at the front. As she goes past Claudia's group table, Claudia interrupts her painting work, stands up, picks up her painting and follows the teacher. On the way she calls, "Mrs. Kasek!" Claudia stands in front of the teacher, who has now turned around to face the class, looks at her and says "I'd like to sit here. When it's time to do writing I'll go back to my place!" At the same time she points her left hand first at the empty place at the small table which is adjacent to the teacher's desk and not occupied and then at her own seat further back. Mrs. Kasek points her right index finger at Claudia's seat and says something briefly (unclear). Claudia takes another step towards the place in front, points at it again and says, "Yes, but I want to sit at the front!" She lets her hand drop to her upper thigh, shifts from one foot to the other and looks down for a moment at the floor. The teacher points firmly at Claudia's seat and shouts, "You'll sit in your own place". With a quiet whisper Claudia turns away, returns rapidly to her group table and sits down on her chair, eyes fixed on the side of the table next to the window. She calls out the name of her neighbour (out of camera shot), leans back, while the fingers of her right hand, almost forming a fist, are pulled back. Again she calls, "Excuse me, excuse me!" and waits for a moment. At the same time the teacher's bell rings several times. Claudia and the person sitting next to her sing out in short staccato notes: "Na-na-na-na-na," and Claudia makes the sign of a piece of paper

with her hand on the last syllable. Then Claudia waves her hand in a dismissive gesture, "Hey, I haven't yet..."; she pushes her chair back, picks up a pen and turns back to her painting which she has now put back on her table.

The children are following the directions set by the teacher in preparation for the lesson: *getting on, on their own in their own seats*. Claudia asks the teacher if she can sit in a different place. By taking drawing material with her she shows her readiness to continue with her individual task there. It also shows that she expects the teacher to acquiesce in her request. Claudia tries to make her request sound reasonable by assuring the teacher that she will return to her seat as soon as the lesson begins, in other words, when the rule structure that governs *lessons* is most binding.

The teacher rejects Claudia's request. Claudia's repeated attempt to assert herself, both verbally and through her body language, fails. In expressive gestures and with clear behavioural instructions regarding the seating plan, the teacher puts an end to the negotiation. The power relationship between teacher and pupil clearly proves to be one-sided. The most obvious power differences have to do with the institutionalised rules of the lesson, which it is in the power of the teacher alone to enforce or suspend. Claudia carries out the instructions, but not without some gestural resistance (a whining whisper). Having returned to her seat, she fails to get back to the task at hand, and instead turns towards her neighbour and plays a quick game and sings a song (part of a particular playground ritual), all in a tone of somewhat provocative resistance. This implicitly reactivates a playtime situation, in that there is a certain resistance to the lesson despite the fact that the seating plan, which is laid down by the rules, is adhered to. However, this moment of distraction does not last long. Claudia turns away from the game again and—after the teacher has rung a bell to signal the beginning of the lesson—pushes up her chair (i.e. she corrects her physical position and at the same time her stance to the lesson). She then resumes her drawing, returning to the process of being ready to take part in the lesson.

A fixed seating plan is an important condition for the lesson and a basic element of the transition ritual. Suspending this plan to cater to the individual needs of each pupil would seem to endanger the school rule system. As demonstrated in the example, any attempt to relax this rule by claiming an individual need is immediately rejected by the teacher. One way to relieve the resulting tension is by means of a performative act of resistance (however partial), involving a measure of rejection of the institutional rules and regulations.

Despite the significant differences between the two examples above, the framework is the same. The liminal phase from peer group-structured playtime to the institutionally-structured lesson allows for playing with or negotiating a partial suspension or postponement of the latter. In the last scene this threshold character is also revealed in the fact that after Claudia's attempt to sit elsewhere is rejected, she immediately has recourse to the typical form of interaction within her peer group: a shared game.

The seating plan facilitates the teacher's supervision of a large number of children, makes it easier to register those who are present or absent, and communicates the ethos of the school to the children. Depending on the class as well as on the school's educational policy and ethos, the seating pattern can vary from a system where all the desks are facing the front board to a decentralised pattern involving group tables. Moreover, the extent to which children are free to choose their own seats in relation to other pupils, as well as in relation to the teacher and the lesson, may also vary widely. Thus from the seating arrangement we can see the children's social relationships within the classroom in terms of both the way they are organised by the school and also peer group interaction systems.

Clothes as personal accessories

Just as there is a variety of ways of coming into the classroom we also note that pupils have a variety of attitudes towards their clothes. It is possible to roughly differentiate between two main approaches. Some children take off their coats, jackets etc. upon entering or when they are inside the classroom, and immediately take them to the coat area and hang them up. Others, largely corresponding to those who remain in the door area, keep their outdoor clothes on for longer after they have entered the classroom, and in some cases until the teacher has entered the room. The first pattern can be interpreted as a procedure that is part of preparing for the lesson and is thus school-affirmative. The second may be regarded as an attempt to postpone or delay the lesson and is thus school-resistant. A third and special point is some children's attitude towards headgear. Those who wear caps or hats treat them in terms not only of a particular youth culture, but even of rituals in the narrow sense, since this does not only involve repetition but also mimesis and a process of making something sacred.

What taking off a coat says about a pupil's attitude to learning

Tutor Group 5x, 10:22

The door opens. Jeanette, Uzman, Martina, Ulak, Sabah, Jana, Stefan, Andy and David walk towards the coat area. Some children are taking off their jackets as they go. Jeanette comes back quickly from the coat hooks without her jacket and goes to her place. Uzman walks to the coat hooks with his jacket on his arm. David, with his jacket on, goes to the shelf which separates the left from the right hooks and begins to take off his jacket and scarf. Uzman comes back from the coat hooks without a jacket.

Tutor Group 4y, 10:26

The door is unlocked from the outside and opened. Within the following thirty seconds the children enter the room in a continuous stream. Birgiel is the first to enter (in a coat). She goes to her seat, takes her coat off and hangs it over her chair. Cennet goes to her table, opens her coat, takes it off, goes back, and takes it to the coat hooks by the door. Upon entering the room, Lisa turns immediately into the aisle that leads to the coat hooks, between Paul and Sören's table and the wall, takes off her coat, hangs it up and goes to her place. Samuel goes to his table, takes his coat off, turns round, goes back, takes the coat to the coat hooks next to the door, hangs it up there and goes back towards his seat. Sabine, who has gone to her seat with her coat still on, goes back to the coat hooks, takes off her coat in front of Sören, standing at his table, and hangs it up.

Common to these two examples is the fact that two clear actions (taking off one's outdoor clothing, hanging it up on the hooks) take place in rapid succession immediately upon entering the classroom. There is a close connection between clothes-related movements and the space-related movements leading towards the coat hooks and towards one's own place in the classroom. Common to the patterns of action in each tutor group is the fact that four sets of movement are connected (two are clothes-related and two are space-related). What we have here is a ritualised connection of movements rather than a ritualised sequence of movements, which is found in both tutor groups to the same extent. For indeed the sequence, which characterises a ritualisation in a narrow sense, varies between the two tutor group groups observed but remains relatively uniform within each individual tutor group.

This activity pattern can be interpreted as an affirmation of the rules and regulations of the institution. The fact that the children take off their outdoor clothing shows that they expect to stay in the classroom for a significant period of time and accept this, thus showing that they are ready for the lesson to begin. Taking off and hanging up their outdoor clothing within seconds of the classroom door opening limits the playtime mode of activity to an absolute minimum within the classroom. At least with regard to clothing an attitude of lesson readiness is brought about instantly upon entry to the classroom.

There are, however, perceptible differences between the two tutor groups. In Year Five more children take off and hang up their outdoor clothing as soon as they enter the room than in Year Six. Age difference or the different stages of child development possibly play a role here. More ten-year-olds enter into the set ritual and thus comply with the rules and regulations of the institution than eleven-year-olds (and those Year Six pupils who do so seem younger than their classmates).

The strikingly visible difference between dominant sequences of action is more difficult to explain. While those children from Year Six who have a positive attitude to school generally go directly from the door to the coat hooks to hang up their outdoor clothing and then sit down, Year Five children tend first to go to their own place, then to the coat hooks near the door and finally back to their seat. Two possible interpretations seem to make sense here. Firstly, the route to the coat hooks in the Year Six form room leads across the room itself and therefore not only do some of the children have to walk past their places to get there but they have to walk across the expanse of the room to get to the coat hooks. This in itself allows the playtime mode of activity to be sustained and sets a lively tone in the room. In Year Five, on the other hand, the coat hooks are situated next to the door, which prevents such a threshold period and enforces an abrupt end to the playtime behaviour directly when the children enter the room. Secondly, however, the fact that Year Five tutor group members tend to go straight to their places can also be interpreted as expressing an affirmative attitude towards the institutional ethos. The observation that the class seating arrangement is already mimetically implied upon entry by the Year Five pupils supports this interpretation. Several desk pairs, pupils who sit next to each other during class, go through the doorway next to each other and enter the room at the same time.

Keeping on one's coat as an extension of break-time
Tutor Group 5x, 10:23-10:26

> 10:23: Ömer and the older girls who have come in behind him, Ayla, Hatice and
> Medine, remain near the door ... 10:26: Ayla, Medine and Hatice come back in.
> Mr. Maier comes in. ... Ayla and Hatice take off their jackets, walk towards the
> cloakroom and leave the camera line of vision. Ayla comes back into view without
> her jacket and goes to her place ...

Only at second glance can what happens here be recognised as a ritualised
removal of clothes. What strikes the eye at first glance are the three girls' diverse
activities near the door, their peer group interaction and their frequent going
out and coming back into the form room. These activities take place between
10:23 and 10:26 and the events in the door area can be interpreted as a form
of anti-school ritual. This can also be detected in the attitude displayed here
towards outdoor clothing. The behavioural pattern of Ayla, Hatice, and Medine
is characterised by them not taking off outdoor clothing until the teacher has
entered the room and shut the door. This shows a negative attitude towards the
learning situation. Those still wearing their anoraks after the teacher has come
in give an impression of unwillingness to remain in a certain place, let alone
sit in a specific place and work. The beginning of the lesson is delayed by this
attitude towards outdoor clothing.

We were also able to identify intermediate practices, when a child slightly
delays taking off and hanging up his or her outdoor clothes. Thus, children may
be seen taking off their jackets particularly slowly, or a child may first turn to
a fellow pupil and communicate briefly before hanging up their coat. However,
these kinds of delaying behaviour vary too much from day to day and from child
to child for us to be able to speak of ritualised behaviour. Moreover, they do
not seem to function as ritual knowledge, for they do not attract the attention
of other pupils and are not an object of mimetic activity.

Headgear: The ritualised treatment of an everyday object

A particularly interesting ritual has to do with the children's attitude to headgear
(caps or woolly hats). There are not many cap or hat wearers in the tutor groups
observed. But those who are stand out in the strikingly reverential manner with
which they treat their headgear, so much so that one could certainly speak of
their behaviour as a ritual in a narrow sense. In a performative way, and not least
in the many ways in which they pick up each other's headgear-related actions

mimetically, this ritual contributes not only to individual but also to collective identity. Headgear is a personal possession and is protected as such, but those children who wear hats have something in common and can locate each other and interact more easily. Headgear constitutes a stylistic expression of a certain peer culture.

Tutor Group 5x, 10:25

> Ayla, wearing her jacket and cap, goes along the wall from the door to the coat area, leaving the camera's line of vision. Shortly afterwards she reappears (with jacket and cap) in the camera's line of vision, places her cap on the desk, turns round and goes back towards the coat hooks.

Tutor Group 4y, 10:26-10:31

> In rapid succession, Martin, with his coat still done up, André and Binol, with a red cap on his head, enter the room. (Five minutes later, the others have long since hung up their coats, the teacher has already been in the room once, and has left to go and get something.) Binol, standing at his table, takes off his cap, runs his hand through his hair and, holding the cap in his hand, answers Birgiel who is speaking to him. When Birgiel goes back to her seat he puts the cap back on his head. When Mrs. Kasek enters the room again, Binol takes his cap off again and puts it on the desk.

It is obviously common practice that you keep your cap with you. This suggests that a high value is attached to the cap as personal property, possibly even as a sign, either of belonging to a particular group of classmates who are already showing teenage characteristics, or as a sign that, at least as far as headgear is concerned, you are ready at any moment during the lesson to be dressed to leave the room.

Another striking feature is that caps are not placed on the desks until the last minute, just before the teacher starts the official lesson. This suggests that cap wearing tends to have a lesson-delaying function and is thus a school-resistant practice.

Finally, we may note that the descriptions reproduced here do not contain detailed information on the way in which the caps are placed on the desk. However, the notion of 'placing' implies clearly that it is not a question of carelessly throwing or dropping, but of a quiet and dignified depositing and that where the caps are put is precisely on that taboo surface, which, during the lesson, is officially reserved for lesson equipment.

Lesson equipment

The liminal nature of the transition to the lesson makes lesson equipment important, i.e. pens, books, and other objects needed for the lesson. As long as these have not yet become integral parts of a lesson that has officially begun, they may acquire anti-structural significance (e.g. take on a ludic dimension) or assume a meaning that relates to another structure (e.g. the peer group). Three patterns of behaviour with regard to lesson items may be distinguished: 1) lesson-preparatory behaviour, including showing or giving lesson items to the teacher; 2) peer group-related behaviour, including taking other children's lesson items; 3) how individual pupils play around with lesson items.

The ritual of showing or giving the teacher something to
indicate a positive attitude to the lesson to come
The phase between playtime and lesson allows for two-way interaction between individual pupils and the teacher to take place. This form of communication is very different from formal lessons, which are mainly conducted from the front, yet it can be viewed as affirming the lesson to come in that, by seeking one-to-one interaction with the teacher, the pupils express and openly confirm their acceptance of the teacher's authority to solve problems, supervise work and to recognise, accept or reject the pupils' achievements.

This two-way interaction usually involves a particular lesson item being shown, given, handed over or taken. In transition phases it is mostly the children who show or give the teacher something, although in some cases a teacher may hand out something to a pupil. The teacher's part in this obviously familiar and routine pattern of interaction usually consists in making a comment of acceptance or rejection of what the pupil presents.

Tutor Group 5x, 12:17
With an exercise-book in her hand, Jana goes over to Jeanette's table, where Mr. Maier is sitting talking to Jeanette and Nina is standing listening. She stops half a metre away and follows the events. As David goes past, Jana takes a step back, looks to the right for a while, and then goes back to Jeanette's table. Mr. Maier continues to explain something to Jeanette. He nods his head and keeps eye contact with her. Some time later David moves over to the group with Jeanette, stands next to Jana and looks over Jeanette's shoulder onto the desk. Jana raises her book to chest height with both hands, lowers it again, looks at the desk or at

Mr. Maier, and takes a step forward when David approaches. David bends down to Jeanette and speaks to her. Mr. Maier straightens up. Jana speaks to him and holds her exercise-book out to him. Mr. Maier looks at it, shakes his head, stands up and goes towards his desk, followed by Nina. Jana goes back to her seat with her exercise book.

Although the event takes place before the official start of the lesson, Jana finds Mr. Maier in a lesson-type situation, since he is explaining something to Jeanette. Jana approaches the teacher gradually, moving forwards and backwards in a balancing act between approaching and distancing. This shows that she respects the relationship between the teacher and the pupil, which contributes performatively to instigating a lesson-like structure before the official start of the lesson. Jana raises and lowers her book in search of eye contact with Mr. Maier. This is a rather timid and weak signal, to which Mr. Maier does not appear to react. The fact that Jana does not respond to the teacher's non-reaction underlines the fact that she subjugates herself to the power to make decisions that lies in his hands. It is not until another pupil speaks to Jeanette and Mr. Maier does not protest, but straightens his upper body to declare an end to the conversation that he was engaged in at the desk, that Jana speaks to him and holds out her book to him. It is not just the fact that what she offers is a lesson item, but it is the very act of beginning to present him with something that affirms the teacher's authority or rather the rules that enforce this authority at school and in lessons.

A ritualisation is at work here insofar as it is possible to recognise a fixed sequence that occurs in the same or a similar way everyday. The initial situation is dominated by the teacher, the pupil in question approaches the teacher respectfully and presents something to the teacher, the teacher makes a positive or negative comment, in some cases the object is handed over, and finally the pupil returns to their seat. There is, moreover, a kind of 'sacred' dimension to these ritualisations. It is recognisable in the pupils' respectful manner of approaching the teacher by which they show a practical knowledge of taboos, as well as in the lesson item itself, which by its school-relatedness legitimises the pupil's approach towards the teacher.

Provoking fellow pupils by taking their things
Another everyday ritualisations of lesson equipment involves using the item as a means of provocation in at least two respects. On the one hand, the provocation

may be directed a personal possession of a particular pupil. An attack of this kind is aimed at establishing a relationship between peers, giving rise to a particular hierarchy either between two classmates or, if spectators are present, within the tutor group 'community'. On the other hand, it can also be directed at the item as what it represents, i.e. something that is needed for the lesson. As such the aim of the attack is to disrupt the school ethos because the item and where it is placed (e.g. pencil case on desk, pen in pencil case) are implicitly part of this.

There are essentially two different ways in which this type of interaction occurs. A pupil either objects or does not object when another pupil grabs something that belongs to him or her. In the following, both types of interaction will be illustrated.

Tutor Group 5x, 10:25

Dursum walks slowly towards the coat hooks. As he passes Ulak, who is already sitting at his desk, he has a word with him and then suddenly pulls Ulak's woolly hat right over his head from behind. Ulak frees himself, stands up and goes to the neighbouring desk. Dursum then takes a pair of scissors out of Ulak's pencil case, plays with them, turns to Ulak smiling, holds the scissors out to him and gesticulates with them (pretending to cut off his hair). He goes back to Ulak's table, motions across the desk to the window, snips around with the scissors, turns around and holds the scissors up to the camera for a moment. Ulak moves back to his table. Dursum puts the scissors back in Ulak's pencil case. Ulak sits down at his desk again.

Tutor Group 4y, 10:27

Binol approaches Martin's desk and takes a pen out of the pencil case which is lying there. Martin, who is rolling up a (break-time sandwich) paper bag, packs it in his bag, drops onto his chair, says something to Binol and points to the milk bottle with his finger. He then takes a small ruler from the pencil case. They both talk, while Binol busies himself with the pen and the lid and Martin fiddles around with the ruler, sliding it to and fro on the table. Then Binol turns away, takes one step to the side, looks over to the window ..., looks towards the board, then to the door, where Samuel is passing on his way to the coat hooks, then back to the pen, with which his hands are constantly occupied. Binol looks over to Samuel, then ahead; he then walks down the middle aisle, stops and leans on the front of the overhead projector, and observes the events in the board area, still with Martin's pen in his hands. Martin, still busy with the ruler, stands up, moving backwards, and goes over to the overhead projector. He stands behind it, leans on the glass surface with his arms crossed, and looks at the surface and the tin containing pens. Shortly afterwards, Binol turns away, walks down the narrow aisle where the projector is, to the back of the room, past Sybille (coming towards him) and Martin. He quickly puts the pen down on Martin's table and carries on. Martin looks at him and follows him later to the window area.

In the first scene the formation of a hierarchy within the tutor group is extended to the attitude towards an item used in lessons. Dursum, who is bigger than Ulak, takes a pair of scissors away from him, without encountering protest. This interaction shows, both to those involved and to potential spectators, that a 'big versus little' relationship exists between the two boys on both a physical and a social level.

The dichotomy between identifying with the peer group and complying with the rules of the teaching group is also played out here. Ulak is among the first pupils to come back into the room after break and to immediately take off his outdoor clothes and sit down. It is therefore no coincidence that Dursum chooses to take Ulak's scissors out of his pencil case. This is an attack not only on Ulak's territory but also on the particular group of children that have a positive attitude to the lesson. This is recognisable in the behaviour involved in the way Ulak enters the classroom, his tidy desk and his well-organised pencil case. The end of the sequence nonetheless suggests that Dursum finally accepts rules of possession (he places the scissors back on Ulak's table) as well as the rules of the classroom (he places them in the pencil case). The scene thus demonstrates provocation but not rebellion.

The second example can be understood in a similar way. Here too power and hierarchy within the tutor group are established. Binol demonstrates his affinity with the anti-school crowd by means of his cap, his provocative behaviour with the milk bottle etc. even more than Dursum in 5x, where there are several pupils who wear hats or caps. Inversely, Martin, like Ulak, is among the children who return quickly to their places after break and are the most absorbed in the week's learning activities and the quickest to immerse themselves in the lesson-related work mode. Here we are not only confronted with the establishment of power relations between children of the same age but also with an attack on the rules of the classroom and on Martin's positive attitude to lessons. Like Dursum, Binol does not carry his action beyond a certain limit.

Both examples differ from each other in one significant respect, however. While Ulak seems intimidated by Dursum, and his lack of resistance appears to be justified by fear, Martin's lack of resistance appears to be more of a concession. The mimetic aspects of Martin's behaviour support this interpretation. His game with the ruler emulates Binol's game with the pen. When Binol goes to the projector and leans on it, he follows suit. When Binol plays with the pen there, Martin looks into the pen tin. When Binol goes past Martin's table to the window, Martin follows him again. This is backed up by observations of Martin and Binol's interactions in other situations. Binol is obviously more important for Martin than the pen. Although Martin has a positive attitude to school and is one of those who contribute well to lessons, he allows Binol to continue for a short while and seeks contact and commonality with a child of the same age.

Other forms of interaction may be observed in which the taking away of an item used in lessons gives rise to resistance.

Tutor Group 5x, 12:17

Ömer enters the classroom behind Ayla, wearing a cap turned to one side. He walks quickly along the wall on the right hand side of the classroom, and holds a narrow, black piece of material in front of Dursum's eyes from behind. Dursum fights this off. Ömer does a small turn around Dursum's desk and sits down quickly at his place, opposite Dursum. (…) Ömer bends down to his bag and rummages around in it. Dursum leans over, looking at Ömer, half on the desk, speaks to him and grabs an object from Ömer's desk. Ömer seizes Dursum's hands, which are holding the object. Ayla follows the events while drinking out of a cup.

Tutor Group 4y, 10:31

Cennet observes the events in the class. When Canel and Samuel finally stand up and go to the middle of the room, Cennet stands up and walks diagonally across the room directly towards Sören. She bends down to him, speaks to him, and motions to something in the open exercise book. Sören finally takes it away and closes it. Cennet tries to grab hold of the book. Sören holds the book closed in front of his chest. When the teacher appears Cennet turns away.

All three pupils involved in the first example are cap or hat wearers and thus associate themselves with the behaviour of the bigger children in the tutor group. And indeed, the children's social position is the main issue in this scene. First Ömer attacks and Dursum counter reacts; then Dursum attacks and Ömer counter reacts. Each attempts to subjugate the other but neither succeeds. It is unclear whether the set lesson ethos implied by the desk area and its items is also being attacked and defended. The scene shows a conflict that occurs within a peer group. It can be interpreted not only as the pupils struggling to gain social dominance over each other but also simply as a game. Ayla has the function of a spectator. Whatever Dursum and Ömer do, it happens before Ayla's eyes. It is a performance. The outcome of the conflict is undecided. Both have preserved their image as 'big' members of the tutor group.

In the second example the players also have 'big' or cool status. Cennet is one of the few who, in the transition from playtime to the lesson, often walk out of the room again. Sören is the boy in this tutor group who is most popular with the girls. Generally speaking, Cennet and Sören are developing into teenagers. Whereas the first scene shows a conflict between boys carried out in front of a girl, here direct interaction occurs between a girl and a boy. The exercise book functions as an anchor for interaction between the sexes. This piece of lesson equipment provides a concrete excuse for them to move closer to each other.

At first sight, what seems different in this case is the involvement of the female spectator. Whereas in the second scene the teacher's entrance as a potential spectator puts an end to the interaction, in the first case the fact that Ayla is watching perhaps even encourages Dursum and Ömer. At second glance, however, how a spectator affects the interaction does not differ greatly in the two scenes. In both examples the interaction is a performance aimed at a female spectator. The first of these (Ayla) indirectly supports identifying with the peer group, and the second supports identifying with the class whose lesson is about to start (with the arrival of the teacher). The fact that the interaction is a performance thus helps define whether the taking of somebody's things is to be understood as a way of gaining peer group recognition or as a way of causing disruption to classroom learning.

Communicating with objects in the classroom

We see our final example less in terms of a ritualisation than as an aestheticisation, or a sensual appreciation, of classroom objects.

Tutor Group 5x, 10:26

Yussif remains standing next to the overhead projector; he embraces it with his hands and observes the surface. The light of the projector turns on briefly, then off again.

Tutor Group 4y, 10:28

Claudia turns away and goes back towards her seat via the middle aisle. Passing the overhead projector she pauses, touches the cellophane slide lying on top of the overhead projector and continues in the direction of her seat.

Tutor Group 4y, 10:28-10:29

After Mrs. Kasek has left the area in front of the teacher's desk, Sybille, who is still standing there, takes the CD which Yussif left there, looks at it briefly, turns it over again and moves her head and upper body as if she is dancing.

The children's behaviour with regard to the projector and the things on their teacher's desk is not especially to do with the idea of a community and its structure, but appears to constitute a game without rules, in which the children communicate, as it were, with the objects. This is an aestheticisation process insofar as such behaviour seems to be aimed at incorporating, extending and intensifying the person's perception of certain objects.

When Yussif puts his hands around the overhead projector, he is making it accessible to other senses beyond vision. At the same time, he embraces the apparatus, as if it is a friend of his. Moreover, the fact that he turns the light on and off indicates his sense of fun for testing, experimentation and play.

Similarly, Claudia not only pauses on her way to her seat next to the projector, she reaches out and touches it, that is, employs her haptic sense alongside that of vision (aestheticisation). She does not embrace the projector but only touches the cellophane slide on top of it. Again, such a strong attraction seems to emerge between the pupil and the object that the pupil may be seen to enter into a physical dialogue with the object.

The extent to which the children's dialogue with certain objects takes on a physical dimension is illustrated most clearly in the third example. Touching and examining a CD is sufficient to generate imaginary music, and to incite Sybille to move her body in dance.

Even if this dialogue with objects cannot be equated with a ritual or ritualisation in the narrower sense and does not amount to social interaction, and even if it is mostly a one-off event, not to be repeated, there is something in this activity that is common to rituals and ritualisations: the event acquires a particular atmosphere, a sacred component.

The creation and confirmation of children's social identities

This chapter has focused on ritualisations of children in everyday school life through which a sense of community is generated in a performative way. The *transition phase between break-time and lesson time* is our focal point because actions overrun from the one into the other. This is where the different positions and attitudes of the children and diverse key situations of school activities are to be seen and where different forms of community emerge. The transition reveals itself to be a *threshold phase*, or a liminal phase in Turner's sense, which is characterised by structural weakness. The organising system of the lesson has not yet been fully established; yet the playtime activity of the peer group can no longer continue uninterrupted.

The actions and interactions of the pupils, as actors within the social space of the classroom, are determined by the way the institution organises the areas within the school, the timing of the school day and various furnishings and requisites. The pupils relate to these elements differently depending on which group they see themselves as identifying with. They include the doorway area, aisles and blackboard area, desks, chairs and seating arrangement, playtime and classroom items and objects and it is these elements that have led us through our analysis of the threshold phase.

A wealth of ritualisations, ritualised sequences and mimetic interactions are apparent. They have a structuring effect on the structurally weak liminal phase. At the same time they contribute to strengthening and forming smaller school 'communities' (with children identifying with a peer group, tutor group, or teaching group). Where they strengthen tutor group and teaching group solidarity, they also construct the ethos of the school as an institution.

The formation of boundaries and differences is stored in such ritual production of community. The way space, time, and objects are used in the ritualisations leads to differences emerging between various peer groups with regard to their collective behaviour and to where their specific boundaries are set.

At the same time, differences in attitudes and behaviour towards school rules are particularly noticeable. They can be interpreted as differing degrees of being pro or anti school. We speak therefore of *ritualisations which demonstrate either a positive or a negative attitude to school* and of peer groups which are firmly on one side or the other.

The ritualised drawing up of boundary lines, which helps to shape the specific community of the tutor group, indicates *ethnic* belonging, belonging to a certain *state of development* (child versus teenager) as well as belonging to a certain *school tutor group*. As regards *gender* and gender relations, we find numerous ritualisations that play with boundaries as well as those that mark out clear boundaries. The threshold phase between break-time and the lesson is particularly suited for such ritualisations. It offers moments of *communitas*, features possibilities for experimenting with new relationships, is pervaded by ludic and staging elements, and has dramatic features.

Certain territories and props give rise to ritualisations of *sacred spaces and objects*. Thus, in the boundary that frames ritualisations, the door can become a taboo threshold for children from other tutor groups. The performative entry ban carried out in such ritualisations contributes to creating a tutor group 'community'. Another example is the children's ritualised behaviour with regard to their caps and woolly hats.

With regard to our focus on the individual spatial or physical surroundings and the ritualised behaviour of the children within and with them, the following are important.

In the *doorway area* essentially two types of ritualisation can be observed. On the one hand, multi-level rituals of expulsion present the classroom door as a threshold that is not to be crossed by children from other classes. With this staging of the doorway as a boundary, the tutor group, that is part of the way the school is organised, is established and strengthened as a 'community'. On the other hand, ritualisations can be observed in which children from outside are allowed to enter. In one case entry is legitimised institutionally, in another it is peer-group related.

In the liminal phase, the classroom *aisle* constitutes a forum for close exchange and interactive involvement among peers. In the lesson context the area in front of the board becomes a 'sacred place'. Occupation of the *blackboard area* by the standing teacher in contrast to the seated pupils is a ritual that marks the beginning of the lesson. The actors' spatial position creates an asymmetrical structure. The board area is used as a space from which institutional authority is expressed.

With regard to the *desks*, there is a difference between the ritualised design of the desks as lesson-related work surfaces and their use as requisites for the development and clarification of relationships within the tutor group. Examination of the latter use reveals three varieties of everyday ritual sequences. Firstly, the desk serves as a place to meet and have a chat. Secondly, it becomes a stage for presenting power or affection within the tutor group (especially boy-girl interaction) and exclusion. Thirdly, and partly connected with this, ritualised interactions can be observed which focus on the desk as a personal space.

Sitting on a *chair* quietly is an important ritual marker in the transition from playtime to lesson. It signals a readiness for the lesson; it has an effect on the establishment of order and it indicates the end of the structurally weak liminal phase. Delaying the process of taking one's seat, or provocatively occupying another child's seat, are ritual ways of coping with and processing difference that contrast with the attitude of pupils who are ready and waiting for the lesson to begin. The arrangement of the seats and the positioning of the pupils in relation to each other and to the sacred place of the blackboard area, enables a performance of the school class to take place, both as a part of the whole school organisation and as a collection of peer groups who may all have different interests.

The children deal with their *clothes* in the transition from playtime to lesson in a way which, in view of its everyday repetition, its performative structure and the fact that the clothes sometimes take on a sacred quality, can also be described as ritualisation. Particular differences are to be observed between children who promptly hang up their outdoor clothing in a school affirmative spirit of being ready for lessons and those who, in a school-resistant attitude, will not relinquish their outdoor clothes. Finally, some children's attitude towards their headgear was noted, which has a ritual character not least insofar as it assigns these objects a sacred quality.

Essentially three approaches to *classroom objects* can be identified in the liminal phase. To show or give the teacher items that have to do with the organisation or relate to the lesson before the lesson starts, is a school-affirmative ritualisation which contributes to the development of a sense of belonging to a teaching group. The second approach, in which items needed for the lesson are taken away from conscientious fellow pupils, provokes the pupils concerned and is also a statement of opposition to the institution of school. The third approach amounts more to an aestheticisation of these objects, since it is solely concerned with the embodiment of certain things in the classroom.

Although we are aware of the danger involved in summing up our results in a sentence, perhaps, in conclusion, we might say that a wealth of children's ritualisations can be detected in the everyday liminal phase of school transition from playtime to lesson, which is structurally weak. These ritualisations make use of the spatial-physical surroundings in a specific way which lends them also a sacred quality. They contribute to the formation of pro-school and anti-school peer groups and to the development of a particular tutor group identity, which in turn contributes to the creation of a sense of cohesion in lessons.

Chapter 3

GoGo performance in the playground

A primary school playground is where children meet and learn to coexist. If we see schools as places where children and teenagers are taught according to didactic concepts in groups, then the playground represents a space which, compared to the classroom, is less institutionally shaped. A playground in the inner city is a space of high social density and heterogeneity. Children of various ages from different backgrounds, family compositions, countries of origin and speaking different languages meet here. Although we are interested in all that goes on in the school playground, interaction between the children in Years Six and Seven is observed in more depth.

The activities in the playground are largely structured by the children themselves. They do this, as becomes clear in the course of the first field observations, primarily by means of games, i.e. throwing games, ball games, catching or hopping games. This suggests that any one of these games can offer an insight into child culture, their values, rituals and of the way they establish common ground, and it can also shed light on their behaviour and attitudes towards social differences. Our thesis is that socialisation takes place by means of rituals, and we find that the investigation of games reveals a special facet of rituals. Just as rituals contain playful moments, games are strongly characterised by ritual elements. In order to trace the ritual character of games, therefore, we will take the 'GoGo game' as an example and look at it in detail. This game was a favourite amongst the children of the primary school we investigated between September 1999 and February 2000.

First, the children's game is elucidated as an insight into the complex events in the school playground. The main part of the analysis reveals two aspects of the complexity of children's games through empirical examples. First of all we examine the GoGo game as part of a social exchange system among children, where we see the game as relating closely to the practice of exchange and giving, and secondly we look at the community-forming aspects of the game. We also introduce the different forms of participation in game events and describe the different ways in which boundary lines are drawn up by participants, both between themselves as players and also between players and spectators. We will now look at the subject of child culture which helps us draw together the main strands of the project.

Playground

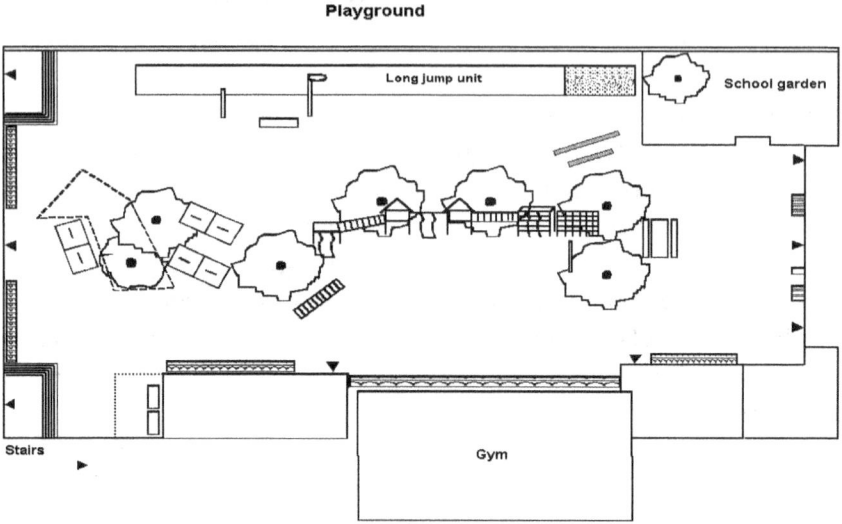

Figure 1: The school playground

Ethnography of the school playground: observing a playing 'crowd'

The school corridors are a popular place for the children's throwing games. A lot of them play the GoGo game in the school building when they are waiting for the lesson to begin in front of the closed classroom door, or when they come together in the stairways, after the autumn holidays have begun or during the Christmas Bazaar. However, the children's favourite place for this activity is the playground, which is surrounded by walls or fences, and serves as a space for recreation and relaxation in between lessons for the approximately 360 pupils in the school. The teachers spend break in the staff room. All communal activities take place in the playground in a very confined space. Each child must learn to find his or her way under these socially crowded conditions. The ethnographer of primary schools, Philip Jackson, talks about 'learning to live in a crowd' (Jackson, 1968: 10). For a child it is impossible to be alone in the playground for a long period of time without incurring a loss of prestige. The children generally master this situation by developing social activities; in many cases they play games and are in constant physical motion.

The playground 'corners' are favoured by the children for chosen games. The 'prisoners' of the girls-catch-boys game (and vice versa) are brought into and held in the covered entrance to the gym. Games take place in larger groups on the basketball field. Games such as French skipping and other hopping or throwing games which are obviously defined by clear rules are played near the school; the climbing apparatus is included in catch and all sorts of boisterous games; play fights take place on the only non cement-covered area. The children play at chasing each other around the table tennis table, and nearby, clapping and singing games take place. Many games, especially the catching games and chases around the table tennis table, are played by girls and boys; others, such as French skipping or football, are more often played in gender homogenous groups. Football is almost exclusively played by boys, although sometimes a girl is brought in as goalkeeper.

School as an institution consists of four levels of school event. First, there are the official lessons and school framework, secondly, negotiation processes between teachers and pupils, thirdly, there are the unofficial lesson activities of the pupils which contribute significantly to what the lesson actually is, and fourthly the actions among the children in which everyday child and youth culture takes place (see Helsper, 2000: 663). The children's school world is differentiated within itself and cannot be described fully on either the macro or the micro level. The GoGo game, the focus of our study, is part of the last level. However, it does not prove to be an isolated activity since all the other levels of the school world are involved in it.

Playtime events offer a context in which the children claim a space 'of their own' within the school yet at the same time are still part of the institution of school itself. Thus, to the extent that with regard to *space, other children* and *time* the GoGo game takes place in the context of school, it is closely connected to *school culture*. The children's *culture of play* is established in this particular place at school and is expressed differently in other places. Game culture is a relational construct that remains related to other surrounding cultures. The intensity of the game and the children's craze for the game is possible because free time in the school is limited. A school provides good opportunities for transforming this free time into playing time. There are always other children of a similar age group around to join the game. And the building itself has a lot of suitable places on offer to stage this game. Many children try to bag the best area in the playground as soon as they can and immediately begin to play, in a quest to fulfil their passion for GoGo. In the following example, that refers to the ingredients of space, players and time in the game, we show the relation between school culture and game culture. The version of the GoGo game we describe is the one most frequently played by the children.

Absorption in the game

> On the landing directly next to the door of entrance A at the beginning of the long break eight children, mostly in Year Seven, are playing GoGo. They got out onto the snow-covered playground early and were thus able to occupy the staircase for their game. The door next to them is open and other children, of whom the players take no notice, stream onto the playground. The GoGo players set up between three and five colourful GoGo figures at a distance of between one and four centimetres between each other in a line and take turns to throw a figure. The person who hits one or more GoGo figures is allowed to keep them. The place where they are playing is now surrounded by spectators. Other children continue to come through the open door onto the playground. Suddenly there is a loud sound of breaking glass and all the children nearby stop what they are doing and turn around. A child has dropped a glass containing pasta in the middle of the doorway and it has broken. The staircase is covered with pasta and shards of glass. Some children gather next to the broken glass. The spectators of the game move over to stare at the disaster, but the players resume their game. A child comments, "Someone's gone and done it!" After a few words have been exchanged about the incident, the group breaks up again. Those children who go into the building or leave it see the scattered pasta, glance at it briefly, then turn round and continue on their way. A teacher arrives with three children from the younger classes. She goes up the stairs and sees the broken glass. She asks, "Why isn't anyone picking up the glass?" She kneels down in and picks up some pieces. The children accompanying her follow suit, while the players continue their game. An older boy comes running up. He claims responsibility and is sent away by the teacher to fetch a dustpan and brush.

Door and landing at the top of the stairs represent the transition from the educationally and architecturally rigid space structure of the school building to the less structured playground and become the cramped location for school events. After two hours of lessons in which they have been with their own form group, the children usually enter the playground, where they meet children of different age groups. The crossing of this threshold thus constitutes a transition from classroom events to the activities in the corridors and on to the game events in the playground. The activities within the peer group are not connected to a certain place on the school site or in the school building, but the spatial and institutional conditions of these activities differ according to the context.

The players are situated in this transition, without, however, really being aware of what is going on around them. They are immersed in a special game world to such an extent that the events around them are simply perceived as a tinkling of glass. The teacher notices the broken glass, seems surprised that no one has reacted and endeavours to get rid of it or have it removed. She lets the children on the landing carry on playing; she does not even talk to them. The stability of the community of the players and their identity as a group is formed through their concentration on the game and by the fact that they do not let anything distract them. It is the teacher with her 'escort' of six to eight year-old children who ensure that the pieces of glass are removed. She asks the child who dropped the glass to fetch a dustpan and brush. The players, who she can assume will continue to play despite their proximity to the broken glass, are not asked to do anything.

While the teacher removes the glass, the constellation in the game changes. The large number of children in the playground means that there is no shortage of new players and a game rarely has to be interrupted. The GoGo game is open to new children and offers great flexibility because its pattern of play allows players to be changed frequently and is thus correlated with the demands of the playground. Since the children are in an almost homogenous age group for the GoGo game and for most other games on the playground—the GoGo game is enjoyed most by children from Years Five and Six –in contrast to games in the local community, the school offers ideal opportunities to quickly form a group for playing.

Game participants

Four children remove themselves from the game without saying goodbye. The other three continue to play alone. One of the children who was originally playing is now only watching. Ayten is the last of the players on the landing. She looks around and then looks over to the landing at entrance B where GoGo is also always played at break-time and goes over there slowly. There she meets some of the boys who were watching the game that is now over, and she continues to play with them.

All this takes place without a word of explanation. When two other children leave the game, Ayten is left on her own. She immediately looks over to the other landing because she obviously knows from experience that GoGo games also take place there and she then wanders over. She meets some boys with whom she has not yet played but who know her as a GoGo player from the row of spectators of the first game of eight. Spectators from the previous game now become GoGo players themselves. Ayten, an impassioned player, thus profits from the packed playground. A group of players forms without much delay at the beginning of playtime and when this breaks up other children who have tuned into the game through watching it are ready to join in. Ayten thus plays GoGo throughout break and only wastes time not playing when she has to move from one landing to another.

The length of time they have for the game is defined by the general time structure of the school day which is divided into lessons and breaks. The framework of the school break provides a certain amount of time which the children use in different ways. In this school the children eat the contents of their lunch boxes in their classrooms after the lessons before going out into the playground. The division of time varies according to what classes are doing. When the children in a class have finished their food their individual class goes out into the playground. They often remain within the class group for their playground games but also often enter into new constellations. There is no central school bell, instead a portable gong is sounded at the end of break by either a member of staff or a child on the landing, which is close to the staff room.

When the gong is sounded at the end of break a lot of children raise their heads, turn towards the school building and start moving towards it. The sounding of the gong coordinates the movement of the children with the sound. Everyone stops their conversations or games briefly and almost simultaneously turns their head towards the source of the sound. The central electric school bell was done away with in this school in favour of a manual gong so that the time at which the end of the break is signalled can be varied and a completely 'different' school time established. The sounding of the gong of course generally takes place as part of a binding, mechanically measured organisation of time but it can be adapted to particular events in the school and used flexibly. The school gong structures the school community's time and establishes a connection between general and individual time.

Another quick game

 The school bell sounds and the players pause. A teacher comes out of the entrance
 in front of which Ayten and the others are playing and strikes the Chinese gong
 again. The players look at her, speed up and begin a new game. Three children

break away from the game and enter the school. At the end, only Ayten and a boy are left, and they start a new game. The teacher who sounded the gong at the beginning of the break turns to the players and points out that break is over. They both rush forward to pick up the figures that they have set up, put them in their pockets and enter the building.

When the gong sounds this time all the children gradually walk towards the building. Only one group of GoGo players remains; their game is taking place one or two metres away from the teacher on duty. When the teacher strikes the gong again in the immediate vicinity of the playing area, the players turn their heads to her and nonetheless continue with their game and even begin another game at greater speed. The gong adds a certain dynamic to the game but also reduces the size of the group. Three players leave the game. Only Ayten and Stefan play on until the teachers asks them explicitly to go into the school, which they do, and the doors to the playground are then locked.

Ayten and Stefan use the game to extend playtime for as long as possible. The clearly structured game of GoGo, with its own division of time into games that have to be played to the end, is aligned with the time division of the school as an institution, which increases the excitement. Extending their 'own' time is thus possible, without them being threatened by sanctions even though the children sometimes draw out playtime so much so that school time is reduced by it. The following section analyses the immanent complexity of the game with regard to its equipment, the different ways the children have of swapping their equipment, and the way a sense of community is formed in the game.

How a children's game is played

The GoGo game with its colourful figures known as 'Crazy Bones' incorporates different traditional throwing games which, over many centuries, have made use of a range of objects to be thrown. In ancient times people used to play with sheep bones, but pieces made from metal resembling bones were also used. The 'Crazy Bones' of the GoGo figures draw on the old pieces in that they are reminiscent of animal bones, but they come in shapes and a material that appeal to children at the turn of the twenty-first century. The section of child culture examined in the following is grouped around the small GoGo figures that are marketed by a toy company which uses them to represent similarities and differences.

The game involves the following five elements:
– *coming together* in selected places,

– *swapping* figures,
– a *strict order* of turns in the game,
– the *pragmatics of shared rules*,
– and a common *movement and game style*.

Forms of social exchange in play: swapping, giving and winning

Our first step is to examine how the GoGo figures are passed on from one child to another. The GoGo figures are a person's entry card into this system of exchanging. They can be acquired in different ways and at the height of GoGo fever many children possessed them, though by no means all. This game has a special attraction, as has already been indicated. Even on the last day of school before the autumn half-term holidays, on which all classes only have three hours of lessons and the children can then go home, all over the school building, although the lessons are over, children can be found playing the GoGo game with theses colourful figures. One group plays on a landing on the third floor of the school building. Whatever version of the game the children play, there is always a clear pattern. A game begins with each player setting down a playing figure and ends with all the figures disappearing into the bags of the owners, who are sometimes new owners. The figures are thus embedded into a specific form of economy.

'None of mine are bought'

Vladimir, Binol and David have figures in their hands and take turns to throw them against the wall. The children aim briefly and throw their figures fast and decisively. None of the boys says much. The player whose figure lands closest to the wall gets to keep all the others. When I ask where the figures come from, I am told, "From the paper shop". Binol, however, proudly adds, "None of mine are bought". Vladimir rushes over and says, "Nor are mine". The three boys continue to play. Petra comes out into the school corridor, walks across the playing area and bends over a range of figures which Binol has laid on the table. Binol joins her and also bends his head over the figures. Petra asks, "Binol, can I have one?" His answer is short, "No!" to which Petra retorts, "Oh! But you've got so many doubles!" She looks at the figures again, picks them up one by one and examines them. Binol exclaims emphatically, "Please don't touch them!" and Petra counters once more, "But you've got so many doubles!" Then she goes back across the playing area down the corridor in front of the class rooms where she came from.

During the game the figures can be won by all players in the same way. These children play a type of game which is not often played at this school. All the players throw a figure against a wall and the person whose figure is closest to the wall is allowed to keep all the figures. Each player may therefore lose the figure he or she staked or he or she may win more. The game produces a framework in which skill certainly plays a role but so does luck. When asked where the play figures come from, Binol says from the newsagent's. But he hastens to add that he did not acquire his by this conventional means and Vladimir claims the same. Both imply that it is less honourable to buy the play figures in a shop than to win them in a game.

Later we observed that many children place a figure in the game and borrow a 'throwing GoGo', which they return to its owner after winning a game. It is theoretically possible, therefore, for a child to 'hit the jackpot' using one or two borrowed figures. This form of luck, however, can only succeed when GoGos are bought by some children and put into circulation. The circulation of figures that are brought into school is based on particular exchange practices among the children, in which the setting down of a GoGo acquired through winning carries high social prestige.

Petra's argumentation and negotiation indicate social practices which, like play practices, also belong to the GoGo world and constitute part of the appeal of these figures—collecting and exchanging with a view to possessing different figures in order to own the most complete collection possible. Petra shows that the value system of swapping connected with the figures is not congruent with the value system in the game. In the game the figures acquire a value by being won or lost, whereas in the system of exchange their value is determined in relation to the other figures a person possesses and in relation to the type of figures which are in circulation. In the value system to which Petra refers, the value of a figure relates to an individual child's ownership of it. And it is precisely this argument that Binol alludes to. Petra's absorbed scrutiny of the figures ultimately causes Binol's exaggeratedly polite and modulated request, which adds additional emphasis to his negative answer. Binol obviously interprets Petra's examination and fingering of the figures not as mere viewing but as a theatrical performance corresponding to her request for a GoGo.

Petra requests the social practice of giving something away, which she sees as being her right because of Binol's 'wealth'. Since Binol has not bought any of the figures, his wealth is not connected to a certain social status but to his personal position within the swapping system among the children. Giving is always associated with a voluntary desire, even when it is embedded in an economic cycle of give and take (Gebauer and Wulf, 1998: 160; Mauss, 1990). The game, on the other hand, with its clearly regulated framework, creates a supposedly identical initial position for all participants. Each person puts down a figure, the sequence of throwing is established, and in each new game there is a new chance to win one or more figures. Whilst the game, with its new matches, emphasises the equality of the players, giving, especially if it is limited to a one-off act, underlines the contrary. In the process of giving, the giver and the taker, the active and the passive are determined. Binol is willing to lose his figures in a game. Indeed the particular version of the game he plays offers an even higher chance of losing lots of figures, and also of winning them, than other versions children play.

On the same day in another group a similar negotiating manoeuvre occurs in which an exchange of figures is transformed into a GoGo game that is modified by the conditions of the exchange. Here too the children can be seen to be processing the topic of equality and inequality.

Duel

Ayten looks at the figures which Ersin has in his hand. "Hey, would you like to swap the 'king' for this one?" Ayten holds out a figure from her collection. Ersin shakes his head. Ayten increases her offer to two figures, but Erwin's answer remains negative. She then offers him three figures. Ersin answers, "Yes, but mine has a broken foot." Ayten now says, "Okay, I'll leave it then." After a short pause she turns to David and asks him if he would like to swap the king. He declines and she offers him two and then three figures. Ersin calls out, "Don't be so tough on girls!" Ayten and David do not react; but then Ayten proposes a duel. David is to put down the figure she wants and she will put down two others for it. He immediately approves of this suggestion. They place their figures in front of the wall. Both throw a few times without speaking. Nobody hits. Then David hits his own figure, rejoices, picks it up and puts it in his bag. Both children continue to play while Ersin watches. Next, Ayten hits one of her figures, puts it in her pocket quietly and continues to play. Both have another go until Ayten hits her second figure.

In the middle of the game Ayten offers Ersin one of her figures in exchange for his, but he does not accept, offers another figure and, when she offers a third, her trading partner approves with a brief "Yes", adding that his 'king' has already lost a foot. Ayten then loses interest. Ayten initiates an attempt to exchange the same figure with the other player, David. Ayten continues to successively raise the stakes although the value that the figure has for her is obvious to David. The suspense between the high number of figures placed in the game and the individual figure at stake, which Ersin defused as a result of his honesty about his figure missing a foot, is now broken up altogether by his patronising call on his 'gender peers' not be too tough on the girls.

Ersin acts twice at the very moment when Ayten puts three figures down for one and draws attention to the way the numbers are unequal on both sides. The swappers pause after Ersin's comment until Ayten makes a practicable suggestion for both parties. She suggests a GoGo game played in the same way as before, but with a modification of the rules. David puts the 'king' down against Ayten's two figures, thus abandoning the rule that all players have to put down the same number. The children combine this form of exchange with the game.

The suspense in the exchange, which is generated by the inequality between the person who possesses a craved for object and the person who would like to possess it, makes a conclusion of the swap impossible twice. It is not until the swap is carried over into a game by the children that an appropriate form of exchange is found. In contrast with swapping, not only is the game designed by the mutual agreement of those who are trading the figures, but it is subjected to the conditions of the game, its framework and its moments of skill and good luck in particular. The large difference in swap trade, which is obviously hard to deal with, in which three figures are traded for one, is transformed into another form of difference. Firstly, the number of figures used by Ayten is reduced to two, and secondly, the *modus* of the swap is altered. Furthermore, the person who has put down more may win the desired figure, as well as the figures of his or her own which were placed in the game and maybe even all three figures. The number of figures placed in the game is indeed unequal; the chances of winning however seem to compensate.

The GoGo game itself makes a decision by facilitating a competition and thus artificially generates equal chances of winning. Compared with the other swapping practices which the children involved might engage in, the game makes all the participants equal and similar to each other, but at the same time it offers the chance for differences to be worked out in a practical way. The strict framework of the game and its ritualised forms are especially suited to this. In this game, however, the original situation is re-established—David hits his 'king' and Ayten eventually regains her figures. Both accept this outcome without question.

This turning to the game and its ritual dimension does not always succeed however. If the regulated forms of exchange are transgressed, the loss of a GoGo can be extremely painful for individual children. If a figure is lost within a GoGo game then it is not so bad, for a high number of GoGos are exchanged among the children during playtime. However, if someone loses a GoGo outside the described ritualised forms, not only is the plastic figure at stake, but also—as is shown in the next example—the status of the child among other children.

Theft

Opposite the entrance to the staff room a First Year boy with a freezer bag full of GoGo figures sits on a bench crying. A teacher comes out, asks what has happened and is told that so and so stole a GoGo figure from him. She places a hand on the boy's shoulder, pulls him towards her and asks, slightly annoyed, how this could have happened. He claims that the person in question simply took his bag away from him, delved into it, took out a GoGo and ran away. The teacher asks why the boy didn't leave his figures at home in safety. The conversation stalls, and the adult and child part company.

This boy participates in the social practice of exchange and with his GoGo figures very visible through the transparent plastic bag, he enjoys a certain status among the children. The fact that the exchange of GoGos means so much to him makes him particularly vulnerable. He experiences this personally as a result of the boy's attack on his bag of GoGos. Although it does not threaten the way he presents himself as an owner, it threatens him as being unable to defend his property. For, if another boy was able to take away one of his GoGos, he obviously wasn't able to defend himself adequately. The 'attacker' does not steal all his figures, therefore accepting the rules of ownership to a certain extent, but by only taking one GoGo figure he shows that he would be capable of more. The thief not only gains a GoGo but also demonstrates his power over the boy. Whether he shows this off in front of the other children or whether the attack remains secret and only the victim gets to feel his power we cannot tell.

The teacher, who initially comforts him, now suggests that he leave the figures at home, saying that this would stop such situations arising in the first place. The teacher's argument fails to acknowledge the personal status that is at stake in presenting the figures. The teacher seems to ignore the fact that showing other children his GoGos is so important to the boy. The conversation draws to a standstill at this point and the encounter ends. The teacher's failure to acknowledge the social status that the child attaches to the figures does not mean that she does not understand the importance of the figures for the children, but that for educational reasons she does not include this in her discussion with the boy. Her practical suggestion that the boy leave his figures safely at home and thus not risk losing them focuses solely on the possible loss of these figures. It only embraces the material value of possessing them and thus omits the cultural practice of collecting these figures which is so manifest in the transparent bag. It is not the figures themselves as a mere possession which bring status but putting them on display.

The GoGos which have been bought and can be passed on via different social practices from one child to another give rise to a framework which allow children to participate in a cultural exchange system resulting from the possession of these figures. Participation in this makes other children vulnerable to attack and can demonstrate inequality—as in the example of theft—but also equality—as in the game. In principle, practices that demonstrate a relationship between equals seem more popular than those where there is an unequal balance of power, at least on the surface. The game is preferred to other forms of exchange because it involves both luck and skill and allows the children to regulate their exchange practices through the rules of the game. The figures form a specific exchange system which, in most cases, is transferred to the framework of the game. Through this game, differentiated communities are established.

The forging of a sense of community in the game

A sense of community is formed through mutual ritualised practices from which other groups or individuals differ or even consciously exclude themselves. Players form a temporary friendship group in which the inclusion of participants and the representation of boundaries to the exterior succeed above all through an amicable performance of the game. Brian Sutton-Smith, a specialist in games in different cultures, considers the beginning and the end of a game to be the areas upon which the players' belonging hinges. A game does not simply begin, but is initiated by specific practices which model the entry and the exit from the game for the players (Sutton-Smith, 1971: 103). We describe next a practical entry into the game which is of particular interest because it does not succeed until the second attempt.

When the children find themselves in the regular GoGo playing area first of all they set their figures up in front of the wall and then they stretch out their arms in the middle and sing a song. This practice, which decides the entry to the game, takes place in the form of a game. All the children perform a chanting song: 'Cliiiick Clack Cluck ... Cliiiiick Clack Cluck'. In the repeated sequence of the tune the extension of the vowel *i* emphasises the first syllable. This syllable is repeated twice without elongation, but the vowel *i* is replaced by *a* and *u*. The singing remains constant: a broken triad, which starts with the third, is followed by the tonic and ends with the fifth. The children's movements run parallel to this repeated tune. On the first syllable all the children in the circle stretch out their favourite throwing hand and remain in exactly this position on the second syllable while they pull back their hands a little. On the syllable 'Cluck' all hands are moved forwards quickly and demonstrate one of the three favourite stylised gestures in the school, a fist for 'stone', the simultaneous stretching out of the middle and index finger for 'scissors', and the formation of a circle with all five fingers for the 'well'. The first syllable thus gets the group into the right rhythm, and there is a moment of concentration and a slight hiatus before the second and the third syllables are performed.

To ensure that everybody has the same chance, all players have to carry out a gesture simultaneously and incorporate it into the rhythm, which is also performed physically. This does not mean, however, that all the children have to complete the rhythms and movements perfectly. Instead, when the group has tuned into it, the common rhythm also allows for participation without the precise performance of the movements and the rhyme. After the start of each match, which is indicated by the setting up of the figures, this activity serves to establish the throwing sequence. Furthermore, it makes it possible for the group of players and those joining the game to enter into a mutual rhythm and thus to mark the transition from not playing to playing. The transition ritual (van Gennep, 1960), which makes non-players into players, requires that those involved stand side by side in a tight circle.

The circle is the ultimate model of an egalitarian community. All participants position themselves at approximately the same distance from the middle so that hierarchies in this representation of the community become insignificant. The act of standing in a circle for this transition ritual is mainly functional. All those involved can keep the gestures of the others in sight and quickly gain an overview of which gesture loses and which gesture wins. If someone walks through this inner circle and obscures the view of those involved they are told 'Wait!' or 'Hey!' and sent out of the circle, and the ritual is immediately interrupted. The following example illustrates the extent to which physical and aesthetic dimensions play a role in the way in which friendship groups are created.

"I'm playing too!"

Three children are playing in the staircase entrance of the school building, a place where people constantly have to walk through the playing area. As soon as a game has finished, Kolja, who is sitting on a chair next to the playing area, calls out "I'm playing too!" At the same time he stands up and moves his hands to his belt and opens his bum bag full of GoGos. The other three are already kneeling on one leg in a semicircle in front of the wall and are busy setting up their figures. While Boris is still kneeling and Fuat and Mohammed have already stood up, all three begin with "Click Clack Cluck". Kolja, who is still standing apart, then distances himself from the other children and sits down again. When all the children hold out their arms, Mohammed, in the middle, forms a fist with his hand, Boris stretches out his index and middle finger and Fuat's hand cannot be seen. Mohammed then leaves the circle in which the three are standing and performs his first throw. The other two repeat the counting game once more and then follow him. He skids a GoGo into the set up figures, hits and goes to the wall to collect the figure he has won. Fuat does the same. As Boris throws his third GoGo and hits he moves forwards on his knees to take his figure. At this moment both the others set up their figures. Kolja is standing by the wall and quickly puts a figure there, calling out, "I'm playing too." As he is already near the other players he can immediately join in with "Click Clack Cluck".

It is not until Kolja's second attempt to join in the game that he is successful, although he is present as a spectator on a chair in front of the row of figures for a long time. When he first declares his intentions to play, he obviously uses the wrong medium to make himself understood. His call is not in tune with the common rhythm of the others. Kolja does not voice his intentions to play very loudly although he is quite emphatic and indicates them clearly by means of a small performance. While Kolja is occupied with the preparations for his entry into the game the three other players have put down a GoGo and started the transition ritual. Kolja therefore has to wait for another match before he can enter the game. When he puts down a figure at the same time as the others he becomes an equal player. He repeats his statement somewhat more quietly "I'm playing too!" but his participation only succeeds when he has tuned in with the common rhythm and performed his *practical knowledge* of how to enter and participate.

Kolja has now joined in the game and throws his figure in a similar way to the other players. Each player stands with his legs apart approximately four metres from the wall in front of which the figures are set up, bends his upper body and lets his throwing hand swing backwards between his legs. They throw their figures at floor height without taking a long time to aim. Even if there are other forms of throwing among GoGo fans, e.g. some throw from above or from a side position opposite the horizontally set up figures, a common *style of movements* can be elaborated. The movements in the game are clear, fast and do not require a lot of thought. This game shows that all players display a similar throwing position without being consciously aware of it.

Whether a child can participate or not is determined by his or her knowledge of the physical style of the group playing, his or her performance of this style and his or her knowledge of and keeping to the rules. The group which emerges can be described as a 'group which is based on a common style of movement' (Gebauer, 1998). Movement—like language—is a medium which enables specific communication. The scene vividly demonstrates the performance of the game in its mimetic function. Participation in the game is only successful for those who yield themselves up to the game and enter into its fast rhythm. The style of throwing movement, the opening ritual accompanied by a song, the marking of the playing area by the players' and spectators' physical presence, and the common rhythm of the game combine to allow a temporary friendship group based on the game to emerge on the basis of shared practical knowledge.

If we look at its form, a GoGo game includes at least two players who are situated in a suitable place. The marking out of the playing area is established not only by the place but also by the bodies of the players and the spectators who frequently stand on the edges of the playing area. The spectators form the framework of the specific, unrepeatable events and thus become a part of the game group. They follow the game silently, comment on its events or join in. After Kolja has selected the appropriate form of entering the game he can move from a spectator to a player role. The game offers those standing around the chance to participate as spectators and to learn the game mimetically whilst watching.

The following scene is taken from a different game constellation. Boris is the first on the landing and pushes the snow lying there to one side. As soon as Ayten comes out of the door he speaks to her and both of them begin a quiet game. Although spectators frame the game, no one comments on the individual throws. Kolja keeps to the back. Suddenly the game stops.

Watching the game

Everyone who is on this landing suddenly moves to the other landing, not together but one by one. Boris speaks briefly in Russian to Kolja, who is just behind him on one side. Five figures are quickly set up a small distance away from each other and five children form a circle and play 'Click Clack Cluck'. The children's hand movements are very fast and take place in a common rhythm, their arms and hands are tense and their faces very concentrated. The whole group on the landing consists of nine people. Ayten, Stefan and Andy are among the players. Three boys are standing on the edge and are following the game. Boris has not set down anything but stands near the figures while the three other boys stand near the throwers. An argument develops among these about who is next. Boris puts a leg in front of the figures. When the throwers have agreed, a child throws. One of the spectators demonstrates a throw with his hand, aims from a slightly bent position, while making a wrist movement and saying, 'That's how to throw.' The other spectators nod. Tips are offered by those standing around and discussed while the players continue quietly with the game. Those who have only demonstrated their throw make room for the players to throw. A boy runs without any obvious reason towards Kolja, grabs him from behind underneath the shoulders and pushes him in front. Kolja tries to release himself from his grip. He neither protests nor indicates annoyance. After twenty seconds the boy lets go of Kolja. When Ayten wins a GoGo she gives it to Boris, without a comment, who then encourages her by cheering joyfully every time she has a successful throw. After each turn Ayten and Boris briefly exchange a few words.

A group of nine people is on the right landing. Five of them are actively playing while the others are watching the game. After they have decided the sequence of throwers by means of the transition ritual, those who have put down a figure quietly play one game after the other. Suddenly an argument about the order of play arises. Observations show that only two points of conflict in the game are solved by confrontational dialogue—on the one hand, the implementation of special rules which have to be negotiated at the beginning of the game, and on the other hand, throwing sequences in the game. Being first means from game to game having increasingly more chances of winning than fellow players because a greater number of figures are up for grabs. Boris, who is not one of the players but participated in a game with Ayten, places his foot in front of the row of figures and thus in the way of a potential thrower.

Boris therefore has a special role in this GoGo game. He is not an active player but is allowed to watch over the course of the game. In contrast to an umpire, who is defined by the ability to judge and survey the game independently, Boris increases the players' reactions and by his physical action prevents anyone from getting around the agreement that the group adopts. He thus personifies the rules. According to our observations, rules are never explicitly discussed but are generated throughout the course of the game. It is only when rules are violated that the contravened rule is discussed. Boris clarifies the compliance with the rules and behaves like an advisor who supports the events in the game, without deciding what they should be. He thus assumes a special form of participation in the game. Boris took part in the previous game and now finds himself in the position between player and spectator which is accepted by the players as well as by the spectators. He remains close to the row of figures because this spatial position is not that of the spectators, who stand at the edge of the playing area. Secondly, he enters into an alliance with his previous game partner, Ayten. He encourages her, expresses his pleasure loudly when she wins, confers briefly with her after she has thrown and gets the figures she wins.

The five children actively playing are surrounded by a group of spectators who give tips and confer over throwing styles. By performing this in a theatrical way and supporting the represented style they demonstrate several types of throwing. The players, however, do not allow themselves to be influenced by the spectators' comments. They do not look up and continue undisturbed. The activities of playing and watching form two different groups whereby the spectators mimetically refer to the players but the players take no notice of the spectators. Both groups direct their concentration at the same game.

The fact that it is not the players alone who form the centre of attention is demonstrated by the small scene which takes place on the edges of the playing area. Kolja, who at the very beginning of the game kept slightly out of it, is suddenly grabbed by another boy from behind and slowly pushed forwards. Kolja attempts to release himself, yet does not protest. He plays along, so to speak, by not showing any annoyance. A protest by Kolja would not relate to the actions of the boy alone but disturb the entire event and draw attention to his plight. His scope of action as a spectator of the game is not extensive, i.e. he can only either participate by means of watching—even if this is made more difficult by the boy's attack—or disturb the course of the game. He finds himself, with the players, on a stage where he has no choice but to play along.

This framework makes it impossible to tell whether the boy's attack is playful or not. There is a potential for power concealed behind the aesthetic dimension of the event, its strictly regulated course and the fact that the bodies are so clearly on display. It is hard to do anything about this because it is so overt. The attacking boy also abides by the spectators' rules. He designs his attack in a way that does not disturb the game and only pursues his aggression, whether playful or not, to the extent that both bodies remain focused on the game and both boys can still be regarded as spectators.

The different power constellations in the game are illustrated in the following scene. The emerging physical competitiveness favours exclusion and differentiation within the group.

Dancing for joy

Cihan, Fjodor, Boris, Nalan, and Kolja are playing together, and Boris and Fjodor form a team and have a common pool of figures which Fjodor carries in a bum bag. When it is Fjodor's turn or someone else is congratulated, he turns his head, spits and quickly turns his head back to the game. Mostly he spits down the stairs but sometimes he also goes forwards to the figures and spits next to them in the corner next to the door. When Fjodor wins several figures with one throw Boris rejoices loudly. On one occasion Boris even performs a little dance and accompanies it with a panting-like 'Hahahahahahahahahaha', the first 'ha' of which is emphasised and the second not. He swings his hips to the beat and moves his head to the right and left in the same rhythm. At the same time he draws up his right and his left leg in turn and hits each ankle respectively with his hand on the same side. This movement is carried out at medium speed. When one of their opponents misses, either Boris, Fjodor or Kolja shout out 'yeah' or some other word that intensifies their joy. The three boys hold short conversations in Russian, speaking to each other more quietly than they normally would. Nalan speaks to Cihan in Turkish. Such exchanges are, however, rare, quiet and accompanied by few gestures. German remains the general game language used for rule definition and play.

This small scene is shaped by the children's enthusiasm but also by the competition between them. The children act out the competition on a completely physical level. Brothers Boris and Fjodor form a team which shares a common pool of GoGos which is kept close at hand on the body of the younger of the two. Both make joint figure settings in the game and take turns to throw. When Fjodor wins several figures with one throw, Boris laughs enthusiastically in a stylised and spiteful way. The stylisation consists in his repetition of the syllable 'ha' which he sings to himself and which is quite different from a real laugh. His movement underlines joy rather than spite, however. He swings his hips and head in an exaggerated manner to the beat of his own singing and throws his right and then his left leg in the air while slapping his ankles. Boris thus converts his joy into a dance while Fjodor selects a different form of movement which, instead, represents his commitment to the whole game and his impatience for a turn. He distances himself by about two metres from the playing area between goes, turns around briefly and spits over his shoulder. Fjodor's marking out of the external borders of the territory clearly marks the playing area.

Fjodor and Boris have different ways of working themselves up into a state of frenzy: they enjoy playing and winning. The team of brothers co-operates closely with Kolja and they react to his successful throws with encouraging calls as if they were their own winning throws. Inversely, the success of the two boys is also met with enthusiastic shouts from Kolja. Although the language used in this game is German, and this remains the case for all-important questions regarding the course of the game, the conferences between the three boys at the time of most of their wins are held in Russian.

Group formation occurs this time on two levels: by means of the boys' physical performance and by means of the communication between the Russian boys in their common mother tongue. Enthusiasm for the game is displayed by an increase in movement intensity, and especially by the physical performance of excitement in the form of dance and spitting. When excitement reaches a climax in the group that considers itself to be winning, their language changes to Russian. Nalan and Cihan also suddenly start to speak in their common native tongue, Turkish, but they accompany this with less exuberant gestures. They find themselves in the position of losers from several points of view. Firstly, from a completely material perspective they lose their figures to the others; secondly, they do not support each other or their own commitment to the game by means of an enthusiastic physical performance; and thirdly, they find themselves together in an alliance of fate. As a defence mechanism they resort to the simplest of possibilities to present themselves as a group, when, like their fellow players, they also demonstrate their belonging together by means of a common mother tongue. At this point two teams can be seen to exist in the game; they communicate with each other in German but speak amongst themselves in a language that the 'rival' team cannot understand.

The switch from one language to another emphasises the team of three children not only as a successful group but also as a group with a common linguistic identity. Because their mother tongue offers a clear differentiating characteristic, a group with a common linguistic identity emerges within the game. Their physical gestures as well as their use of their mother tongue fuels the game, at least for the three winners, and allows not only the group that desires cohesion, but also the other two to form their own group within the playing group. Here intentionality with regard to the representation of identity becomes relevant: linguistic and cultural difference does not appear as a characteristic which *should* be presented, but on the contrary, it simply comes about as a differentiating feature in the game and is performed by the children.

Nalan and Cihan only reluctantly communicate in Turkish and altogether show less enthusiasm for the game situation in which they find themselves in a coalition of Turkish speakers, and, at the same time, on the side of the losers. The situation is different for the group of winners. Even if their sharing a linguistic identity is no doubt unconscious, and merely slips out in their joy at winning, they do in fact profit from the course of events. Even if it is as a result of different situations, both groups refer to a reality outside of the game, namely to their own respective cultural background. Whereas in this example cultural identity can be seen being performed, the next section focuses on the performance of gender and discusses this in connection with the formation of community spirit.

Ritual games as an insight into child-culture

The GoGo game, with its competitive spirit, elements of chance and clear rules, has a strictly regulated form in which the children participate with full concentration. Despite the fact that it allows for lively and excited forms of play, creativity in finding solutions to individual problems and moments of suspense and surprise, in other words despite its wealth of ludic elements, the sheer seriousness with which the children engage in this game is quite baffling. No doubt, it is precisely this seriousness which enables the children to access the frenzy of the game. The players waste no time discussing controversial rules or even searching for suitable playing areas. They immerse themselves in the game as often and for as long as possible, in playful self-abandonment. The clearly regulated sequence forms the basis for a very fast pace of play. Characteristic of the performance are the ritualised body movements of the players. Every passionate player displays a recognisable style which relates to the results of the game: concentrated, controlled movements, long aiming, sparse communication, loving handling of the pieces and routine adherence to the rules which are only discussed when someone violates them.

The starting point of the game involves setting down the plastic figures called GoGos like the game. The children carry these figures close to their bodies, so they are always at hand, ready to be played with and protected from attack. The children take care of their figures so that none get lost except in the course of a game. Losing a GoGo figure outside of the context of the game can severely harm the owner's status within the children's culture. The figures are embedded within a spectrum of social exchange practices; they are swapped, given as presents or sometimes stolen. Winning figures in a game is clearly the children's preferred way of exchanging. In the cases we have described, giving away GoGos as a present is rejected; an attempt to swap game figures is transformed into a duel; and a theft which goes against the rules of coexistence leads to bitter sorrow.

The system of cultural exchange activities that allows one to acquire and display GoGo figures prevents the display of too great a degree of inequality. In the game, the purpose of exchange can at least be partially forgotten. When it comes to swapping or giving away figures, however, the inequality between participants is emphasised. The game thus assumes a ritual quality which, for a section of the children, regulates social exchange activities in school. Because of the arguments and unfortunate situations it can induce in the playground, some inner-city schools in Berlin have forbidden the GoGo game. In this school, however—in addition to a host of other activities in playground—the game is an important ritual and something that creates social cohesion. The ritual element in the game processes the topic of difference in a particular way. Differences are carried into the clear framework of the game and suppressed for the duration of the game and even reduced.

The GoGo game provides a small insight into child-culture. The system of GoGo exchange allows social differences to be performed by being shifted onto values in the game. The children make use of these ever-changing materials not only to assert their own personalities but to regulate the activities within their social group. Children thus acquire a practical knowledge of the game and, at the same time, experience competition and the formation of a sense of community, as well as becoming aware of social differences and vulnerabilities.

Chapter 4

The creation of peer group identity through TV adverts and popular shows

Media performances as framework for ritual group action

In both research on socialisation and research on youth and media it is unanimously assumed that—besides the family, school and peer groups—the media are an important factor in socialisation. We propose here to describe how, especially with regard to the visual medium of television, the creation of a sense of community in groups is furthered by media-related processes of ritualisation, which in themselves represent an essential aspect of media socialisation. We will focus on processes of how a sense of community or group identity evolves in children's peer groups, since the influence of the media seems to play a particularly important role in such groups. Children between the ages of ten and thirteen are on the threshold between childhood and adolescence, at a time when they are beginning to move towards independence from the family.

While media usage is generally associated with a low level of consciousness and reflexivity, peer group activities are defined by a certain spontaneity and informality of action. We do not therefore assume that children consciously use media-related processes of ritualisation in a peer group context. They do not intentionally employ ritual gestures to establish their own positions and those of others. Rather, our research is based on an open and dynamic concept of ritual as is found in ethnography, the social sciences and in media ritual research. We will begin by taking an empirical example to explain our understanding of the relationship between the media and community producing ritualisations. The performative character of social action is of central significance, since the media enact social reality by means of ritual forms of display and representation. Through processes of mimetic learning the children incorporate these media performances into their practical knowledge and then draw on them as they create their social practice. This recourse to media models in everyday activities is evident in *ritual media performances*, which are only coincidentally and sporadically enacted in peer group interactions. For the empirical analysis of such practices we have developed a quasi-experimental method, which was employed in the context of video work groups in a Berlin primary school between May 1999 and March 2000.

'Guildo loves you'

Let us begin by elucidating the significance of ritual media performance for the construction of community by means of an empirical case. The first of the *video workshops* that were put together for the purpose of this research comprises a motley group of children some of whom do not know each other. Towards the end of the group session the six participants, Güley, Lisa, Maria, Binol, Murat and Vladimir prepare for a final performance in front of the camera. There is no planning or discussion about what is to be enacted. The children equip themselves with various requisites and consider their different options—until Vladimir, half addressing the camera and half addressing Murat, calls out, "I'll do Guildo Horn!"[3]

> Murat, whose gaze, head and body are turned towards the camera, begins to sing the first verses of the hit *Guildo*[4] and then breaks off again. Vladimir, spurred on by Murat's spontaneous entry, breaks into song and Güley and Maria join in at the top of their voices. A full song and dance performance develops, led mainly by Vladimir. Other children join in and come up with variations. The children sing *Guildo loves you*. The children dance together to the rhythm of their song, and at the same time each one of them puts on his or her own performance. After the first verse has been sung the individual performances gain in strength.

The well-known song and its performance on television provide a frame for the group's collective action. This commonality, or acting as a group, arises not by way of a cognitive or intentional plan of action but *performatively*: in a spontaneous and creative *re-enactment*, a repetitive 'tuning-into' a media model, which results in a harmony of bodily movements and voices. Mimetic adjustment to a media product enabled the children in our video group, who had previously had only little to do with each other, to find a common platform for their action. The media can thus be seen as creating a field of learning and experience which is both independent of and connected with various realms of life and interactions between family, school and peer group in diverse ways. This field plays an important role in how adolescents shape their everyday forms of sociability and social practice.

In our view, this re-enactment of a well-known media performance is ritual in character. By carrying out this 'cultural performance' (Geertz, 1973), which

3 Guildo Horn is a German singer, famous for his eccentric stage persona, which includes outrageous clothes and very extroverted antics.
4 *Guildo hat euch lieb!* (Guildo loves you!) sung at the Eurovision Song Contest 1998

involves momentarily suspending the flow of everyday action and spreads through 'mimetic infection' (Gebauer and Wulf, 1995), the children signal their participation in a media culture. This enactment was a formal scenic arrangement, by which a relatively heterogeneous group transformed itself into a community of action for a limited period of time. Although the event was not anchored in a firm tradition, it did, however, display ritual characteristics. Instead of falling back on cultural tradition, the children drew on the constantly changing repertoire of media presentations available, which suggested open and dynamic processes of ritualisation and enabled them to introduce their own ideas and creative transformations in a playful way. We call this kind of activity *ritual media performance.*

Virtual or concrete community?

Within the field of media studies the question of how media rituals play a part in constructing a group identity is a widely debated issue. Television is generally regarded as the main media, enabling the transition from everyday routine into realms of experience that are pre-shaped by rituals, in which transient, imagined or virtual communities establish themselves. Until now the ritual element of television has been studied solely in terms of the media itself. Thus, processes of ritualisation take place on the level of what the media has to offer, and the cultural form or the social structure of the media. Individual media products can be designated as rituals if they have characteristics such as repetition, a formal style, performance, framing and a connection between canonical and indexical elements. 'In their relative self-containment and unity, the individual programmes perform particular rituals. As a result of the organisational designs of individual rituals, distinct patterns of form and content have developed which are commonly described as types or genres and have a variety of coordinating functions' (Thomas, 1998: 504).

If we limit a study of ritualisation processes to those that originate in the media we divorce these processes from the concrete practice of social groups. The community-creating effects of rituals are simply a 'secondary' ritualisation, which constitutes virtual communities in the framework of media presence (cf. ibid., 442 f.). Ritualisation remains on the level of a mere potential, a ritual delivery that cannot be guaranteed. Media studies focusing on young people in particular have pointed out that there is a discrepancy between the way media programmes are produced and the way they are received by groups of young people. The notion of an 'active recipient' has been underlined, suggesting that, people make choices between media freely, depending on their personal and social background, media here being a whole range of consumer activities and products on offer (cf. Vollbrecht, 1997). In this view, media-related behaviour depends on the recipients' subjective processes, i.e. how they choose to react to the media, and becomes part of the way they normally behave in society. In view of the ever-increasing role played by the media in recent times, 'media competence' has come to be important, an approach which emphasises the individual's ability to use media in a purposeful way. This ability has been declared to be one of the tasks of education.

In our view, the perspective of youth media studies underestimates the extent to which individual media action is embedded in collective practices. It is true that the media have come to assume the role of giving young people a sense of direction in their social interactions, leading to a media related 'stylisation' of adolescent acts of 'self expression' and to similarities in their everyday actions (cf. Vogelgesang, 1999). Especially for the age group of ten to thirteen year-olds, which we are most interested in, reference to the media plays a crucial role. To date, however, little research has been done into how such media-related processes of creating group identity operate.

According to our thesis, the creation of peer group identity relies substantially on media-related ritualisation processes. However, we must look at more than the ritual aspects of what the media offers and the way individuals react. As well as this, we ought to be able to prove that media-related processes of ritualisation take place in the social interactions of peer groups. For indeed, only when the rituals on offer in the media are made real by recipients in their own social interaction can a concrete community or group identity be seen to emerge from a virtual one. Thus, media-related processes of ritualisation are linked to the social practices of concrete groups which are already in existence.

Our investigation proceeds from the assumption that there is a tension between the ritual character of the media and the media-related ritual or ritualised practice of social groups. As well as concrete media usage, there are ritual media performances in peer group interactions, which, through mimetic processes of creative imitation, performatively create a relationship between media models and the social activities of peer groups. This does not involve a mere imitation or taking-over of media shows or extracts but, in line with model of recipients being 'active', it has to do with a creative and constructive process leading to media models being constantly transformed and reworked. Drawing on the examples of the children's largely ironic reworkings of commercials and chat shows, we will present this process in detail here. Central to our investigation is how, through collective ritualisation processes, such a staging produces collective practical knowledge and 'appropriate action' (Jennings, 1998) as a basis of creating a peer group identity.

Our research method: provoking the performative

Little research has been done into how people's group identities and performance practices are affected by television. In our view, previous investigations, based on qualitative and quantitative methodology, have not taken sufficient account of the effects that practical knowledge of action and community creating processes have on social actors. It was with a view to broadening these investigations that we developed the qualitative investigation method of video performance in cooperation with Anja Tervooren. In explicitly provoking the performative, this method directly addresses the 'practical media knowledge' that social actors possess. Television is studied as a medium that encourages social cohesion. Its community-creating effects can be seen in concrete activities.

The method of video performance involved us offering individual children and existing peer groups the chance to participate in a video workshop. In these workshops the children are shown how to use a video camera and are given a space for spontaneous and independent performances. During the workshops the children's performances are filmed by the children themselves (video performances), and also by a fixed standing camera, which continuously records the entire group-event within the video workshop (video-based observation). In this way the end result can be seen on a screen, which is also the theme and the presentation method of the whole activity.

The video workshops were initially offered to Years Five and Six of a Berlin primary school as a voluntary afternoon activity that was open to all. Four video workshops were created, consisting of five peer groups of ten to thirteen year-olds. The workshops were made up of between three and thirteen participants and involved between four and ten sessions of about three hours each. All the groups were same gender, whereas the ethnic and religious backgrounds of the children varied widely.

The children were free to design their recordings and we were careful not to emphasise that we were focusing on 'media rituals'. The children made use of this freedom in choice of themes to make their own versions of well known television genres. It is striking that in all groups the children perform almost exclusively commercials, chat shows, action movies, news reels and music clips. This confirmed our assumption that by its very nature the method of video performance suggests to the children a treatment of themes and ways of presentation, which they are familiar with from television. The method thus works like a magnifying glass. In front of the camera, which they themselves are in charge of, the children develop performances that are based on particular media genres. In so doing, they performatively demonstrate their practical media knowledge. The fact that all the groups chose to produce particular media genres demonstrates the extent to which these genres affect the children's imagination and the way they act, and how they are creatively processed in the children's performances. They invest them with contents of their own, which have a particular significance and meaning for them. No games of schools or shops are performed, but what we found was commercials, newsreels and chat shows.

The data obtained—video performance and video-based observation of the four video workshops—is analysed in a four-step procedure, which is a further development of the 'documentary method' applied to film analysis (Bohnsack, 1999, p. 34 ff.). In a first step, which involves the rough analysis of one afternoon, the thematic development of the performances is reconstructed in the light of the whole session. It is at this stage that we look out for the performances that are based on particular television genres. In a second and third step, selected performances are taken down in writing, undergoing fine analysis through description, and analysed by means of a detailed interpretation. On this basis, and in a fourth and final step, similarities and contrasts of genre within the performances are identified in an interpretation that summarises the whole, using the method of comparative analysis. This procedure may be seen as a spiral, in which individual steps are related to each other time and again and thus further consolidated.

In what follows we will present the two genres most often appearing in video performances: commercials and chat shows.

Commercials: presenting the world and expressing the self

Of the fifty-three performances of the four video workshops, twenty were commercials. We assume that the omnipresence of advertising in the modern world and its unmistakable form of presentation account for there being so many. We will now analyse this phenomenon more closely.

Advertising is, by its very nature, pure performance. As a way of increasing sales, its purpose is to promote products and services and, to this end, it strategically makes use of performative means of composition in order to bestow meaning on them. Advertising methods include either presenting the effects of a product (product campaigns) or linking products to a specific image (image campaigns). The latter is achieved by means of lifestyle campaigns or by associating a product with certain values. 'Advertising sells images of an ideal life, it sells notions of what is good, right and desirable; in short it sells values' (Schmerl, 1983: 14). In a commercial the image of a product must suggest the fulfilment of a dream: friendship, peace, love and success. The implication behind an advert is that if the offer to purchase is not accepted—if the laundry, teeth or evaporated milk are not quite white enough—then there will be social repercussions. With its emotional impact this association between product and effect or image is meant to anchor the product's label or brand deeply within the unconscious of the particular target group so that it will emerge in the form of a decision to purchase soon after. The way the product is displayed, with all the suggestive power of its image, is meant to persuade us to purchase the product, by engraving itself into the inner world of our imaginary. In today's world the media message we hear is, 'Happiness in life will be yours if you buy, buy, buy!'

Rhythm and aesthetic refinement are used to create alluring atmospheres and desirable social settings which appear in the audio-visual images and catchy jingles of ubiquitous commercials. Adverts often contain successful elements of surprise and, more often than not, are completely detached from the functional value of the acclaimed product. These images capture a certain longing which the product on show promises to satisfy. In the interest of sales, the dreams and myths of modern man and woman—his period of tranquillity over coffee at breakfast in the presence of brand X, her toned and sexy stomach after diet Y, their relaxation over beer Z—are forged into short scenes and then produced and kept alive in the form of images and stories.

Advertising increasingly influences the patterns of our actions and needs; it presents models with which we identify and it is an essential phenomenon within the competitive capitalist economy and consumer society. Scientific studies of television advertising tend to consider the consumers of commercials to be independent, responsible individuals or merely consumers seduced by something attractive. Advertising creates a certain tension between individual freedom and responsibility on the one hand and collective seduction in the context of a capitalist social order on the other.

Children are regarded as a particularly endangered group, who, to a large extent at least, are not capable of distinguishing between fact and fiction, nor between commercials and the actual programme. Thus they seem to be especially susceptible to the machinations of the producers and the images of advertising. According to numerous studies (e.g. Schell, Stolzenburg and Theunert, 1999), the contents of the media and commercials appear in the imagination, the play and the consumer desires of children. Today, growing up in a media and consumer society turns childhood into a period of life that is dominated by the media, consumerism and commercials. And indeed, as initially mentioned, scenes from commercials are by far the most popular genre to be enacted by the children in the video workshops. This choice is mostly spontaneous and appears in ever new variations. In our study we regard these advert enactments as telling us a great deal about how consumerism dominates the way children, in whatever socio-cultural context they live, lead their social lives.

Just as there has been a shift of emphasis from a discussion of the effects of the media to a discussion of media reception, or from the power of the media to the creativity of its user, within the controversial debate about the effects and use of television commercials special attention is now being paid to the issue of active reception. In this view, the effect of the advertising message is—still carefully but explicitly—formulated as being 'to a certain extent' self-produced, that is an individual creation of the person. This takes place through a communicative exchange.

It is the children themselves who, through their performances of commercials, reveal the community-creating dimension that commercials provide. In the following, we will introduce and analyse two selected performances of commercials. The analysis shows, on the one hand, that a standard presentational style is adapted in all of the children's performances of commercials, and on the other hand, that the product presented is indexically charged. This means that as they perform the presentation of a product, by using the framework of a commercial, the children negotiate themes that are relevant to them.

Our analysis is not about the way commercials especially geared towards children persuade them to buy products, nor is it about children's advertising competence. Rather, what we are most interested in is how the children's performances are executed in their reference to the presentational world of television and how this contributes to creating a community identity. Our guiding thesis is that spirit of community is created in ritualised sequences which involve mutual reference and mutual reactions to each other. These take place in a situation where repeated and creative, accepted and indexical elements interact. With this in mind, we are especially interested in how dramatic and expressive gestures that are rooted in practical knowledge have the effect of creating a sense of community.

The ambivalence of femininity

The first child commercial presents the new 'Basic', a brand of blue eyeliner. It is introduced by Dunja, an eleven year-old girl of Romanian descent, who is one of three participants in a girls' video workshop. Lydia and Claudia act out the scene whilst Dunja is behind the camera. (Lydia is ten, Claudia is eleven, and both are of German origin).

Lydia and Claudia are sitting on two chairs, half turned towards each other and half turned towards the camera. Lydia is wearing everyday clothes, a tight dress with jeans underneath; both her feet are on the ground. She is holding a little make-up box in her left hand and a powder-puff in her right. Claudia is sitting with her knees crossed, her hands folded on her knees. She is wearing a white unbuttoned lace blouse over her sweater. Lydia's gaze and body are turned towards Claudia. She gesticulates with swinging elevated arms, "And here we have the new model, Korinna Kannbie!"

Claudia, alias Korinna Kannbie, holds her head at a slight angle. During the introduction she opens her mouth a bit and swings forward with her upper body. At the mention of the powder she nods her head and grins. Lydia turns toward the camera and offers her little box of eye-liner. "And, and, and of course she uses the new Basic." Korinna Kannbie smiles distinctly and turns her gaze upwards to the camera while slightly lowering her head to one side. Lydia: "It's, it's, it's easy to apply." (Continuing to speak she applies blue powder to Korinna's eye-lids with a small brush. Korinna holds her head towards her, her hands still crossed over her knees), "It doesn't itch and is nice and powdery so you can spread it everywhere. So, how does it feel?" Claudia, alias Korinna Kannbie, opens her eyes. "It feels ni ..." Lydia continues to apply powder. Claudia, alias Korinna Kannbie, speaks with closed eyes. "It makes me feel great." Lydia, "Yes! This is the new Basic! You must recommend it to your friends!"

She stops powdering. "Done. You look beautiful!" she says quickly, and turning to the camera, "Doesn't she?" Korinna Kannbie opens her eyes and mouth, stands up, walks a few steps towards the camera holding her hands at chest level to the open buttons of her blouse, speaking clearly and looking straight into the camera, saying, as if it were a matter of course, "Of course! Beautiful with Basic! Keep that in mind!" She grins, closes her eyes and moves her head, that is still tilted back,

from side to side. Lydia stands up. "And if you think so too," she holds the little
box towards the camera, "then buy the new Basic now!" She looks at the price tag
and announces: "Only four Marks forty-nine! (…) recommended price as long as
stocks last." (…) Showing the new Basic to the camera again, "You just try it, too!"
She proffers the little box to the camera. "In your make-up shop now!", and walks
out of the frame. Claudia sings out loud, "BAAA.......SIC!" and laughs.

In this spontaneous advert performance, two girls and a make-up box
advertise 'The new Basic!'—a subject area that comes up in about half of all their
video performances: beauty, femininity and physicality. The advertised product
is epitomised by an authentic and exemplary representative of these qualities:
the model Korinna Kannbie, played by Claudia. The model as an epitome of
beauty, publicly recognised as such, personifies the effects of the product she
demonstrates.

With the words 'and here we have…', the model is introduced. In this
adaptation the advert presenter Lydia thus picks up a gesture of praise from
the world of advertising and amplifies it by applying it not only to the product
but also to the model Korinna Kannbie. In a de-personalising performative act
the possessive verb 'have', used in the first person plural, turns the model into
something of an object. It is not that 'she is' the model, nor 'is she' Korinna, and
instead of the model herself saying 'I am' Korinna, the presenter displays her
as something that 'we have'. In uniting the owners, the 'we' in effect emphasises
the 'otherness' of the model: the model is counterpart to the 'we' and thus, in a
sense, 'opposed' to us; she is not part of the community, and cannot be, for 'we'
only come into existence through 'our' ownership of the model.

At the same time, possessing what is still the 'other' remains desirable and
out of reach. If the option for ownership of the highly praised model in reality
vanishes, the only option that remains is to own the image and with it the values
it stands for—youth, well-being, happiness, beauty, recognition, attraction
etc.—(all of which the girls enact in the subsequent scene of the commercial).
In other words, these rhetorical gestures are in fact performative statements.
They do not procure ownership itself but merely call on the spectator's desire
for ownership. Thus, imaginary ownership of the values portrayed can be
achieved by means of owning the powder, which, as the scene shows, serves as
a link between model and owner: the product represents the bridge between
the owner and the highly desirable quality of beauty—entry into the sphere of
beauty is achieved by purchase.

In the children's commercial, the potential possession or quality that is striven for is given a name, indeed even a 'family' name—something which in the business of beauty and the beautiful is a privilege reserved for the most exquisite. And the possession is 'new'; it is the 'new model, Korinna Kannbie', a new face in the realm of beauties. 'New' points out to the viewers what is up to date, hip, the 'latest fad'. As a description for the model it emphasises freshness, youth and vigour, the hope for more, the potential for great success. Yet, not only is the model 'new' and therefore fresh and successful. So too is the powder. 'Basic' is 'the new Basic', fresh on the market, cheaper and better than previous products: the powder is presented as a real best seller. Moreover, 'new' not only refers to the model and the powder, but also to the pressure of competition as well as to the notions of modernisation and progress in a capitalist society to which the economy responds with commercials that advertise ever new products. It is precisely all of this novelty that the girls pick up on with their 'new model' and their 'new powder'.

The two girls enact a whole succession of ritualised elements taken from stereotypical commercial performances. The bargain price of the product ('only') is emphasised, a 'price recommendation' is uttered, the scarcity of the product is pointed out ('as long as stocks last') and the immediacy with which it can be bought is indicated ('in your make-up shop now!'). At the same time Lydia repeatedly inserts imperatives into the performance, pressurising the imaginary audience to do things, thus making explicit what in many real commercials on television is usually only implied: 'You must recommend it, it, it to your friends!' 'Buy the new Basic now!!' 'You just try it, too!' Claudia, alias Korinna Kannbie, puts it all in a nutshell by saying 'Keep that in mind!' Finally only the name of the product is presented with a rather shrill but catchy tune. The whole performance is laced with the presentation of the little blue powder box being repeatedly held up to the centre of the camera lens, that is, to the imaginary audience's centre of attention, the centre of the gaze.

The teamwork between Lydia and Claudia, alias Korinna Kannbie, is predominantly led by Lydia who, as the advert presenter, presents the product with all its advantages. Using the 'new model' as a guinea pig, Lydia demonstrates the qualities of new Basic ('easy to apply', 'doesn't itch', 'nice and powdery') and vaunts its effects (the compulsory 'it makes me feel great' and 'you look beautiful!'). Enacting a chain of cause and effect, in her appraisal she links the quality of the product with well-being and beauty.

As the girls present the product verbally, at the same time they always handle the powder box, performing the standard presentational gestures of a commercial. We may wonder at this point what it is that motivates the girls to present the positive sides of the product in front of the camera with such verve. In doing this they in fact demonstrate mastery over the subject area that they are performing, i.e. 'self-confidence through beauty through well-being through make-up'. The girls generate and conjure up a product image that will endow us with beauty and self-confidence. Thus, the actual effect of the product becomes suffused with the images evoked by the way it is advertised, which suggest that a woman can only be attractive if she uses it. This message endows the product with 'performative magic', i.e. the promise of salvation and security. This is particularly important for young girls who are still rather insecure. The advertising suggests that this product will not only fulfil a functional need but that it will also turn you into an attractive woman. (What young girl of this age could resist?) At the same time, conjuring up such an effect remains a specifically female presentational strategy in a society where the cultivation of femininity, with the aid of the cosmetics industry, is part of a normative gender performance. Thus, by processing the topic of beauty the girls are in fact rehearsing specifically female presentational strategies and acting out their own femininity, which they do through the set performance practices of our particular culture.

Names are important. The name of the powder (Basic) also points to the 'basis' of this performance of being female. For 'Basic' makes up the material 'base' of the performance, from which both beauty and self-confidence spring. 'Basics' are to be found in everybody's handbag, wardrobe etc., the everyday necessities a woman simply can't do without. The girls add the 'Basic' powder to these many general 'basics' by giving the product its name.

The name of the model (Korinna Kannbie) is also more than an alliterative name for a beautiful woman. Indeed, the 'Americanised' name condenses the performative possibilities of self-expression. 'Korinna Kannbie' is of course Corinna Can-Be. She is what she can be through 'Basic'; she is able to design herself performatively. However, this 'Can-Be' is not a 'Must-Be', the performance is not compulsory, but merely possible; it can be but it does not have to be. A 'Can-Be' necessarily asks about what limitations there might be to what 'can be' and raises questions about the insecurity of existence. All this is sought to be understood performatively and possibly carries within itself a fear of the 'Cannot-Be'.

By varying and repeating a positive presentation of the product and reiterating the fact that it brings a sense of security with it (i.e. you are sure to be more beautiful) in a world of possible existential insecurity, the girls perform and express themselves in a way that is aimed to bring them recognition. In so doing they are training themselves in the social skills involved in advertising and presenting products. This is achieved by linking product presentation with self-expression. By closing her eyes and offering her face up to Lydia to be 'painted' (in the sense of 'describing' or 'inscribing' her), Claudia, alias Korinna Kannbie, enacts a general approval of being painted, or rather, performs a trusting and pleasurable bodily act of self-discipline and subjugation to the product and to Lydia's authority as advert presenter.

In terms of space, because of the physical intimacy, the process of being made up can be understood as an act of bonding between the two girls, as a performance in time it represents a transition: the transition from an un-made-up condition to a made-up condition, from an un-painted to a painted state, from an undefined state of being to a defined state of being. This transition can be interpreted as an initiation rite, as an act of initiation from girl to woman, as a change of state. This all takes place within the light-hearted context of the commercial performance. Before and during the make-up procedure, Claudia, alias Korinna Kannbie, sits quietly and still on a chair, opening her mouth when her name is uttered, with her upper body swaying forward at the same time, quite relaxed, and her arms enfolding her knees. (At the mention of the powder, however, she grins, nodding affectedly and affirmatively.) As a model she expresses herself as being both passive and 'on offer': the open mouth, the doubly crossed body (both her arms and legs are crossed) swaying towards the camera and the imaginary viewers. After the make-up process is over, however, she stands up; she strides confidently towards the imaginary audience and speaks, gazing straight into the camera. Both of these states of being that she enacts are connected to each other by the transitional phase of being made up (a connective act) as well as separated from each other (transition/threshold).

In his studies on initiation rituals, Victor Turner (e.g. 1982) focuses in particular on the liminal or threshold phase, which is characterised by vagueness, insecurity and crisis, which lays the foundations for the transformation. This type of insecurity is manifest in the halting speech of Claudia, alias Korinna Kannbie. Her answer to the rhetorical and expectant question of the presenter during the make-up procedure: 'So how does it feel?' marks the transitional phase of this little initiation by the clumsy words, 'It feels ni-... It makes me feel great!', which she utters with her eyes still closed. Her initially reserved, restrained and expectant sitting position with legs crossed, hands folded over one knee, head slightly tilted and mouth open, changes into an act of 'resurrection' after the make-up session, and culminates with her standing up. Claudia, alias Korinna Kannbie, opens her made up eyes, holds her head upright, stands up, walks a few steps towards the imaginary audience, her hands fingering her buttons like Napoleon, and speaks emphatically as if it were a matter of course. And then, grinning contentedly with her eyes closed and her head back, she shows her blue eyelids from all sides. Korinna enacts the effect of the product by taking on a new self-assured identity: self-confidently standing on her own two feet, speaking into the camera emphatically and with a firm gaze because she is 'Naturally! Beautiful with Basic!' 'Keep that in mind!'

The last sentence signifies the new found authority of Korinna Kannbie. She decides, indeed commands, what the audience has to keep in mind. Her firm gaze leaves no room for doubt: it is a gaze that speaks of self-confidence and security. Grinning with self-assurance and with her head tilted back she then presents the source of this security, 'The new Basic!' Her 'resurrection' implies that the act of disciplining the body is really an act of creation, the origin of a new identity. Physical subjugation to the product and the act of being made up open up new options to Claudia in performing her role as the model Korinna Kannbie. At the same time, they contain the draft of a very particular role enactment: a role which enacts gender and the idea of being female and feminine. Concepts of being female, as imaginary concepts, require creative performances to bestow them with effective reality (Butler, 1993).

Claudia's, alias Korinna Kannbie's, affected grin not only demonstrates her pride in this new role. It also contains an act of distancing herself from her role, which is evident in her ironically exaggerated smile, thus establishing a distance between her role and the way she is performing it. At this point, Claudia's performance becomes ambivalent, and the direction it is taking only becomes clearer again when she can use the powder box again.

Lydia performs her role as advert presenter as a figure of authority who prescribes social norms, who not only exacts social expectations but also seeks reassurance from the imaginary audience as to whether or not the norms have been fulfilled. She evaluates the effect of the make-up procedure as positive with the words 'You look beautiful!' and then amplifies this evaluation in her rhetorical question to the audience behind the camera 'Doesn't she?!' In this powerful act of giving her approval, the presenter consolidates her own power. For when she appeals to the audience they cannot fail to agree with her—they have no choice. The model adopts this positive evaluation from the advert presenter—naturally. If everybody else finds her beautiful, then why should she not? At the same time she basks in the compliment, as her closed eyes and contented leaning back suggest. The acceptance of the evaluation of her looks, which has been imaginarily confirmed, bestowing her with collective approval and a touch of power, initiates the unfolding of her new self-confidence. She fulfils the norm in accordance with Lydia's expectations, which represents a social norm: she is found attractive—and can lean back in a relaxed way.

The norm represented by Lydia is not just any norm. In it resides the social norm of a male gaze, with which women and girls have learned to look at themselves—brought to a point in the now famous sentence by the cultural critic John Berger: 'Men look at women and women look at themselves as the ones who are being looked at. This mechanism not only determines most of the relationships between men and women, it also determines the relationships women have with themselves' (Berger, 1980: 47). According to Naomi Wolf, this gaze that determines the relationship draws its power from a beauty myth according to which in order to be 'woman' a woman must be beautiful (Wolf, 1991: 10). The effect of this beauty myth on socialisation is that women see themselves in comparison with the norms of aestheticised images. In their performance of their chosen theme complex 'make-up—well-being—beauty— self-confidence', Lydia and Claudia enact the seemingly 'successful' social positions as women in commercials. They emphasise this by their casting: Lydia as the knowledgeable make-up expert and advert presenter who introduces and praises the product and Claudia as the model who is beautiful *per se* and even more beautiful with 'Basic'. They thereby act out the ambivalent elements of power and subjugation, for the self-confident woman who stands on her own two feet and holds her head up high only comes into being in a procedure by which the body is disciplined.

Interestingly, it is not beauty that is the girls' first and foremost concern but well-being. This is what presenter Lydia's first question refers to ('So, how does it make you feel?'). It is only afterwards that there is a remark about beauty ('You look beautiful!'), implying that if you feel good you are beautiful. In the girls' performance beauty is therefore not reduced to mere looks but brought about by well-being, which is caused by the blue powder. The former remark is formulated as a question, albeit not a very open one, the latter as statement of confirmation. In the performance, the feeling (of well-being) evades the efforts to conjure it up. The privacy of how one feels, since this is an emotional inner space is more protected than what is visible on the outside. From a different angle, one could also conclude that now one also has to feel good to be considered beautiful—mere looks are not sufficient: the need for well-being can become just as much of a straitjacket as the cultivation of one's looks.

At this point we may conclude that the transition from girl to woman, which is still half playfully performed in the Basic-advert, only repeats, with the aid of culturally cultivated techniques, what happens to women generally and on a daily basis as they look at their reflections in millions of mirrors, as they move from the private sphere to the public sphere where social recognition is important. The normative ideology of beauty and the ideals propagated by it are negotiated by girls and women in collective processes and then taken up and prescribed in the interests of advertising.

In the 'Basic' advert performance, Lydia and Claudia can be seen to be acting out and recreating a standard presentational style: in the presentation of the product they are presenting themselves in their female gender roles, in particular as those who make up and are made up. In the ritual genre of the commercial, here especially the cosmetics commercial, and by the bonding act of touching as they apply make-up for the advert performance, they are enacting a ritualised transition from girlhood to womanhood. Thus they enact a concept of being female, that is full of potential and also ambivalence—'Can-Be', the idea of having to suffer to be beautiful, well-being, pride of approval, self-confidence. In their acceptance and creative reworking of their roles, which have been laid down for them by the media but which are taken up and acted with gusto, in the bonding act of applying make-up, Lydia and Claudia are also performing an act of disciplining the body along consumerist lines. This is a ritual initiation of a self-confident and disciplined woman who feels good and is motivated by the thrust of gaining social recognition on the level of the imagination.

Pleasure in obscenity

A similar presentational style, but with additional issues of body and gender is performed by the actors of the following advert performance, which is intended as a comic act.

> After a brief agreement among all participants, the commercial is choreographed under the direction of Maria, who coordinates the movement of the boys and marks the beginning of the act by clapping an imaginary clapperboard. The advert

presenter Murat, standing to the left of Binol and Vladimir's swinging behinds, shouts into the camera: "THIS IS THE PERFUME FOR THE ARSE!" holds the spray-on deodorant out towards the camera with his right hand, brings it to his nose, smells it and shouts out the product name printed on the can, "ROXAAAANNE!" He then generously sprays Binol's and Vladimir's backsides, which are rhythmically moving next to him and shouts out again, "ROXAAAANNE!" Binol and Vladimir continue to proffer their behinds to the camera, moving them rhythmically while singing laughingly, "Waggle, waggle; waggle, waggle". At a sign from the director, the advert presenter jumps towards the camera with outstretched arms and thumbs up, and yells out "YEAH!" This is immediately followed by the two other actors who turn around in a jump and also yell out "YEAH!" loudly laughing with outstretched arms and thumbs up.

In its form of product presentation, the children's performance fits into the accepted rules of screen commercials: in a presentation (spraying of the behinds) the product ('perfume for the arse') is repeatedly held up to the camera with a name ('ROXAAAANNE!') and a positive connotation (three times 'YEAH!'). At the same time, the commercial contains the rhythmical group movement of the two 'waggling' behinds. This is a parody of commercials which attempt to reinforce the positive presentation of a product by using well-orchestrated and celebratory group movements.

In this scene, however, the boys are not advertising a conventional product but a 'perfume for the arse'. In the performance, the spray-on deodorant is used for the same purpose as such products usually are, not in the usual place. The behinds, otherwise known for their unpleasant odour, are liberally sprayed by the presenter Murat, with a product, whose purpose is to neutralise body odour and make it smell better. By the degrading shift of the product being not for the armpits but the 'arse' the children are presenting a region of the body, which is even more intimate and taboo than the armpits. The boys move their bottoms in baggy jeans, 'waggling' them in an attempt at rhythm. Even though, there are graphic portrayals of this region of the body in TV-commercials, the social sciences and cultural anthropology pay it very little attention. Also in the realm of school, which is where the video workshop takes place, bottoms are certainly more usually objects of taboo than of conversation.

No doubt the attraction of this obscenely staged body part has to do with its taboo status, which in turn has its roots in the taboo sexual connotation of the arse as well as in the sexual and dirty connotation of its orifice. 'Open body' is the term used by Mikhail Bakhtin (1968) to describe an aesthetics relating to the body which emphasises acts of transgressing the boundaries of the body and thus especially to the body's orifices—like those relating to excretion, eating, sex and birth. The aesthetics of the open body is presented by Bakhtin as the grotesque; an aesthetics which plays with body taboos and sexual fears and thereby shifts and transforms conventional ways of presentation. It is precisely this open body that the children stage in their advert scene, parodying the presentational form of commercials like that of the body by their grotesque performance. For, unlike what we are used to from body-care commercials, the use of the deodorant is not presented as a discrete and aesthetic procedure. Rather, the product is praised by a person who presents its use on two exaggeratedly swaying bottoms. Here, an intimate act of physical hygiene is replayed by the children and transformed into a collective movement of bottoms. They thus turn a commercial for a body-care product, the aim of which is normally to promise refinement and individuality, on its head. In the history of civilisation the subject of hygiene is a particularly sensitive one. The area of body politics is full of tensions between anti-hedonist moralising and hedonist sexualisation. In the children's performance, however, it is amusingly lampooned. Also, the deodorant, which, like many other body-care products, was initially developed and marketed for women, has nothing of that association here. On the contrary, as a body-care product for the backside it no longer fulfils its task of differentiating between the sexes. It is also presented by boys.

By taking over roles that are traditionally equated with femininity, the boys may perhaps be indicating their interest in the other sex, or in that which is alien to them and, considering their age, is probably also exceedingly exciting. The gender-specific roles, as presented by the media, are not rejected but taken over and parodied by replaying them in a fun way. At the same time, by means of this parody, there appears to be a difference from the female gender role, for in the term 'perfume for the arse' there is the hidden connotation of a 'perfume for an arse-hole' (i.e. they are being disparaging about the person for whom it is intended). Thus, the very act of naming the product sabotages it. Its use as a traditionally more female 'scent', evoking ethereal substances, which is usually portrayed in TV-commercials with an erotic whiff of success, is 'arsed around with' by the initiators of the scene so that it appears as something that is hopelessly unsuccessful.

In their 'Basic' commercial the girls dare to utter what in real advertising only exists as a non-spoken subtext ('Keep that in mind!'). Similarly, in the deodorant performance the children present the open body, which is barred from body-care ads. But the performance goes even further: by the ambivalent setting of what they are enacting—the bottom as an attractive object, the ironic hip-rolling movement, the product 'perfume for the arse' as 'perfume for an arse-hole'—not only do the children parody the use of a perfume or deodorant as being 'for arse-holes', they also ridicule the marketing efforts of advertising. At the same time, it is precisely this pastiche of spraying the deodorant (associated with being female) and advertisement that allows the children to touch on the partly taboo themes of sexuality and physicality, that are constantly shifting, and playfully appropriate them in the performance. The form of the commercial, albeit a grotesque one, provides a creative and safe space for this.

Through spraying the deodorant, shouting and 'bottom waggling' the children's performance follows the standard presentational style of advertising—the product is presented on the backsides, which present themselves simultaneously. The movement of the backsides emphasises the fact that the whole subject area cannot be pinned down. In the bonding act of rhythmic movement, the bodies become united in a hedonistic way into a single group. Because of the parody that is being enacted there is no subjugation of the bodies to the product, the purpose of which, aside from the pure pleasure of using movement in the performance, is not further elucidated by the children. In their enactment of the subject 'perfume-arse-sexuality' they pick up on the sexual connotations present in many commercials and parody them by their disparaging, degrading and irreverent attitude to the product and the performance of open bodies. In this derisive manner, rather than through dry discourse, the performance of the advert 'perfume for the arse' proves to be a travesty of this type of commercial.

How the standard presentational style is subverted

In the video performances of the 'advertising' genre presented here, the children mainly interpret (1) items as products on sale, by using (2) the standard presentational style of advertising, and (3) they bond into groups as they perform myths upon which society is based as they work through social differences, by means of rhythmical physical interaction. They do this by using the material of their performance, through the message that they are trying to convey and their presentational style. We can elucidate these three aspects as follows.

1. In the girls' advert scene the product presented is linked to its effects. 'Basic' is associated with beauty. By establishing this link, the girls are primarily

performing a commercial for a product, which, in their advertising presentation, exhibits the effects of the product. In other words, the material is presented in a performative way that emphasises its effects. In contrast, the boys' workshop is less concerned with linking product and effects than with emphasising the realm of body and sound—'perfume' with a swinging of the bottoms and a communal chant. This presentation, which emphasises movement and body, is primarily a brand-image commercial. Brand-image commercials create an association between a brand and an atmosphere which is staged and created by a group of people or by using nature or technological images. These do not focus on the product itself but represent moods, status etc. which are associated with the product that is to be bought. For the boys these are hedonistic group movements, and their joy in movement is a purpose in itself. The effects of the products and the purpose of their use remain unclear.

2.   Even without any prior agreement all the children who performed these scenes were clearly familiar with the accepted style of advertising and the standard presentational style associated with it. Whilst the first advert performance (Basic) is most closely in line with the ritual rules of advertising, the 'perfume' performance distances itself from accepted rules by employing parody and subversive elements. While the girls process the topic of beauty and being female in an affirmative manner, the three boys in the 'perfume' commercial break the approved presentational form of advertising by making use of indexical shifts in their style of presenting the product and staging the subject area 'body and hygiene' in an obscene way.

3.   Within the framework of commercials there have been seen to be many processes whereby children bonded into cohesive groups through playful creativity. The first example (Basic) deals with the social myth of beauty. On the one hand the ritual treatment of this creates a group identity in the bonding ritual of putting on make-up; on the other hand, in the transition ritual from young girl to grown woman, it also produces the ambivalence of a self-disciplined and self-confident woman. In the second example ('perfume') the boys take on a group identity in the rhythmical movement of their bottoms (a bonding ritual). On the other hand, the way they present their bodies, trampling over taboos and satirising the adult concepts of body and hygiene, contains a ritualised treatment of the generation gap.

The children form a group identity through the framework of their commercials. This is achieved in a performance that is not (only) affirmative but (also) ironic and subversive. The presentational style is the practical knowledge that the children have. They conform to this style by presenting indexically charged products and in so doing they process their own issues and concerns. Additionally the presentational style is performative: it becomes creative by being enacted. This style catches the audience's attention; it is a 'bridge' between the actors and viewers who are present in the room or imaginarily present through the eye of the camera. The children perform by using a form of communication that is not based on dialogue, as is always the case on television. This form of communication has nothing to do with the performers. The group bonding processes that they undergo are based on their practical knowledge of what constitutes standard presentational style, which they act out hedonistically. They may ridicule the intentions of advertising, by sabotaging it. The presentational style is part of the habitual presentational world of the children, but they are not oblivious of its intention.

The chat show: a ritualisation of real life

Amongst the TV genres most often taken up in the children's media performances chat shows rank close behind advert performances. Indeed, three out of four children's video workshops chose to perform chat shows, and in these performances the children displayed a detailed practical knowledge of the performative characteristics and peculiarities of the genre. The children's chat shows can be divided into the two types: 'confessional chat shows' and 'celebrity shows'. The children's interest in chat shows seems surprising at first glance, for this kind of programme is not usually considered to be designed for children and young people. The relatively drawn-out format which usually lasts an hour or more and the non-fictional and verbal emphasis that characterise chat shows would seem to go against the viewing preferences of the age group that we are studying here.

The 'chat' that occurs in chat shows must of course be clearly differentiated from argumentative conversation or from the notion of talk as the verbal transmission of information. Indeed, in the talk that takes place in most chat shows it is not 'what is said' that counts, as much as the 'relationship' that is presented. As an entertaining performance of 'socialising' this 'talk' has become a central component of a general trend towards a greater emphasis on speech in television, a TV of 'talking heads', which takes up more and more space in the image world of this medium (Plake, 1999: 18, 47 ff.).

Like other media analyses, previous empirical studies of chat shows have focused largely on the structure of programmes on offer, how they are presented and the contents of individual broadcasts as well as on their reception in terms of viewers' habits and how often they watch programmes. In contrast to this approach, our purpose is to show the ways in which chat shows in the re-enactments of the children appear as ritualised media productions and how they can be linked to ritualised processes of creating peer group identities. The re-enactment of ritual media performances is evidence of consumerism also being creative, as it transforms and converts media models in order for us to rehearse an 'art of action' on the level of physical action and habitual social practices (see Mikos, 2000: 74). Through staging or recreating the ritual aspects of actions, through mimetic adaptations and creative imitations a sense of community is established.

Chat as a show

The emergence and the ubiquity of chat shows can be seen as a mark of social change. Chat shows are described as the product of a 'reflexive modernity', in which self-reflection has increasingly become central in society. Chat shows enact a 'negotiation society'; they show that, beyond binding norms and values, everyday life is accompanied by a permanent discourse of negotiation. The ritual of the chat show consists in portraying social life as full of complexity, as a 'ruptured' world that cannot be depended on and is full of 'irritations' (Kade, 1999: 154 ff.), in which finding a direction and a sense of community identity come about through 'endless talk'. 'Constant talking ... prevents us from going mad because of ourselves and the world. At the same time it strengthens the social community in the widest sense, that is all of those with the same interests, with whom we can talk in that way' (Plake, 1999: 21).

Chat shows of a confessional or celebrity show variety that are related to everyday life form a counterpart to the TV-commercials that are also related to everyday life. While commercials attempt to performatively enhance everyday life by stylising them, by evoking associations and having a particular presentational style, chat shows obscure their performative character behind a form of chit-chat that could in fact be going on anywhere or everywhere in a similar way. The proximity to everyday life aims to transfix social reality from outside the realm of media performances onto the screen, in order to reveal people as they really are and portray their conflicts in an authentic way. In this respect, TV chat is similar to the discursive ritual of 'confession', which, according to Foucault, is diametrically juxtaposed to the sovereignty of the standard presentational style. What is being presented should not demonstrate its power and competence, but should be urged to reveal hidden truths and articulate weaknesses and passions (see Foucault 1978: 61 ff.). Chatting to celebrities is intended to liven up their carefully crafted public image. The 'celebrity show' is supposed to cleverly undermine itself as a show in order to let the 'spontaneous' life of the participants shine through. In so-called 'confessional talks', ordinary citizens discuss incidents that are extremely private and personal in front of the TV camera, thus creating an atmosphere of shared sympathy and concern among the participants and viewers.

This approximation to everyday life brings to light the fact that, due to its performative aspects, everyday socialising already contains elements of enactment and performance. Everyday performances and informal everyday conversations are doubled in the chat shows and ritualised by the particular performative character of television. Thus chat shows encourage a 'theatricalisation of everyday life', which is similar to our method of video performance, insofar as it provokes the performative side of everyday practice.

Chat shows are not merely continuations of everyday socialising but 'conversational performances'—a hybrid of 'verbal/acoustic' talk and a non-verbal/visual show that is designed to appeal to the emotions. Moreover, because they are broadcast on TV, chat shows have to fit into the dramaturgical frame of television which is characterised by brevity and terseness, the construction of tensions and climaxes as well as by commercial breaks and fragmentation (see Kade, 1999: 157 ff.). The whole programme is broken up into short episodes and individual appearances of people who often come together completely arbitrarily and hardly make any coherent sense. Daily repeated performances contain a multitude of ritual standard elements, which are varied on the indexical level by using diverse themes and participants. This structure of the genre—which includes a high degree of ritualisation and short individual sequences as well as suggesting an affinity with everyday performances—is obviously ideal for the children to re-enact. For indeed, in re-enacting these shows the children do not seem to have to make any particular theatrical effort and the genre allows them to create numerous references to their own lives.

The choice of topics of the children's performances are based on those in these kind of shows. Like on television, the enacted confessional shows are largely about social relationships, beauty and style. In the celebrity show, famous pop stars appear and, because of the very individual make-up of the participants, the way the stars present themselves follows an unusually confrontational course. We have selected two performances for detailed analysis.

Confession and healing: the ritual of 'confessional talk'

In the middle of the room an empty chair is placed in front of the camera. Lydia, the camerawoman, points the camera straight at the empty chair. The performance begins.

> Microphone in her hand, Claudia, the presenter of the chat show, steps into the frame from the right and places herself next to the empty chair. She looks into the camera and says in a clear, lively voice:
>
> Presenter: So, welcome to Talk, Talk, Talk … Tonight our theme is, 'Everybody laughs at me because of my clothes'. And our first guest is … (she raises her voice and indicates the door of the room in a presenting gesture)
>
> … BRITTA.
>
> Dunja, dressed up as Britta, enters the room in a colourful wrap-around skirt, a poncho-like cape and a knitted hat with earmuffs. In a slightly crouched posture she walks into the frame from the left and sits down on the empty chair, looking into the camera.
>
> Presenter: So Britta, why does everybody laugh at you?
>
> Britta: Because I wear such pre…tty clothes (she points at herself).
>
> Presenter: Well you want to have a make-over with us today, don't you?
>
> Britta: Yes.

This brief introductory scene leading into the chat show performance *Everybody laughs at me because of my clothes* runs both spontaneously and smoothly. Just before their performance began the three girls involved agreed on the scenario. Dialogues and actions were not discussed.

The apparent routine course of the performance results from a strict concentration on the standard elements of the confessional show: greeting of the viewers by the presenter; announcement of the theme; and presentation of the first guest etc. The indexical elements typical of chat shows—the presenter's remarks and explanations about the programme's theme—which define the particular cases more closely, are completely absent in this performance. The children's re-enactment condenses the ritual dimension of the media model and thereby elucidates what constitutes this particular genre.

The scenic arrangement—the fact that the guest sits facing the camera, and the presenter stands next to the guest with her gaze half directed at her and half at the camera—shows that the children are well acquainted with the performative characteristics of TV chat. The chat takes place between presenter and guest and not between several people at once. It is asymmetrical, the dynamic presenter standing above the passively sitting guest. The children's performance thus repeats a hierarchical structure that is typical of confessional shows: the presenters always remain sovereign and dominate the scene. They 'keep their cards close to their chests' while the guests are 'put on display' (Plake, 1999: 97-100). Thus, the scenario reveals a power imbalance, characteristic of confessional rituals, in which 'the agency of domination does not reside in the one who speaks (for it is he who is constrained), but in the one who listens and says nothing; not in the one who knows and answers but in the one who questions and is not supposed to know' (Foucault, 1978: 62). Finally, the whole happening is geared towards the audience and television viewers. By turning towards the camera, both the presenter and the guest make it clear that this is not a private conversation but is actually a performance in front of others.

At the centre of the conversation there is a 'victim-performance', in which a concerned guest makes a confession about her experiences and the presenter offers advice and assistance following the model of 'healing speech'. In Mikos's view, the 'victim's narration' represents the 'main narration of chat shows, in which individual fates are merely sub-plots of the narration' (Mikos, 1998: 439 f.). Tholen, on the other hand, detects a 'basic therapeutic dimension' in confessional shows, which allows the presenter to appear as a 'mixed character, something between therapist, social educator and sensationalist journalist' (Tholen, 2000: 146). The talk resulting from this constellation is performed as a 'discourse of concern', in which both participants and viewers are emotionally involved and in which the presenter functions as a disassociated 'higher authority'. Even though the children are unable to fill the victim's performance with a confessional narration that is verbalised with any clarity, they do express the victim-therapist constellation of the guest and presenter roles on a performative level. In the second episode of the 'clothes' chat show, Dunja and Lydia switch roles; Dunja takes over the camera and Lydia appears as the second guest 'Ingrid'. In her performance, Lydia emphasises Ingrid's victim status by appearing with a croaky voice and a cramped and anxious posture, thus making a pitiful impression.

The last ritual element of the introductory scene is indicated by the announcement of the make-over. The media ritual gives a visible form to what could become just an everyday conversation so that it can be grasped by the senses. In the course of the programme the guest has to undergo a visually perceptible change. He or she is expected to emerge from the programme visibly 'healed'. Changing outfits or cosmetic surgery are therefore popular topics for the children in their performances. Another option is for the chat show to be linked to a 'live life-drama' genre (the live presentation of a life drama), in which relationship problems and conflicts are acted out live in front of the camera and in the end carried over into a 'reconciliation', which is relevant to the everyday life of all participants, even outside of the context of the programme. In this way, television has a clear life-improving function, which goes beyond its own boundaries to become social reality (see Kade, 1999: 158 f.).

In TV chat shows, after the theme and guest have been presented, a conversation between guest and presenter takes place, which introduces the narrative element of confession. The guest's particular fate is laid bare, opening up a space for them to give a picture of themselves. The special nature of the media arrangement often provokes the most intimate revelations, which would normally only be revealed in an intimate social context because of the barrier created by embarrassment (see Mikos, 1998: 443 ff.). The peer groups do not transgress this barrier in their chat show performances. Because the children meet each other in an intimate social space outside of the performances as well, the anonymity brought about by a media appearance in front of an unknown mass audience is not guaranteed—a self-revelation would have concrete social consequences. This explains why the narrative element, the performance of the confession, is absent from the children's enactments. Instead there is a dialogue about body performance and body awareness, which articulates a mimetic and graphic 'intertextual knowledge' about visual clichés and role patterns (see Mikos, 2000: 86 f.; Gebauer and Wulf, 1995).

Returning to the children's chat show, immediately after the introductory greeting, a dialogue develops with each guest about their clothing. The guest remains seated with the presenter speaking into the camera while standing or walking around the guest, inspecting her. The following conversation develops between the guest, Ingrid, and the presenter:

Presenter:	And where did you buy these?
Ingrid:	Some I got out of the rubbish and some were hand-me-downs.
Presenter:	From your family?
Ingrid:	No, the Red Cross gave them to me.

Presenter:	I see (loudly). And did you buy any of them?
Ingrid:	Yes, the trousers. They were very expensive.
Presenter:	How much were they?
Ingrid:	Twenty Marks.
Presenter:	Twenty Marks? That's VEEERY expensive. Well, (walks around Ingrid), (into the camera) Ingrid also has the problem that she often gets laughed at because of her clothes (slight grin) and this makes her very sad. So, today you would like some helpful hints from us, is that right?
Ingrid:	Yes, please (whimpering). (...)
Presenter:	Well, the scarf looks OK., but it's more like a bed cover.
Ingrid:	Yes, but ... I do feel good in it. All it needs is some jewellery to go with it.
Presenter:	I see. Have you got any jewellery?
Ingrid:	No (a short laugh). I've got an earring. My boyfriend gave it me (voice still whimpering).
Presenter:	So you have a boyfriend?
Ingrid:	He left me.
Presenter:	Strange ... (looks into the camera) So, Ingrid wants to have a make-over today; so we'll send her out straight away (walks around Ingrid, looking at her). OK, Ingrid, so you'll have a make-over, I'd say.
Ingrid:	Thanks.
Presenter:	OK, that's the way out (points to the door). Bye ... and that was Ingrid.

Applause from offstage. Ingrid gets up and walks to the door with tiny steps.

The dialogue about Ingrid's clothes expresses her failure to present and dress her body with style. In obvious contrast to real TV chat shows, here both the price and the origin of the clothes are mentioned. Ingrid's lack of style is clearly identified as a material deficiency. Her lack of financial means prevents her from meeting the demands of dressing with style. The deficient outfit causes social exclusion and isolation ('everybody laughs at me because of my clothes', her boyfriend has left her) and thus becomes the central criterion for the organisation of social relations. In his studies about the connections between social class and social interaction among pupils, Wexler (1994) states that especially among children of the working and lower middle classes, image and physical dress play an important part in their self-esteem and social identity. Accordingly, in the inner-city borough of Berlin in our study, which has a high proportion of workers and immigrants, stylish dressing is an important means for young people to find an identity in a peer group. Those who cannot keep up face social exclusion. While the children re-enact the ritual standard form of presenting used in the media in a creative and ironically detached way, on the level of performance we see a process of creating or reinforcing a peer group identity that is crucial for the group.

In their transformation of the chat show format the children come up with a theme that brings to light the group dynamics of the girls' group. The three girls Lydia, Claudia and Dunja are part of a peer group which also exists outside of our video workshop and in which Lydia has the role of leader. From this position she is able to enact the status of victim with superior style and with an appropriate distance to her role. Dunja, however, who is not as well integrated into the group and lives in difficult social circumstances, cannot bear to play the role of victim. Thus, the ironic and humorous re-enactment of a media show that the children initially intended, in fact becomes a highly serious performance of group norms and hierarchies within the girls' peer group.

The staging of Dunja as victim is linked to the allusion to poverty as well. However, she breaks out of this role by suddenly wearing an expensive hat (500 Marks/250 €) and a jacket she bought at the High Street store Hennes and Mauritz. The very confused presenter tries to re-establish the initial allocation of roles by accusing her guest Britta (played by Dunja) of theft and thereby emphasising her poverty with the allegation of a socially deviant criminal act. As a result, Britta shifts back to her role as victim in the performance:

Presenter: Well, … and … did you buy them or did you steal them?
Britta: I bought them, of course!
Presenter: I see (looks into the camera). None of us can believe that she really did buy them. (Turning back to the guest) Yeah, well … but you have said the clothes were sooo … cheap.
Britta: Well they were … errrm, … in the box.

In the children's version, the sympathetic discourse of concern is replaced by an argument that touches on the foundations of their own friendship groups. Displaying who one is and achieving a rise in status by means of one's outfit are subject to limitations and social norms that are clearly expressed in the performance of the children. 'Outfit' is linked to individual body awareness, creating a relationship between body performance and self-confidence. This is indicated by Ingrid's remark that she feels good in her clothes, which are rejected by everyone else. While Ingrid, who is socially more privileged than Britta, can at least imagine feeling good despite the critical opinion of the other, for Britta the value of her physical appearance remains tied to the material value of her clothes. Good looks are not only a question of style and taste, but primarily a question of money. Someone threatened by poverty, however, also comes under pressure with regard to taste and style, thus jeopardising his or her group affiliation. Thus, although they do not consciously play the role of victim in a confessional show, what they do have is the involuntary confession of fear of the threat of poverty and social exclusion, which declares Claudia to be the real potential 'victim' of the group.

On the one hand, chat shows present the deviations, problems and unusual phenomena of everyday life, which dissolve notions of normality in favour of a confusing plurality of means and options. On the other hand, they tie the performance of the extraordinary to a code of conduct aimed at dismantling irritations and reconstructing the performance of social consensus as discursively affirmed normality. Kade therefore describes the confessional shows as a modern form of 'people's education', as an 'educational trash-world' (Kade, 1999: 151 f.; 171 f.).

Chat shows have an educational effect not so much by rational discourse which tells children how to behave but through the actual performance involved in the ritual process which causes children to adapt and 'act appropriately' (see Jennings, 1998: 65). Thus, a compulsion towards complying with norms can be observed, which is consciously reflected by the children. In the following scene the guest Ingrid appears on the stage anew after having undergone an extravagant make-over procedure by the group and her outfit having been changed into fashionable everyday clothes.

> Ingrid slowly enters the room, turning round several times and showing herself
> to the camera from all sides. She then sits down on a chair.
> Presenter: So Ingrid ... how do you feel?
> Ingrid: (in a lively, clear voice and a dynamic posture that is no longer
>   hunched) Well, I feel much better now.
> Presenter: I see, could you get up and take off your jacket?

Ingrid gets up, takes off her jacket and looks down at herself.

Presenter:	And have you asked about how much it costs?
Ingrid:	Yes (smiles in embarrassment).
Presenter:	And, how much?
Ingrid:	350 Marks.
Presenter:	But looking like this you'll be sure to get a job. You can find yourself a job and make money. Then you'll be able to afford it.
Ingrid:	Yes (smiles into the camera). Yes, thank you.

After her make-over, Ingrid complies with the dress-code of her peer group. Her appearance, which complies with the norm, is cemented by the comment on the appropriate price of her clothing (350 Marks/175 €). The fact that this outfit is not only accepted by her peer group but also articulates a social consensus that goes beyond it, is expressed by the suggestion that she could get a job and some money. In this way, the girls confirm their perception of the pressure of normalisation: a person's outfit is perceived as central to their social identity. Through what they wear social integration and status can be achieved. In the face of the healing re-socialising change that has been performed on her, Ingrid shows her gratitude towards the presenter. At the same time, she demonstrates with her voice and posture that fitting in socially on the level of how one presents and styles one's body brings with it a feeling of fitting with oneself. She now feels better and enacts this by having an appearance that is appropriate to her gain in status.

Britta, on the other hand, refuses to comply with the social consensus. Instead, she highlights a further compulsory aspect of the chat show ritual by rejecting her role as victim because she is different and challenging the roles of both victim and presenter.

Presenter:	And Britta, how do you like your new outfit?
Britta:	Not very much.
Presenter:	So you don't feel good in it?
Britta:	No.
Presenter:	But you'd stand a chance of getting a job for once, looking like this.
Britta:	Yeah (looks down at herself) … you're right.
Presenter:	I like the way you look now, and what does the audience say about it?

Lydia:	(intervenes as camerawoman) Oh yeah, I like you like that, it looks really nice.
Britta:	(turns to the presenter) Can I say something else too?
Presenter:	Yes.
Britta:	I would like to say something to you (points at the presenter). .... I think you're looking a bit scruffy. If I were you, I would definitely have a make-over.

The presenter is speechless and obviously perplexed.

Lydia:	(outraged) WHAT A CHEEK!
Britta:	I don't think so at all.
Presenter:	(interrupting) I agree, what a cheek! How rude!
Lydia:	Will you please leave the room now, yes, this is not allowed.
Presenter:	That was ... BRITTA...

Despite her protest, Britta is kicked out of the room by Lydia and the presenter.

At first, in the context of the ritual performance, Claudia the presenter acknowledges Britta's refusal to accept a make-over by recognising the discrepancy between social norms and individual creative preferences (feeling good). As the performance runs its course, the presenter emphasises the pressure to conform to norms in two different ways. First, with reference to the job argument she brings social consensus into play which also affects the peer group. Second, she tries to secure the peer group consensus for herself by addressing the viewers, who are only present in the form of the third peer group member, the camerawoman Lydia. Lydia accepts the invitation to speak straight away and immediately sides with the presenter by signalling her agreement.

At this point, Dunja breaks the ritual performance. She turns the roles around and begins to radically question the sovereignty of the presenter as a role model. The presenter Claudia thus loses the superior position that had allowed her to steer the show until now. She is helpless and at a loss while Lydia takes over the situation. As the dominant person in the group, Lydia sees her own status jeopardised by the attack on the normative standards of the group. She leaves her role as camerawoman and acts as presenter herself by expelling Dunja from the room. At this moment, Claudia re-enters the scene; she supports Lydia in kicking Dunja out and gradually returns to her role as presenter ('That was BRITTA').

Dunja's attack on the pressure of the chat show ritual to be 'normal' ties the ritual media performance to the peer group's process of bonding and interacting as a group. By refusing to approve of her new outfit, she presents the compulsory nature of the practices of bonding at work in confessional shows: her allusion to social consensus as well as to the agreement of the group taking part in the chat show become evident as a lever against acting differently. The questioning of the role balance between victim and presenter finally topples the basic principle of the ritual performance—the power imbalance between the superior presenter who is well acquainted with the practices of the show and the inferior guest. This transformation of the media model elucidates how the children not only repeat the rituals offered to them, but how on the level of performative action they are capable of a 'media analysis', a form of critical reflection on the media practices of creating a community identity.

The moment the ritual performance is broken, the girls swap their roles in the performance (presenter, guest, camerawoman) for their roles in the peer group. The performance is not given up in favour of everyday communication but is shifted to a mimetic sphere that switches between media interaction and peer group interaction in order to act out an unspoken conflict within the peer group. While the chat show continues on the level of the actual staged scene, the relationship dynamic within the group is expressed on the level of performance. For a short time, Lydia takes over the dominant role that she normally occupies in the group and Claudia reveals herself to be the slightly inferior ally.

In this way, the children's ritual media performance amounts to a staging of the group dynamics within their friendship group. It brings to light the group's 'ritual knowledge' about the chat show ritual, which consists not only in their ability to make a faithful copy but also in the ironic act of distancing, their playful reworking, and the performative analysis of the ritual process. At the same time, the action that is carried out in a creative sphere that falls in between ritual re-enactment and peer group interaction permits the group structure to be renegotiated and reconstituted. In the sketch, an unspoken competitive situation erupts into a 'mimetic crisis', which according to René Girard (1989) expresses the violence inherent in the process of the construction of a community.

From star to self: finding an identity through rituals

The second example of a chat show performance is based on the model of the celebrity show. Two rows of seats are set up diagonally in front of the camera so that the guests can sit half opposite each other and half facing the camera.

The presenter sits in the back row in the middle, microphone in her hand, and looks into the camera. In front of her there is a small table with cans of drink on it, suggesting a relaxed conversational atmosphere.

Presenter: Welcome to Interactive. We would like to introduce a new guest today. The first I would like to welcome are... um ... the Spice Girls, yeah, today we have Mel B and Emma.

Mel B and Emma enter the door side by side. Applause from offstage. They both sit down to the left of the presenter.

In the course of the performance, Missy Elliot, Emilia, Tarkan, Foxy Brown and Tupac join the circle one after the other. They are all stars from the world of pop music who are well known to the children even if they are not all liked to the same degree.

The Stars Chat Show differs significantly from the confessional show described above. Presenter and guests sit next to each other on a level of relative equality. The seating arrangement is such that a conversation among the guests can develop and the relaxed atmosphere is supposed to promote the well-being of the guests. The children's performance is in accordance with the main characteristics of the celebrity show: there is no central theme apart from the guests themselves. The guests are not introduced by a presenter who is in any way superior to them but are given room to display their own personalities. The host is presented as an acquaintance or friend, and is well informed about the backgrounds and biographical details of all her guests.

The children make use of this model of the celebrity show and apply it to the kinds of celebrities most relevant to them and the way they see themselves: music and pop stars. In this way an individual performance is created for which there is no direct ritual model on TV. The experimental character of the programme reflects the group situation: the eight participating children (six girls and two boys) do not belong to a fixed friendship group but to different cliques. They have met in the course of the video workshop, and the celebrity chat shows are the culmination of their work as a team. It is thus a decisive element of a process in which a community is formed, the course and outcome of which are open. The show to be staged by the whole group is therefore not based on a fixed ritual; there is only a relatively loose frame of heterogeneous ritual elements, all of which are taken from the media arsenal of 'TV talk'. At the centre of the ritual process are ritualised performances of the self, which the children sometimes play in a cool or ironic way and use to say something about themselves. Thus, a mimetic sphere comes into being, a tense constellation that is full of conflicts, which alternates between acting the role of the stars and expressing and asserting their own personalities. To begin with, the conversation in the chat show performance is about the stars themselves—their songs as well as gossip about their private lives. Thus, the Spice Girls Emma and Mel B are questioned about why they split with Geri; Missy Elliot is asked about her liposuction; and Emilia talks about her new song and her fans. What is most interesting here is not so much the concrete course of the conversation but the way 'media knowledge' is expressed. In turn, the children contribute their knowledge of 'their' stars.

The stars' ritualised performances of themselves produce a variety of types with distinct abilities, giving the children a range of identities and skills to choose from. Identifying with one particular style is a way of distancing oneself from other styles. By articulating their interest in a particular type, the children are able to secretly explore, through performance, aspects of consensus and difference within their group relationships on the level of taste, chosen style and feelings. In this way they are able to use ritual action to act 'appropriately' and at the same time negotiate heterogeneous group-styles and group formations in a more individual way. Our method of video performance encourages in particular the enactment of habitual styles that are evident in the re-enactment of ritualised performances by pop stars. Thus, Emma and Mel B appear as a girlie-group, with Emma behaving in an affected manner and Mel B in a more down to earth and reserved way, while both of them make nasty remarks about Geri. Missy Elliot, on the other hand, appears cool and relaxed, with her jacket slipping casually off her shoulders. As he talks she gazes ahead of her in a bored and phlegmatic way. In contrast, Emilia appears excessively exuberant; she stretches her arms out to the audience, greets the presenter with a kiss on both cheeks, and generally exudes a positive charisma. Finally, Tupac struts into the room in typical hip-hop style, wearing a back to front baseball-cap.

Since the only ritualised model the children have to base their performance on is the way the guests are introduced, after this there follows a rather chaotic situation in which two distinct processes of community bonding occur that we think are particularly important. The first process makes the group more stable through a 'them and us' scenario which entails the 'sacrifice' of a performance participant. From the way she greets 'Emilia' it is clear from the start that Norma, the presenter, who is quite dominant within the girls' clique, is no fan of Emilia. Although she is very knowledgeable about the other stars, she reveals that she knows nothing at all about Emilia who enters the conversation, joining the Spice Girls and Missy Elliot who are already present at this point.

After her expansive entrance Emilia sits down on the right, opposite the Spice Girls and in between the presenter and Missy Elliott. She takes the microphone from the presenter and opens the conversation.

Emilia: (to the presenter) I like you a lot, you know.

Presenter: (takes back the microphone) Well, Missy Elliot ... what can I say (touches her forehead)? Emilia, your new song, what is it called?

Emilia: Good Times (smiles).

In the course of the 'show', no further conversation develops about Emilia and her music. Instead, the presenter asks the others 'celebrities' what they think of Emilia.

Presenter: (turns towards the Spice Girls) What do you think of Emilia?

Emma: Well, Emilia, I think she's a ...

Mel: Well, I don't like Emilia, her songs, eh, her new song, well, she's just gets chatted up on the beach or something.

Emilia: No, they like my legs.

Mixture of shouting and howling.

Presenter: (takes back the microphone) Well, I'll bring in a boy now, he knows about these things... and it is Tarkan ...., Tarkan.

Tarkan enters wearing shades. There is applause as he reaches his arms out to the audience and the camera, sits down to the left of Mel B with his legs apart and raises his shades.

Presenter: We were just talking about Emilia, and wondering whether she really has such good legs. What do you think, Tarkan?

Tarkan: Well, she's just my type.

Until this point the situation seems to be relatively open. Emilia is rejected by the Spice Girls Emma (alias Maria) and Mel B (alias Janine), whereas it is above all Janine who sets the tone for the conversation with her detailed contemptuous judgement. The presenter Norma clearly sympathises with the Spice Girls while Missy Elliot (alias Michaela) appears to be indifferent up to this point. Sabak (alias Emilia) tries to defend herself and receives support from the newcomer Binol (alias Tarkan) who is unaware of the undercurrents in the girls' clique. In his answer, Binol bases himself on the character he is playing who is well known to be a womaniser and will therefore generally try to please any woman. In what follows he is explicitly briefed on the 'right attitude' while the attack shifts from the star Emilia to being a personal attack on Sabak herself.

Emma: Tarkan, well ... you're really not well informed here.
Tarkan: Well, I only know Turkish women.
M. Elliott: Hey, Tarkan, do you ever watch Viva or MTV?
Tarkan: Yeah, sometimes (holds his shades in his hand).
Presenter: Well, this here is Emilia (points at Emilia).
Emma: This one, the ugly one (also points at Emilia).
Emilia looks affectedly and in a theatrical manner to the side while raising one leg.
Presenter: Well, we have another guest today. Because we also have Foxy Brown here (with a raising animated voice; everyone claps and howls).
Foxy B. comes into the picture, sits down between Tarkan and Spice Girl Mel B.
Presenter: What do you think of Emilia?
Foxy B.:   Well, I have to admit that the music she makes is tasteless (shakes her head disapprovingly).
Emilia begins to cry fake theatrical tears.

Tarkan's briefing extends from the remark about Emilia's star performance in the music programmes Viva and MTV to a comment on her 'ugliness', which is probably directed personally at Sabak. When Esther (alias Foxy Brown) also emphasises Emilia's 'tastelessness', Sabak sees only one way out: she puts on an act; that is, she seeks to distance herself as a person from the star she is portraying. However, the following attack by the hitherto passive Michaela (alias Missy Elliott) is 'below the belt', that is, she steps out of role to attack and humiliate Sabak as a person.

Missy Elliott: I have a question for Emilia (suppresses a laugh), ... why do you stink?
Everybody laughs except Emilia.
Emilia: (stands up, takes the microphone and raises her head and nose in a huff) No comment! (in an accentuated voice).
Emma: Well, I have to say, I can smell Emilia from right over here, and yeah ... umm ...

Presenter:	(claps her hands) Can you all calm down please, please. We're in a live show, here.
Tarkan:	(grabs the microphone) Well, now I want to say something to Emilia. There really is a smell around here, like a gorilla's bum, no shit!
Emilia:	(stands up and throws a can on the floor outraged). THAT'S IT. I'VE HAD ENOUGH! (She leaves the room and the workshop for good.)

With this turn-around by Binol (alias Tarkan) it becomes clear that the whole group has now formed a united front, displaying an attitude that the core group of the girls' clique had previously held. It is the ritualised dispute about star images and preferences of taste that creates this common bond. Sabak's attempt at self-assertion by making a distinction between playing the role of a star and playing herself remains hopeless, since by ganging up on her as the star (who some of the participants in the chat show performance probably do not even know) they are actually ganging up on her personally. So, after Sabak's futile attempt to make the distinction clear, the attacks are aimed directly at Sabak personally.

By means of the ritualised game involving images of media stars, the unstructured children's group develops the idea of someone being 'different'. It introduces a 'structuring principle', which distinguishes between 'them and us' (see Bourdieu, 1977: 22 f.). The outcome of this group process is the constitution of a community—of a performative harmony between boys' and girls' cliques at the cost of the sacrifice of Sabak who becomes the focus of negative projections. By using taste and habitual style, and basing themselves on media role models, groups create their own criteria for participation and who should enjoy privileges, rejecting the 'tasteless'. Sabak, who stands out at school because she is conscientious and works hard, is therefore subjected to these processes of exclusion, which can go as far as bullying. In this context, it becomes clear that these ritualised practices of creating a group identity produce a social reality that can have serious consequences for those concerned.

The second group process concerns Murat, alias Tupac, who performs himself. Tupac is a well-known rap singer from the Hip-Hop scene, who had been long dead at the time of the chat show performance. The cause of Tupac's death has never been officially established. The spectacular nature of the appearance of a 'dead' star is further intensified by the presence of his former partner Foxy Brown among the talk guests.

Presenter:	Tupac is supposed to be dead. Why are you alive again?
Tupac:	Well (mumbles), they wanted to kill me with a matchstick ... Then I sent out a couple of blokes and they both got it. They told them to come back tomorrow (barely comprehensible inarticulate language).
Presenter:	That was cool.
Emilia:	So what are these photos?
Presenter:	Yeah, what about the photos of the corpse? It's been proven that you're dead!
Tupac:	That's because of that millionaire. She thinks she killed me ... (incomprehensible).
Presenter:	You mean Foxy Brown, well she's here today (points at Foxy B.).
Tupac:	(disinterested) Well, she's as good as handicapped (stammering).
Foxy B.:	(screaming) THIS IS NOT TUPAC!
Tarkan:	(positions himself opposite Foxy B., screams even louder) THIS IS THE ORIGINAL TUPAC!

Commotion, performance is interrupted.

Murat blurs the boundaries between a re-enactment of his favourite star and a ritualised performance of his own self. There is only little difference in Murat's portrayal of the role 'Tupac' and the way he presents himself every day as a cool Hip-Hop star with the status of an outsider. Murat does not enact an individual person but a role type, a specific media image. He revives a dead media star, taking ownership of him by blurring the edges and using him for a ritualised performance of his self. While the girls proceed on a theatrical level by bringing the legend of Tupac into play, Binol, alias Tarkan, comes to his friend's defence. He does this by shifting the dispute about whether Tupac is fake or real to a different level, whether this is a successful portrayal of Tupac's style, so how good a mimetic 'adaptation' it is. As the performance continues, the argument about Tupac erupts anew.

Tupac:	(interrupts the ongoing conversation by not participating; grabs the microphone) I am not here because of your stupid drivel. I'm here to ... show you ... (falters)

Emma:	To prove to us that you're alive, right?
M. Elliott:	(to the presenter) Are you so poor that you can't even afford a real Tupac?
Presenter:	THIS IS THE REAL TUPAC.
Foxy B.:	(stands up) THIS IS THE REAL TUPAC! (turns to the presenter, points at Tupac with a stretched out arm)
Tarkan:	(stands up, walks over to Tupac, Tupac stands up too) THIS IS THE REAL TUPAC (takes off Tupac's cap, point at his shaved head), this is the original Tupac. (outraged, Foxy B. gets in between, Tarkan positions himself protectively in front of Tupac) This is his original shaved head. (puts Tupac's cap back on, shouts) … AND THIS IS HIS TATOO (points at Tupac's chest) … of his mother.

The dispute about the self-performance of Murat alias Tupac takes on an existential dimension. Binol alias Tarkan makes clear that Murat is not playing a role but that his whole body actually stands for his media idol, from his shaved head down to his tattoo. Anyone who questions Murat's performance is questioning Murat himself—this therefore really is a matter of life and death. Murat's status in the peer group is merged to such an extent with his ritualised self-performance that without it he would cease to exist for the group. Murat's image in the peer group depends on the ritualised re-enactment of a media image. His performance is aimed at insiders and is designed to confirm his identity as an insider, and it is only their judgement that he seems to appreciate. This is why Murat's performance is hard to fit into the extended group of chat show participants.

In the end, Murat finally succeeds in being accepted. By his unbending consistency and his unconventional attitude, Murat gains considerable prestige and is able to raise his status in the group. By the ritualised performance of his media character as a shady outsider (the assassinated Tupac as gangster rapper) his social position in everyday school life, which is that of a disruptive character on the margins of the group, finds expression. Murat transforms it into a style of his own which brings about a credible relation between 'social position' and the 'disposition' of social action (see Bourdieu, 1977: 17). Although normally Murat is one of a small group of other outsiders, through this mimetic fitting together of model and self he attains social recognition and the chance to be a member of the larger group.

Learning how to live in the world

Advocates of the chat show genre insist that it helps to give people some sort of direction in society. This appears to be because, in a society that no longer has traditions, holding conversations about questions of style and taste has become a central feature of the way we socialise every day with others. Our study has shown that TV chat is not just a simple illustration of everyday socialising but a ritual performance. Although it may not replace the coherent meanings and symbols that are rooted in tradition, nevertheless it does contain a permanent actualisation of collective memory with regard to performative figures of everyday social life.

The mimetic 'assimilation' of media models through ritual action and knowledge does not happen smoothly but—as our examples have shown—with a lot of conflict. The shift from the drama of the TV model to the drama of the group comes about through a performance which contains the important elements of irony and subversion and also involves a distancing from the media show on which it is based. Thus the performance transforms the group. Performing one's own self through the ritual portrayal of a media star and negotiating style, taste and normativity through the ritual re-enactment of a media show enables young people to watch, to reveal themselves and quarrel in a non-overt way. All these are typical of adolescent group interactions. The reference to the media leads to a ritualisation of group action, through which differences and conflicts are acted out. In this way, a concrete reality finally emerges. Here issues of social inclusion and exclusion, status, belonging or being different emerge as important elements in the formation of peer group communities.

'Just try it!' Lydia cajoles us in the 'Basic' commercial. Our attempt to provoke media-related group action in children's peer groups through the method of video performance proved to be successful. The ritual re-enactments ranged from the aesthetic elevation of the world of products and commodities through life-style performances and performances of one's self to the presentation of emotional conflicts and innermost feelings. The media programmes have given the children a platform to act as a group or community. Through ritual re-enactments ways of performing develop that require a repetitive structure and team-work. The oscillation between media models and peer group re-enactments opens up an area of tension, in which the children rehearse an 'art of performance' containing a performative negotiation of social and group-related norms and values. This happens through repetition, subversive resistance and creative transformation. This performance art either concerns negotiations of membership and demarcation lines, as in the case of groups that are put together artificially or whose composition is determined by chance, or, as in the case of groups that already existed as friendship groups before, it deals with power relations within the group and normative standards.

The ritualisation processes found in peer group interaction contradict the thesis of a de-ritualisation of the transition process between child and adult. The place of normative rituals that are tied to traditions is taken up by more flexible, group ritualisations, which establish structures and work out differences in multiple ways. The mimetic appropriation of such structures is linked to violence and force. We do not see any sign of a transformation of collective 'puberty rites' into a more individual way of coping with the difficulties of adolescent problems, because nowadays as children and adolescents grow up, this goes hand in hand with the forming of peer group identities. Therefore they remain rooted in ritualised collective forms of action. Thus, ritualisations continue to be a part of the processes of the transitions of adolescence involving separation and status. In plural societies, however, rather than being binding, fixed rituals processes are variable and differ according to the composition of the group. The media, and television in particular, provides an ideal platform for this.

In heterogeneous peer group contexts, that have no roots in tradition, ritual media performances represent a way of securing social interaction and thereby creating a community identity. Such processes of community creation are often as fleeting as the media themselves. They are limited in time, fragmented and related to specific situations. In peer group constellations, that are usually unstructured or only loosely structured, they do not cause an immediate bonding, but they do supply a way of defining boundaries of inclusion and exclusion, that is, for the performative negotiation of hierarchies and 'subtle differences' (Bourdieu, 1984), which are always a mark of society in its wide social differentiation. The ritualised game with the virtual media-world of appearances brings about a concrete and tangible social reality, a world of competition, winners and victims, conflicts, resistance and compulsory adaptations, which shows that children have indeed learned the 'lesson' of how to behave in society in an appropriate way.

Chapter 5

The role that mimesis plays in rituals

We will now turn to the question of how ritual knowledge emerges and is acquired. Our purpose is to show that ritual knowledge, as a form of performative practical knowledge, is acquired mimetically, or through creative imitation. At the same time, we intend to show that a reconstruction of ritual action using qualitative methods involves mimetic processes. This has been previously pointed out by both Uwe Flick (1995, 2000) and Ralf Bohnsack (1999) who draw on Gunter Gebauer and Christoph Wulf (1995, 1998).

Little America

Once a year the school from which our empirical material has been drawn organises an 'Activities Week'. Its purpose is to allow the children to discover other kinds of learning experiences than those available in ordinary lessons. During this week, the children take on a more active role in planning, organising and engaging in activities than usual. Their task is to think up different kinds of extra-curricular activities. The idea is to offer the children experiences that cannot, or cannot easily, be provided within the usual school curriculum. Moreover, during this week, the way the school is organised in years and tutor groups according to age is temporarily suspended; children of different ages take part in activities together and are able to enjoy new experiences and different social contacts. Many of the projects involve creating something that will later be shown to parents or displayed to the whole school.

The Little America project, which will be described in detail here, brought together eight girls of different ages and at different stages of development. Their activity involved learning and rehearsing the song 'Mambo No. 5' by Lou Bega, which was at the top of the charts in the summer of 1999, and then performing it on presentation day. The girls got together and began by reading and translating the song's lyrics. Then they practised the movements described in the song. They incorporated a whole range of elements drawn from fitness, aerobics and disco-dance movements into their staged performance; learning the dance steps was made easier by the fact that almost all the participants knew the video clip of 'Mambo No. 5' that was constantly on TV music programmes at the time. 'Mambo No. 5' is performed by Lou Bega, an Afro-German singer who achieved worldwide success with this Latin-American-style number, sung in English.

On the day of the presentation, a decorated stage is erected in the playground. A large number of children, parents, and teachers gather in the playground, moving from one presentation to another. The stage stands out in contrast to the other locations because of its size and height. Lots of schoolchildren, parents and teachers gather in front of it. Standing, sitting, or moving around the stage, they are the spectators of the event that is about to unfold in front of them and that we record using a fixed video camera.

The girls come onto the stage, the spectators applaud, and the Mambo music booms out of the speakers. The girls clap their hands: one, two, three, four, five, and dance the steps they have rehearsed to the rhythm of the music. Throughout the song they repeat the following movements: jump, bend knees, turn body, move head, put hands on the floor, step to the left, step to the right, step to the front, step to the side, clap hands. At the front of the stage to the right, a girl who looks slightly older than the rest of the group dances whilst trying to remove a strand of hair that keeps falling into her face; the other girls follow her; to her left, one girl carries out the steps quite easily; next to her, there is a third girl, and behind her four others. All the movements are synchronised and rhythmical; only a few mistakes occur. Despite these slight mishaps, a synchronised group movement emerges, and as a consequence, a performative group identity is created. The show comes to an end with the end of the song; the audience's applause brings the five-minute performance to an end.

The thirty or so spectators of different ages behave in different ways. Some girls standing close to the stage follow the dancers' movements; a girl sitting further away moves her body to the rhythm of the music, as does a boy standing close by. Amongst the spectators, two boys look up at the stage and then turn to talk to each other; they turn again to the stage and then continue to talk. An older man walks by, holding a camera; other parents walk by who are not watching the performance.

Ritual performance and the way a scene is staged

The ritual aspect of this performance does not have as clearly defined a shape as the ritual celebrations for Christmas or the end of the school year, but there are a number of reasons why this activity can be considered a ritual. For a start, performances of this kind always take place during Activities Week which is organised towards the end of every school year. Like Activities Week itself, these performances are repeated every year. When planning the Activities Week, some of the pupils always suggest a performance of this kind. Although something different is performed every year, everyone is familiar with the opportunity to stage something of this kind within the framework of the institution. This type of performance is therefore a recurrent element of Activities Week, which is itself a fixed component within the school's programme of learning activities.

The performance differs from the other activities that are presented, in the fact that it takes place on stage. This makes the event something really special, that it must be sure to live up to. In order to do justice to the expectations that the stage gives rise to, the performance has to be choreographed and rehearsed. The stage itself is a space where something is enacted to which the attention of the whole school is particularly drawn. It gives a particular frame to this activity, thus marking it out from everything else that is going on in the playground. What occurs on the stage is the result of a dramatic enactment and demands to be viewed and evaluated as a performance. Action on stage is a cultural performance. As such it has a beginning and an end; it is bound to a time frame and relates to an audience. Action on a stage is always based on a certain intention that is developed in the staged enactment and presented in the performance. The girls' rhythmical dance movements are central to the Mambo performance. They are clearly directed towards the spectators. This gives them a certain ostentatious quality.

The ritual character of the performance is essentially created by the frame. This means that the place and time of the event are clearly defined, and this is also reinforced by the spectators' applause at the beginning and at the end of the performance. The ritual applause demonstrates the fact that the performance is an official component of the school event. It is recognised by the institution as being appropriate for the school's public image. This is a school ritual through which the school displays the multiple dimensions of its approach to teaching and encouraging the pupils' development. This school does not only teach children formally in the classroom but also encourages other forms of learning. The spectators' expectations are directed towards these other forms. The fact that the pupils have lived up to these expectations is demonstrated by the spectators' friendly response at the beginning of the performance and their enthusiastic applause at the end.

The performance itself also contains ritual elements. These are to be found in the uniformity and the repetitive character of the music, lyrics and dance movements. The absence of variation contributes to the stereotypical quality of the performance. Everyone has seen or heard this sort of show on many occasions. It does not take long to become familiarised with the music, lyrics and movements. Everyone knows what is going on and how the different stages of the event will unfold; there is nothing unexpected about this performance; its success is guaranteed. The staged event is composed of ritual elements; the girls appear less as individuals than as a group. They perform all the elements simultaneously; a collective movement emerges in which a group identity is displayed.

To some extent this event resembles an artistic performance that is defined by the stage, the way it is used and the spectators. The stage constitutes the concrete setting of the event, its ostentatious, public side, and its fleeting quality. In the way it is staged, other elements that make up the performance are related to each other: the girls' bodies, their dance movements, the Mambo-music, the lyrics, the time frame of the performance, and the fact that it is approved as a school event.

It is not the significance of the lyrics, nor the singers' performance, that is most central to the staged event, but the girls' physical performance. Dancers and spectators are drawn together by the fact that the music, the singer's voice, and the lyrics refer to things that interest young people of their age. In the first verse of the song there is talk of 'boys' who want to buy 'gin and juice'. Instead of getting drunk again like last week, however, our hero would much rather go and flirt with young women. This, he says, would be a much more enjoyable activity! In the chorus, this intention is made explicit: the singer names seven young women, each of whom he would like to have 'a little bit' of. He wants to have something different from each woman, and that something, in the last named woman, is what would make him hers, he claims. In the second verse, potential dancers are told how to move to dance the Mambo properly. After the chorus is repeated, the singer then turns to each young woman and assures her that he is bound to fall in love with her and that there is no way she can run or hide. Then the chorus is repeated over again showing how popular the singer is and what a great chance of success he has with the girls.

The Mambo performance is a central event in the Activities Week. Performed on stage in just five minutes, it is a unique and fleeting show, only to be experienced by the girls performing and their audience. Based on the Mambo video-clip featuring the singer and professional dancers, the girls' show now becomes the basis or yardstick for other performances to come. The video-clip clearly differs from the pupils' performance. In the video, the singer stands in the centre whilst young women dancers prance around him, demonstratively showing off their sensuality. The event is accelerated and dramatised by its media production. This stands in stark contrast to the school children's world. Thus, staging the Mambo may be seen as a way of dealing with the mimetic difference between the schoolgirls and their young women counterparts in the video. By staging their own performance, the youngsters create their own Mambo reality into which they draw their spectators. This presentation shows their capacity to appropriate and reshape other worlds.

The spectators play a significant role in this mimetic process of handling differences. Their participation in the event shifts the appropriation of the Mambo world by the institution of the school. The girls are able to show the other pupils, as well as teachers and parents, that they are no longer children but in the process of becoming young women. Their performance demonstrates that they do not just want to learn what is on offer in lessons but that they are seeking other social and physical experiences too. The spectators' mimetic participation turns the girls' desires and interests into an opportunity for the school community and the parents to witness the fact that the girls are in a period of transition between childhood and adolescence.

Thus, the Mambo performance may be seen as an example of a ritual through which an institution and community such as school organises and deals with transitions. The performance is thus a ritual action that marks the threshold phase between childhood and youth. Characteristic for this situation is the performance's explorative character that helps the young people to find a direction outside their own normal experience. It helps them to find something upon which they can model their identities. Ritual forms of expression are often invented, staged and performed; by performing rituals, young people acquire elements of a new identity which has at first to do with the peer group, the bond they feel between them, the staging of ritual actions and the whole atmosphere of the performance. Through the staged performance, the actors in the ritual portray what is important to them. Physical, bodily staging is central to this enactment. Ritual performances show and dramatise differences, and draw the spectators into participating. They repeat these staged arrangements so that they become recognisable and enable us to identify with them and embody them in a mimetic way. Ritual performances portray something that is unusual and offer a chance to stage contradictions that cannot be expressed and worked through in any other way. Ritual performances are collective happenings that create social cohesion.

They constitute a frame of meaning within which all the scenes, symbols, physical movements, and gestures in the performance can be understood. Spectators identify with the sensual quality and meaning of a staged production, and thus themselves recreate ritual actions. In this process, the expressive and symbolic side of ritual action is revealed. Ritual performances are repetitions and re-enactments in one. They possess a creative and structuralising power that affects both body and mind.

Body, movements, gestures

As in all rituals, the girls' bodies, gestures and movements play an important role in this performance. The girls synchronise their movements mimetically and attempt to resemble each other. This results in a collective movement. Although the girls do not always succeed in coordinating their steps with the singer's words, this does not hinder the spectator's impression of a mimetically related group movement. This is because the girls keep their steps in time with the rhythm of the music even if they sometimes for a moment fall out of sync with the words. What these short moments, in which the coordination of movements fails, reveal, is that even simple dance steps are complex; they are not easily learnt and are difficult to coordinate during a performance. The performative group formation results less from the meaning of the words of the Mambo, i.e. from the semantics of the language, than from the rhythm of the music and the ritual movements of the girls' bodies that are related to it. The girls have practised their steps in several rehearsals and thereby perhaps experienced the fact that repetition never recreates exactly the same movement. Just as a signature is never exactly identical to one that precedes it, neither are the girls' movements ever exact replicas of what was done before. In repetition, every movement is created anew.

A complex mimetic process is at work with every repetition of a movement. When the girls do a dance step, they take an imprint of the world that the movement stands for; and in so doing they shape and mould the movement and their relation to the world that it stands for. In carrying out the movement, the girls turn it and the world that it represents into a part of themselves. At the same time, however, they are themselves captured by the movement that they perform and thereby moulded by the world that the movement stands for. In our case, it is the movements of the Mambo that the dancers appropriate and through which they become 'Mambo dancers'. In performing the dance, they demonstrate their appropriation of the Mambo and the world it represents. Like all movements, the Mambo dance-steps communicate between the plasticity of the body and the shapeability of the world. They are the medium through which body and world are linked. They mutually create and effect connections as well as transformations. This process calls for participation and thereby changes the girls.

The girls become part of the world of media-staged global youth culture through Cuban music and eroticism that they access through the appropriate dance movements. By performing the movements, the girls embody this world, whilst on the other hand, they display their own particular way of appropriating it. Through performing these bodily movements, the girls acquire the modes of behaviour that are associated with them, and by combining them with other experiences, they can turn them into attitudes. These attitudes are expressed in the defining of boundaries, value-judgements, and life styles. Dissociating oneself from one's parents, listening to music, wearing a particular kind of clothing, having a life of one's own, not wanting to be different and standing up for each other are important values within youth culture. By performing the Mambo movements, the girls take part in this world through mimetic processes; they embody it, and demand that it should be accepted in the public arena of the school. By copying the movements and signs of this world, they reproduce it physically and incorporate it into their psychic inner-world.

By learning the dance steps of the Mambo, the girls' bodies appropriate the dancers on whom they are modelling themselves in the video-clip, and the world that they stand for. In performing the movements, the youngsters also draw on movements that they have previously learnt in other contexts. Gestures such as clapping hands, joining hands over one's head or making a step to the front or to the side, for instance, were no doubt previously learnt in children's games. Through them, particular movements were developed that are now actualised in the context of the performance, and adjusted to the new situation. Inversely, new steps and movements are acquired in the Mambo performance that may later be applied in other contexts such as ballet or gymnastics. Through carrying out these sequences of movement, the rules inherent in physical action and the social world are experienced. These rules are followed because it is a mimetic process. Indeed, physical action possesses a regulated structure that functions without having to become conscious. Physical performances create their rules to a large extent themselves, drawing, in order to do so, on previously acquired schemas and bodily techniques. In ritual performances these schemas and techniques, by relating to examples and models, serve to produce the movements that each one requires. Before the individual participants in a ritual performance are present, the rituals themselves have already defined which ritual actions the individual ritual participants may perform.

Applied to our example, this theory suggests that the Mambo contains certain movements, schemas and techniques that exist independently of the girls, but that are embodied in their performance. Insofar as the text, music and movements of the Mambo are associated with imaginary worlds and symbolic meanings, through their physical performance, the girls enter into these worlds and the symbolic structures contained within them. They begin therefore to appropriate independently existing forms that are also taken over by other young people. As a result of this process, elements of a youth culture emerge, which help young people to find their particular position within society. Taking up this position involves a social shaping and control that take place largely outside the realm of language and consciousness. Transcending local, regional, and national boundaries, a standardisation of taste and of the emotions experienced in life occurs. Pop and youth culture is an international phenomenon that shapes young people through multifarious ritual practices. It reduces the insecurity that young people feel because they are in a situation of transition; it provides them with strength and security, and thus ensures their influence.

The girls' movements in their ritual performance are charged with imaginary images, rhythms, symbols, and feelings. By carrying out these movements, the girls are shaped by the movements and the impressions that they call forth. Their performance of the Mambo captures them and draws them in. Each girl becomes part of the collective event. In carrying out the same movements, a kind of mimetic contagiousness occurs by which the girls come to resemble one another. At one point, for a few moments, an intense state of self-oblivion is reached. This form of intense presence can be described as the state of 'flow' (Czikszentmihaly, 1974) during which contentment and a feeling of belonging are created. This 'flow-experience' contributes to the creation of a sense of community. Since it is a pleasant feeling, its procurement in the ritual performances of popular and youth culture is very important.

If we conceive gestures as significant movements of the body, then the girls' performance of the Mambo can also be understood as a gesture through which the young people draw attention to the fact that they are entering the process of leaving behind their childhood. This gesture is used to represent new emotions and interests through body-language. By enacting them, the young people achieve a new sense of meaning and a way of defining themselves. Since the gesture is a collective performance, it contributes to a sense of group identity among the girls. The desires and emotions expressed in this gesture are strengthened through the group nature of the performance. Although these changes are displayed in a staged and ritual manner, because they are linked to an exceptional situation at school in which they are not articulated in language, the girls and their spectators are probably only vaguely aware of them. But this is precisely what makes them effective. They create a new situation and present it without commenting on it or opening it up for discussion. The 'artificial naturalness' of this gesture presented by the girls makes for its lasting social effect in which spiritual content and physical expression combine and work together.

A glance at the etymology of the word gesture emphasises its physical character. 'Gesture' stems from the Latin word *gestus* which, in a general sense, means movement or attitude of the body and in particular a movement of a part of the body, especially of the hand. *Gestus* is the past participle of the verb *gerrere*, meaning to do or to act. From this, *gestire* is derived, meaning to express 'a feeling', in particular a feeling of happiness (Schmitt, 1990: 36 f.). 'Gesture' relates therefore to the moving body in the world, to activities of the hand, to human behaviour, and movements of individual parts of the body that express and represent emotions. Thus, it makes sense from an etymological point of view to consider as gestures both the staged arrangement in its totality as well as its individual elements such as hand clapping, joining hands above the head, taking a step to the side etc. In this example, individual gestures and the performance of the gesture of young people defining their identity as a whole have a strongly figurative character. In order to grasp their meaning, closer familiarity with the popular and youth culture to which this gesture belongs is required. In contrast to gestures with a complex symbolic content, which often only appear in sections of a culture, and which can only be understood if one has knowledge of that particular area, the total gesture of the girls' performance is more easily grasped because of its iconic character.

If someone perceives a gesture, they understand it by imitating it, thus grasping the symbolic-sensual content of the way it is expressed and represented through movements of the body. Although understanding the different aspects of what a gesture signifies is important, what it expresses and means for the body can only be grasped through mimetic processes. It is through re-creating a gesture mimetically that it is possible to really understand it, because it has become part of the body. The girls assimilate the gestures of Lou Bega and his young women Mambo dancers, and thus have the same feeling running through their bodies on stage. Through mimetic processes, the original gestures are literally 'incorporated', or feel natural to the girls' bodies. Thus, by acting mimetically, the girls are able to go beyond their personal limits and enter the physical representational and expressive world of their models. And it is through their perception of this world that the girls' mental world is expanded.

Mimesis, or the role of creative imitation, in rituals

Four phases of the mimetic process are involved in the girls' ritual performance. Indeed, mimetic processes are not only at work on stage during the girls' performance. They are also involved in the requirements of the performance as well as in the way it is received. Drawing on Ricoeur (1984), these dimensions of mimetic process can be referred to as mimesis I and mimesis III. They lie respectively 'upstream' or 'downstream' of the central performance which is referred to as mimesis II. By requirements of the performance we mean the range of bodily skills and symbolic means that are needed. If we look at the show's reception, mimetic processes cause the performance to be transposed and transformed within the viewer. Indeed, circular processes, in which the spectators draw on their own experiences, are necessary for them to understand the girls' performance. Finally, relating to something mimetically is also important in ethnographic reconstruction (mimesis IV). Here, methodical reflection on the mimetic processes of other phases (I-III) distinguishes it from the way spectators participate mimetically.

Central to our reconstruction (mimesis IV) are the mimetic processes that the girls carry out in order to stage and perform the Mambo (mimesis II). Through these, they relate mimetically to models or examples; these processes are not only imitative but also creative to the extent that they differ from mere reproduction. After having chosen to perform the Mambo, the girls draw together the elements they need to perform it. They select these from the elements that are available. This includes the movements that, when carried out in coordination, draw the girls into a group. The girls relate these movements to the music and rhythm of the Mambo, thus synchronising their movements in space and time so that the individual dancers fuse into one collective group. Following the instructions of the Mambo, imaginary images of a group body movement are created and realised through processes that relate to these images mimetically. In addition, the girls relate to the rhythm of the music as well as to one another. It is only when all these various mimetic processes interact that the group of girls becomes a cohesive group of young people. The same can be said of the gestures that the

girls' group creates by moving arms in the same rhythmic way, which intensify
the expression of their performance by their bodies. Here gestures are displayed
whose rhythmic performance expresses the group's solidarity. By performing the
Mambo with their bodies, the girls are participating in its myths, desires and
attitudes to life. By getting close to the Mambo through the process of mimesis,
the girls explore their own feelings about how they stand with regard to this
attitude to life.

It is quite obvious that multi-dimensional mimetic processes play a role in
creating this kind of staged performance. What is less clear, however, is the extent
to which mimetic processes also play a role in establishing the conditions for
ritual performances (mimesis I). For the Mambo, these conditions are significant
insofar as the performance includes many mimetically acquired skills which the
girls must have acquired earlier in order to be able to carry out their performance.
Perhaps certain children's games in which they copied certain movements will
have helped them. The same goes for their capacity to follow musical rhythms
with physical movements. In order to develop practical ritual knowledge, such
generally applicable skills and competences are important.

As already mentioned, mimetic processes also play a role in the spectator's
perception of the ritual performance (mimesis III). As we observe the spectators
of the performance, we perceive a number of mimetic processes during which the
spectators come to 'resemble' the girls. One girl in the audience who is about the
same age as the girls on stage is watching and singing to herself while moving her
body suggestively. She is following the rhythm of the music and the girls' dance.
Not far away, two boys stand together talking; from time to time they look up at
the stage without really registering what is going on up there. No close contact
is made between the girls and these boys; they have blanked the performance
out of their consciousness. Elsewhere a group of girls is crowded together but
one girl has a small space in front of her; she is looking at the stage and dancing
along with the performers. The young people standing around this girl alternately
look at her and then at the performers on stage; they laugh and talk and seem to
be teasing the girl; she laughs too and stops dancing; the performance on stage
carries on. As we have said, among the children, a variety of different ways of
watching and listening to the performance can be observed.

Although they may vary in intensity, watching and hearing are mimetic
processes. By relating to the event, the spectators 'expand' into the performance; it
becomes part of them as they absorb into their own mental world of imagination,
memory and experience the rhythms and movements, the performances and

configurations that the spectacle displays. In this process, they also draw on previously acquired conditions such as, for instance, the knowledge of what movement, rhythms and dancing are, as well as what can be expected of girls at this age. Just as, in order to be able to perform the Mambo (mimesis II), the girls have to draw on general competences and basic skills (mimesis I), so the spectators also have to refer to these (mimesis III) in order to be able to relate to the performance's movement sequences and thus understand the event.

Despite the significant differences that exist between our participatory observers and spectators, they also have much in common. Both watch a ritual performance and contribute mimetically to the event (mimesis III). Like the spectators, the participatory observers also have to refer to competences and basic skills that have been previously mimetically acquired, in order to be able to grasp the performance (mimesis I). In order to turn the staged event into a part of their mental world of perception, imagination and memory, both spectators and participatory observers alike carry out the same body-related mimetic processes. In contrast to the spectator, however, participatory observers are always already thinking about how they are going to reconstruct the event later on. This process of reconstruction is always an attempt to create a 'resemblance' of the observed world (see Gebauer and Wulf, 1998). This does not mean simply reproducing the given event. Rather, the mimetic processes at work also create differences between the world of the girls' ritual performance (mimesis II), the spectator's understanding and following of the event (mimesis III) and its reconstruction in the context of ethnographic research (mimesis IV). These mimetic processes are constructive; they create a reconstructed world and thus pave the way for recognition and knowledge. Throughout all the phases of this reconstruction process of qualitative research, mimetic elements play a role: in participatory observation, in the process of turning a perceived event into language, in interpreting it in a way that both formulates and reflects, as well as in the creation of types and in synchronic and diachronic comparison. Mimetic processes of world-creation with constructive, fictional, and structuring elements are therefore central to reconstructive social research. 'Worldmaking as we know it always starts from worlds already on hand; the making is a remaking' (Goodman, 1978, p. 19), resulting in something new.

Chapter 6

The creation of social cohesion in rituals

Some results of the Berlin Study on rituals

Our main focus of study is the performative nature of rituals and ritualisation. We have sought to investigate this in families, schools and peer groups and in television. The notion of performativity emphasises the fact that ritual, social and educational practice is essentially performative. Thus our interest has centred on the corporeality of those participating in a ritual and the event or the staged nature of their activity. Practice is more than the mere realisation of intentions since although certain practices may have the same goal, the manner in which they are performed differs widely. This variation is due in part to differences in historical, social and cultural background and to particular processes that relate to the actors' individualities. It is the interplay between these aspects that gives rise to the complexity of social practice and the limits of its predictability and intentionality. In the sphere of rituals the following aspects and perspectives arise from the performative nature of social and educational processes and can, in our view, be a source of inspiration for further research.

The complexity of ritual arrangements

Because they are over-determined symbolically, ritual enactments are often ambiguous, since they contain heterogeneous and contradictory elements. If we conceive of rituals as a way of handling differences by means of a symbolically staged event, then one of the important tasks of research on performativity must be to reveal the multiple layers of meaning within the ritual. Part of this complexity involves revealing the limitations of a merely functional interpretation. Performativity refers to processes that cannot be reduced to generalities or specificities. Because social enactments tend to have a purpose in and for themselves and an aesthetic and performative quality of their own, they also have aspects of expression and representation that cannot be reduced to the fulfilment of intentions or functions. Indeed, ritual performances do not merely represent meaning, like a symbol and nor do they merely reveal something (completely) different, like an allegory. They also generate meaning by making reference to their own contexts, the conventions to which they adhere and their effects. Performative action is thus not only productive or reproductive, but above all reflective and self-identifying in a practical manner: it carries out its subject matter and in so doing makes reference to the conditions of its production. Thus the ritual creates a frame that stabilises, explicates, differentiates and channels the form and power of performative interaction and communication. Conversely, it is the performative nature of rituals that enables us to explain those forms of performance that are described in terms of their unity, consistency, intimacy, social cohesion, solidarity, inclusion, etc.

The performative character of ritual practices

Rituals are created in and through the social arrangements through which people portray how they stand in relation to others, themselves and the world, also in a transcendent form. In scenes and ritual arrangements we enact who we are, how we understand our relationships to other people and the world and the implicit knowledge that guides us in an embodied way. Contingencies and continuities of representation play an important role in these processes. When we refer to ritual actions as a staging of social actions, we are talking about recurring events that are limited in both time and space. In order for the participants in the ritual to have a stable and continuous experience, the staging of the ritual creates a deviation from the accustomed every-day order of events. In order to transform an event into a collaborative performance, an appropriate framework is required. This framework includes, in addition to those performing the ritual and a temporal and spatial context, most importantly the spectators, who play an essential role. It is only when the social interaction makes reference to an audience that an enactment becomes a performance. Conversely, a group identity, based on a common social and moral understanding, begins to emerge through reference to a common experience in the ritual that forges an inextricable link between the individuals involved. This experience comes about through performative practices expressed in the regular pattern of interaction that defines both the identities of the individuals and the relationships between members of this particular community or group. In order to demonstrate who one is and how one wishes to be seen, one needs typical frames of action, patterns of interaction and the typical requisites. An analysis of the performative must therefore involve aesthetically reconstructing and deconstructing the event in order to reveal the relationships between excluding, restorative and sequential elements (turn-taking, sequencing, repairing). Special attention must be paid to the rhythmic, scenic, simultaneous, consecutive and staged elements of the interaction, movements, verbal and bodily exchanges, responses, attitudes, gestures, and ways of looking and also to the resulting atmospheres and their transformations, variations, positions and oppositions. Intensities of expression and representation as well as atmospheres also play an essential role here.

The aesthetic and playful aspects of ritual performances

Rituals can be seen as a means of processing differences. While this process is stereotypical and homogeneous and is often carried out in an atmosphere of formal rigidity, it is never quite devoid of ludic elements. Here we are talking about a creative seriousness that respects certain boundaries and is thus able to combine duty and voluntariness, solidarity and individuality and also affirmation, idiosyncrasy and criticism. The ritualised togetherness of the actors (who are also spectators) provides opportunities for spontaneous and creative action during which the norms of the group or community can be temporarily suspended and then reinscribed into the awareness and bodies of the participants. Through the spontaneous incorporation of new themes and forms of practice into the performance staged by the group, new ways of criticising, transforming and subverting established circumstances can also be tested out. In the ludic mode, power and normativity converge with criticism and contingency. Rituals thus have certain staged formal elements that are repeated over and over again and are elaborated by the groups in a creative manner. This creative enactment prevents any reduction of community relations to causal or final or, above all, reflected meanings. This is because reflecting on the conditions that make a social group cohesive tends to dissolve the sense of community to the extent that attempts to establish theoretical certainty always come up against the problem of contingency and otherness—and these are issues that pose a certain threat to social cohesion. Thus, it is important to avoid constantly reflecting on how the sense of cohesion and community was established in the first place. We are therefore suggesting that the creative dimension of rituals has an important role to play in how the group identity is established.

The corporeality and sensuality of ritual actions

When rituals are considered from a performative perspective they appear as mainly bodily forms of practice. Irrespective of the difficult question as to which concept of the body should be employed here, there are several aspects to be taken into account. These include concrete bodily actions, the theatrical aspects of the action or the event, how the situation is staged (the 'props') and the status (roles) of participants who are performing something for themselves and also for others.

These aspects must then be further broken down into (re-)enactments, quotes and repetitions. The bodily actions of each participant towards the others are important for the success of a ritual as they are what convey its effects. Acting jointly, i.e. in ways that are symmetrical, complementary and compensatory or divergent and even confrontational, assures the success of the ritual process by creating a physical, embodied social order. Gestures and facial expressions, as non-verbal forms of expression that reach beyond reciprocal rational understanding, also always play an important role in staged performances of the body. As significant movements of the body and symbolic representations of intentions and emotions, they actively contribute to the socialisation of the individual and to the development and shaping of the social group. In all ritual situations, gestures and facial expressions are creating meaning that support us as social beings as we learn to relate to others and to understand each other.

The role of mimetic processes in the staging of rituals

The performative character of rituals and other forms of bodily enactment is produced by mimetic processes. These are processes of creative imitation that are oriented towards models and other people's practices. Mimetic processes usually are largely unconscious. They are sensory and are therefore mainly associated with the performance of human action. They are what go to make up physical participation, physical *habitus* and the practical knowledge we require for action to develop. To the extent that the community-promoting power of rituals derives from mimetic processes constituted by habitual actions and enactments rather than by a conceptual and reflexive process, Bourdieu's *habitus* theory is relevant here. From mimetic processes we can see how rituals create and stage knowledge and practices that are shared collectively and how social orders can be represented and reproduced by means of (actualised) patterns of practical action. It is possible to distinguish between different qualitative forms of mimetic action, i.e. ways in which a specific individual movement or gesture is carried out, and explicit and implicit forms. Socio-cultural practice always contains a reference to its origins; it expresses what is social at the level of the individual and what is individual on the social level. It is a bodily process, an enactment and a performance at one and the same time. Finally, socio-cultural practice allows for both continuity and difference in social relations and is mimetic and performative in nature.

The power structure in ritual performances

Rituals always contain a normative structure that is guaranteed in and through the formalised and repetitive pragmatics of performance. The various social forms of the performative are defined by the economic, political and institutional and milieu-specific conditions of the society or community and are therefore embedded within its power structures. Without a theory of the performativity of power relations in rituals and the associated norms that constitute social life we would not be able to explain either why only very specific actions are constitutive of social order or under what conditions ruptures and changes within social circumstances occur. Thus, authority and power relations shape the ritual social order and the associated cognitive and affective dimensions of experience, and contribute on an implicit level to our defining the world as 'real' and perceiving it as 'natural' and 'right', without our being aware of the underlying mechanisms and schemata. The normative patterns which influence social attitudes, values and modes of perception are practised, lived and experienced in seemingly insignificant interactions, the management of space and time in everyday life and in consciously staged celebrations and traditions. It is due to the power of performative processes that social structures and hierarchies are incorporated in processes that structure and constitute the world and perception. It creates a *habitus* that is expressed both in specific life styles and in the recognition of authorities and hierarchies. Modes of interaction, language patterns, images and rhythms, spaces and time structures and schemas and strategies are incorporated into the body in physically enacted scenes. The body thus becomes a social memory. The body's relation to itself is defined by performative construction, and a physical geography develops that contains the pragmatics and schemes of sexual experience, role distribution and imposed identities. Thus, to understand performativity as productive mimetic normativity is to view representation by the individual as an opportunity to perform the norms to which he or she is subject. The fact that these norms are applied and how they are applied and embodied would seem more important than legitimizing them theoretically. Individuals are thus drawn into a dialectical process which forces them to recognise the very rule that binds them to a certain *status quo*.

The implicit rules in ritual arrangements

How the rules of ritual practice are defined is one of questions under investigation in research on rituals. This involves using conversation analysis to establish whether general regularities and processes can be identified. This leads on to the question as to what extent rules are applied that possess a concrete meaning for the actors within a concrete interaction. In other words, which forms of 'contextualisation cue' (Gumperz, 1992) clarify and define which boundaries the actors use to orient their behaviour (cf. Sacks, Schegloff and Jefferson, 1978; Keppler, 1995). The methodological approach seeks to identify a generative pragmatics of rituals with which the meaning of actions can be reconstructed or deconstructed (Bouveresse, 1993). Here the following questions arise: to what extent is following rules dependent on a form of practical knowledge that in turn creates rule-boundness? To what extent is the following of rules intersubjectively constituted; to what extent is it a practice? What is the connection between mimetic processes and the establishing and following of rules? To what extent is there a relationship between explicit and implicit rules? To what extent are rules actually constituted through rule-breaking? To address such issues we need to focus on rules governing social representations of internal patterns of meaning and action which are observable in concrete interactions.

The iconology of performances in rituals

In addition to conversation analysis, group interviews and problem-centred interviews,[5] participant observation, video-supported observation and video enactments are particularly useful for investigating the performative aspects of rituals. These procedures produce images and image sequences of staged actions and ritual performances that are extremely helpful when it comes to reconstructing such events. At the same time, they raise the important question of the significance of images and visual material in ethnographic research. Although their importance as sources and media has been increasingly evident in cultural studies and the social sciences in recent years, this is still a relatively new field and the development of methods for handling images and especially films and video recordings in ethnographic research is not yet far advanced. Following initial attempts to develop a visual anthropology (Collier and Collier, 1986; Bohnsack, 2009), we now require an iconology of the performative that does not reduce the visual character of iconic material to textuality, but addresses the specific pictorial character of images (Wulf and Zirfas, 2005) and makes use of the central role that mimetic processes play in reconstructing the nature of images. It is thus possible to reconstruct, for example, the collective image

---

5   Cf. Forum: Qualitative Social Research, Volume 1, No. 1, Art. 22, January 2000: accessible at http://www. qualitative-research.net/index.php/fqs/article/viewArticle/1132/2521

world which is created by mimetic processes, and plays a role in the constitution of actions that establish patterns of social life. It can also be shown how image traditions that are specific to a particular culture as well as those that transcend cultural boundaries have a strong influence on ritualised everyday activities. In this connection we need to revive the methodological discussion on triangulation. We need to consider not only to what extent visual ethnography and video analysis or iconology can be used to complement existing, more discourse-linked methods, but also to what extent more visually-oriented ethnographic methods would be capable of generating a multiperspectival approach which would be more appropriate to the scenic nature of the performative. Thus, qualitative evaluation of video and image recordings, often used only to illustrate material, would be extended to include the systematically controlled development of iconological analysis procedures.

The staging of macro-rituals

The understanding we have gained to date of the connection between ritual action and the performative creation of social cohesion is based on the results of a study on micro-rituals. Thus far we have focused our attention on this form of ritual action, while leaving a number of other forms of ritual action aside. Among these, the macro-rituals fulfil a special function in the creation of social coherence and community. Since they are held in public they provide many opportunities for identification with the community. This is particularly apparent in families and schools. Family macro-rituals such as birthdays and Christmas celebrations allow us to gain insight into a wider variety of ritual patterns of behaviour in families. We sought to establish whether everyday rituals and celebratory rituals are similar in structure and whether celebratory rituals require different symbolic staging and performance practices. These lead on to other questions, i.e. what are the ritual patterns through which families extend their boundaries in larger rituals, what kind of ritual practices do they use in order to reinforce the feelings of belonging and the sense of community and what mimetic processes are used to shape these practices?

A focus on macro-rituals also results in an expansion of perspectives in school life. Whereas in the past the reference points of research have been mainly the pupils and the forms of social cohesion within a tutor group, now we are turning to look at the school as a whole and the school community. Our observations of school macro-rituals such as the first day at school, carnival celebrations, summer festivals, etc. suggest that school communities are also constituted performatively, but that symbolic elements are more important in these processes than in everyday micro-rituals. We still need to look at the organisation of time, space, requisites and human interactions in school macro-rituals. For instance, the particular space in which a school carries out its macro-rituals, as well as how this becomes a 'sacred space' is of interest. Other dimensions to be investigated include the extent to which 'sacred practices' within macro-rituals are connected to professional educational roles such as those of head teacher or teacher and how particular clothing, gestures or incantations play a part in the procedures. Still to be explained is how school macro-rituals fit in, in relation to the everyday micro-rituals that place on the level of the tutor group as well as to the specific micro-rituals surrounding a macro-ritual, e.g. the first day at school. Exploring these questions is of equal interest for school theory and ritual theory (Wulf et al., 2004).

The sacred in ritual arrangements

We already come across the dimension of the sacred at the level of micro-rituals. The sacred, which according to Durkheim (1995) is what shapes and organises the collective reality of a group or community, plays a central role. Max Weber's theory of the disenchantment of the world is only partly true and needs expanding and modifying. The guises in which the sacred appears today are different from those of earlier times (cf. Kamper and Wulf, 1997). This raises a number of important questions whose investigation is of central importance for the study of the performative creation of social cohesion—in both adults and children—in the many forms and areas of ritual action. Thus, it would seem profitable to follow up the hypothesis that electronic communication practices have gained access to those ritual peer group activities in which the electronic devices acquire the performative and sacred power of creating a sense of community. This cult is generated by the media and is embedded in a collective mythology. This raises the question as to what extent the media products used in these ritualised behaviour practices are endowed with a kind of 'cult power' which assures both the interaction within the group and the identity of the individuals. It would also be interesting to examine to what extent sacred elements in ritual interactions provide the groups or communities with an organised structure. Does the sacred still function in our society as a principle of distinction that creates various spaces, times and forms of taboo (Douglas, 1966)? Do ritual forms of the sacred, understood as *fascinosum* and *tremendum* (Otto, 1979), still exist in the life of the modern city, the world of the media, the diverse forms of everyday play and child culture? In what social forms of representation and bodily practices is the power of the sacred expressed (Bourdieu, 1977)? Are forms of civil religion to be found in everyday micro-rituals, and if so, how do they relate to the political, religious and cultural macro-rituals of society? Is there a connection between religious upbringing and education and elements of the sacred in the rituals of youth and childhood? What kind of transitions are there between religious and secular rituals? Do the different religions have an effect on ritual culture and in what way are hybrid effects manifested on the performative level? Studying the sacred in terms of the concrete performance of everyday ritual practices will undoubtedly shed a whole new light on the notion of the sacred in the modern world.

Chapter 7

The city as a performative space

This chapter considers school, which is the main focus of research throughout this book, as being an important part of the social structure of any town, city, or in our case, the new and yet old metropolis of Berlin. Our focus is on the city as a performative space, that is, on the processes and rituals that create the city environment. The phenomenon of the city as an environment for living in, with its own individual architecture, social structure, different cultures and history, is here conceived as a space that is constantly being re-organised, re-created, and re-enacted by its inhabitants. We look in particular at the processes involved in creating the characteristic 'atmosphere' of a city—in this case, Berlin. The concept of performative space is considered in three steps, moving closer and closer in, from city (1), to inner-city district (2), to school (3).

The space of the city and its atmosphere

Conceiving the city as a performative space is in line with recent discussions in social science on the concept of 'space', a discussion which has increasingly sought to underline the fact that space is quite subjective, that it is, in fact, more a *feeling of space*. Although, like the concept of time, space has always been recognised as something that is not in itself fixed, but rather as something that is perceived empirically, space and time were for a long time generally conceived as separate entities. Inspired by Euclidean geometry, space was essentially understood as something in three dimensions that could be objectively defined, described, measured and counted. In the mechanical world-view, space was thus thought of as being rigid, inflexible and absolute: as an objective reality. More modern insights in physics, however, have revoked the strict separation between space and time. The traditional concept of space as a container that is filled with content, or that exists as 'empty space', in other words, the notion of space as a 'given' entity that makes an impact on the world as such, is now obsolete and in need of rethinking (Löw, 1999). Even Georg Simmel, who was one of the first theorists to deal with the phenomenon of modern cities, imagined space as a kind of container. He did, however, conceive of it as being shaped by people. He also emphasized the psychological dimension involved in the perception, and ultimately in the creation, of space. According to Simmel, the shaping of individual, historical spaces reflects the fact that 'space is in fact nothing other than an activity of the soul, a human way of connecting disconnected perceptual impressions and uniting them' (Simmel, 1995: 133). Cities are more than simply functional places, or objective geographical and political realities; they are the products of 'activity of the soul' and of sensual experiences. Richard Sennett (1976, 1990, 1994) refers to this aspect of simultaneity in his trilogy on the development of city culture by focusing on the etymology of relevant words, pointing out that the word city can be traced back to different sources. One is *urbs*, the stones of a city. The stones of a city were laid for practical reasons of shelter, commerce, and warfare. The other root of the word *city* is *civitas*, and this word is about the emotions, rituals, and convictions that are rooted in a city (Sennett, 1990).

Cities are formed, performatively, by the different uses that people make of them. They can be bastions against an enemy outside, or open centres which invite trade, finance and people in transit to pass through them. They have always been locations for mimetically getting to know that which is 'other'. For indeed, cities are places of transformation, where, either through exclusion or adaptation, the foreign is taken up and turned into the familiar. A metropolis, in particular, is the result of a permanent collective imagination. Cities make their mark upon and 'form' their inhabitants, influencing the ways and means in which people present themselves, the way they speak, the speed of their movements, their gestures, clothes, tastes and preferences. Moreover, not only has the city inspired a literature of its own, ranging from Charles Dickens, to Charles Baudelaire, to Walter Benjamin, but also its own science, which was founded in Berlin (Simmel) and Chicago (Park) and is more than simply sociology of the city. The knowledge and traditions of a society are recorded in its cities. Buildings serve as a representation of the cultural level of a given society; yet they also represent the power, or at least the striving for power, of their political leaders.

The sociologist Henri-Pierre Jeudy (1998) is not particularly impressed by Berlin's new centre, the Potsdamer Platz, with its sophisticated glass tower blocks, whose architecture not only represents the hierarchies of power, but also Berlin's claim to be a metropolis in the same league as 'global cities' (Sassen, 1991). Yet, in comparison with other major cities such as Tokyo, Rio and New York, Jeudy sees Berlin as constantly trying to restage its past:

The city is putting on a show of its own guilt simply by attempting to manage its memories. As an endless construction site, Berlin is currently erecting its past anew; even its most recent past is being transformed into an archaeological discovery, so as to give the impression of now looking just to the future. In this way, the city is trying to free itself from the burden of its symbols, which it sees itself forced to preserve. Yet history is so deeply present in the city's architecture, that it is becoming a city with no history.   (Jeudy, 1998: 52)

In their attempt to capture the city's particular atmosphere on the once fallow land of Potsdamer Platz, Berlin's city-planners seem to have hit far wide of the mark. Despite so many famous signs ('The Brandenburg Gate', 'The Reichstag', 'Unter den Linden'), the desired atmosphere which makes Berlin Berlin, still seems to be painfully lacking. No doubt the atmosphere of a city is not something that can simply be planned. Gernot Böhme (1998) has described it as being an everyday feeling, something contributed by the inhabitants through their lives, something only really noticeable to an outsider. An ambience cannot be artificially created. It is not a face of the city that is deliberately presented to the outside world. On the contrary, atmosphere is in fact something that creates a city, making it special and unique, like, for instance, its individual smells and noises. Atmosphere has to be felt; it is linked to the physical senses of those who perceive it. Thus, when a city is felt to be busy, cheerful or relaxed, this synaesthetic character reflects how its inhabitants are feeling physically and how they feel about their lives in that city environment. Berlin is generally referred to as a 'fast' city, a place that attracts 'fast people', whose lifestyles constantly accelerate the tempo of the city. Berlin's particular atmosphere has to do with the attractive contrast between the rhythm of the city as a capital, and the very different 'time cultures' (Levine, 1998) of its various districts and neighbourhoods ('Kieze'). The Berlin 'Kiez' tends to give rise to a typically provincial feeling; city dwellers may even feel as if they are in a village here.

In a city it is always surprising to see familiar faces, and the more this happens, the more you may have the impression of living in the provinces, not really in a city at all. In a village, on the other hand, every outsider stands out, and seeing too many may even lead one to fear losing one's own identity.   (Siebel, 1999: 83)

Yet the city, although it believes it has overcome this, owes much to the provincial.

Berlin's inner-city districts are characterised by an atmosphere of cultivated urbanity, involving the typical city rituals of anonymity. Yet at the same time, a provincial neighbourhood community-spirit is cultivated and defended. Even for Simmel, the figure of a stranger is someone who 'arrives today and stays tomorrow'—an issue which has given rise to much discussion in Germany over whether dual nationality should be allowed or not. In the neighbourhood, people can either merge with the lifestyle that is typical of that particular neighbourhood—as for instance the alternative, multi-cultural lifestyle of the 1980s (Schiffauer, 1997: 122)—or they can hold on to their own culture as newcomers to the area, as immigrants, or people belonging to a different social class. In this case they will have an influence on the atmosphere of the district. However, the inner-city districts also have a different feeling about them. Here we find 'the city's other face', where the less desirable consequences of globalisation find expression. Here, in the city's traditional working class areas, people have tried locally to adjust to the requirements of globalisation and the economics and social policies of neo-liberalism. This, combined with the withdrawal of subsidies to Berlin since the fall of the Wall, has brought about processes of de- and re-industrialisation, which have had one major consequence—unemployment. All of this is reflected in the portrayal of Berlin in the press. Whilst there are views that proclaim Berlin, with its new architecture, to be a lively urban city, at the same time, there is a strong tendency towards another view which underlines the increasingly slum-like conditions of inner-city districts, thus resulting in these areas becoming 'symbolic ghettoes' (Baltzer, 1999). The school that figures in the Berlin ritual project is located in one of these Berlin inner-city districts, in a typical 'Kiez', which grew out of the requirements of industrialisation in the nineteenth century. In the following section, drawing on social data, we propose to describe and analyse the social situation in this district, as well as attempt to portray the atmosphere that is characteristic for this neighbourhood.

Berlin inner-city districts—social data

The district that we are researching is the largest in Berlin, with 9.1% of Berlin's population living here. Density of population in Berlin's inner-city districts, as well as throughout the city, is very high. Whilst in Germany, there are on average 2.3 people per hectare, in Berlin's inner city, there are 37.7 inhabitants per hectare. In this particular district, there are more women than men, and a high proportion of foreigners. According to information from the Social Structure Atlas (*Sozialstrukturatlas*), this area has the highest number of people of non-German origin in Berlin. This figure can be broken down further: in the area that our ritual project focuses on, the proportion of foreigners is significantly higher than in the south of the district. This is also reflected in the primary school statistics for the second half of the 1999/2000 school year: in reception classes in the north, over three quarters of the pupils are of migrant origin, whilst in the south it is only a quarter. Almost a third of Berlin's foreign population is of Turkish nationality, 15% are citizens from countries within the former Yugoslavia, 6% are of Polish nationality, and 6% are from nation states within the former Soviet Union, whilst six thousand ethnic Germans have recently moved here.

The district has to deal with large numbers of its population moving in or out, something that has been happening all over Berlin since reunification. Increasing numbers of people are moving to neighbouring districts, and some to the outskirts of the city. This movement is not part of a gentrification process, in which tenants with low incomes are driven out in favour of high-income new tenants, to symbolically upgrade the area. Rather, it is due to an increase in so-called 'transit citizens', people who move into the district only to leave again soon afterwards. Yet this district also sees a continuous flow of people moving in, especially within the category of single immigrants.

What one may generally observe is that the district is different from the rest of Berlin above all in terms of social benefit payments (almost double the Berlin average) and in the unemployment and income support payments, which are also both far higher than the average. According to the 1999 Social Structure Atlas, one fifth of the Berlin population are not in paid work. This is, however, partly due to the fact that a high proportion are dependent on their parents. Nevertheless, the proportion of minors receiving financial benefits and support from the state is almost double that in the population as a whole: every sixth social benefit recipient is a minor.

Compared with the overall situation in Berlin, our district stands out above all with regard to educational standards, with far fewer people than average having *Abitur* (A Level equivalent), and far more who are without any school qualification at all. This is partly due to the high proportion of foreigners in this area, since, according to our data, there is a high proportion of people without qualifications within this group. Since crime statistics are not published according to districts, we cannot make any definitive comments about the crime situation in this district. However, the educational welfare service is currently involved in a study on 'child and youth delinquency' which is being undertaken at the Technical University in Berlin. The study's first report shows that child delinquency is directly connected to the failure of parental relationships and upbringing, as well as to living conditions and environment. Moreover, accounts from teachers at the school, according to whom many children are faced with difficult conditions at home, seem to be confirmed. These children's parents are mostly single parents who often speak little German and are unable to support their children, neglecting them emotionally and physically.

In the district, 45.5% are married couples without children, 54.5% are families with children, of which 20.3% are single parent families. Of the families with children, 37.3% are therefore single parent families, in other words over a third, which is about the Berlin average (37.6%). According to information from the regional office for statistics in Berlin, there is a clear tendency towards single parenting and unmarried couples with children.

In addition, we may look at the results of the 1999 Social Structure Atlas which summarises social data both in a social index and a status index, and then relates these two to each other. The district we are looking at has both a negative social index (i.e. a low life expectancy, the highest proportion of people on social benefits, people with low incomes, a high proportion of foreigners, high unemployment, low levels of health, and a large proportion of children and adolescents), and a negative status index (a high number of unemployed, low levels of education). Whereas in other districts social structure is either better or worse than social status, in our district they are on the same (low) level.

Data thus reveals a precarious social situation in this district. And despite politicians' determination to restructure the economy towards the post-industrial service sector, a move that can be observed throughout Berlin, prospects for the future still seem bleak. Whilst Berlin is making efforts to specialise in the supply and networking of information in politics, media, culture and the economy, this district, having recently opened Berlin's largest hotel complex with an attached congress centre, is concentrating on tourism, and in particular on receiving business clients. The district's main problems, however, are a lack of integration and the segregation of the foreign population, issues which are reflected in a lack of stability in the population and low levels of education.

The environment of school and the 'life space of city children'

The children's city environment is basically the catchment area of the school. The neighbourhood is clearly limited by four 'quasi-natural' boundaries that surround it: on one side, the *S-Bahn* (city train) tracks form an impassable boundary; on another side, a large cemetery prevents children from venturing in that direction; the third boundary is a busy and dangerous road; whilst on the remaining side, a park is the only boundary that is somewhat more open. Children's movements are therefore largely limited to the block and its side-streets. According to the official rent report, this quarter is a 'simple residential locality', without many green areas or open spaces, but with dense housing, neglected streets and many dilapidated buildings as well as high levels of noise and air pollution. Indeed, the reality would seem to confirm this description, for those who live in the tightly built up streets here are bound not to get much sunlight. And although the side-streets are relatively calm, the deafening sound of regular aeroplanes taking off and landing at the nearby airport, is a further significant disturbance factor to contend with.

The school's newspaper also describes the surroundings of the school as being amongst Germany's most densely populated areas, where many still live in the buildings where houses are packed in one behind the other that were built cheaply at the turn of the twentieth century. Many of the apartments still have coal stoves for heating, and children have very little space in which to play. Many of the buildings are typical four- or five-story tenement blocks which date back to Berlin's expansive industrialisation period, and which were partly converted by the social housing programmes during the period of architectural reform in the Weimar Republic. In sharp contrast to how this typical Berlin workers' area was described at the end of the nineteenth and beginning of the twentieth century, now there are hardly any children to be seen playing on the streets. Many live an isolated life, typical of city children, where after-school activities take place away from the close surroundings of home, and children therefore have to rely heavily on their parents' support and their willingness to drive them to places if they are to enjoy their free time. For others free time is spent at home in front of the television, video recorder or computer. It is only really when on their way to or from school that children are to be seen on the streets, and they are very rarely seen on their own. Children usually either go to school and come home in groups, under the protection of their older siblings, or they are picked up individually by adults or parents. This is clearly a necessary measure, for although the area directly around the school consists of relatively quiet side-streets and a beautiful park, not far away there looms the perilous threat of a seemingly endless, multi-lane thoroughfare with a constant stream of fast traffic. In fact, this major street, with its lack of traffic lights and pedestrian crossings, has already been the object of a school children's protest action, initiated and documented by the school. The children drew attention not only to the fact that the green lights for pedestrians do not last long enough for them to cross the road safely, but also that many drivers ignore them anyway. Moreover, recently an accident occurred in the residential area around the school, which was to confirm the children's complaints about the traffic. When a mother and her two children were crossing the road at a green light for pedestrians, one of the children was very nearly run over by a pickup truck whose driver appears to have been attending to his mobile phone rather than watching the road.

This main street, which has clearly proven to be dangerous for children, represents, at the same time, an enticing invitation to adventure and imagination. There are wide pavements all the way down the road, and an exciting mixture of all kinds of shops, expressing a mixture of multi-cultural and German styles. Here you can find telephone cafés offering 70% cheaper rates for phone calls to exotic destinations, Turkish grocery stores and fast food kebab restaurants, in front of which men holding prayer beads peacefully sit right next to the local German pubs. There is a video shop and a gambling arcade next to a handbag and rucksack retail shop, in front of which enormous sailors' kitbags and chequered plastic laundry bags are just waiting for people about to embark on long journeys to far-off lands. All this is right next to the grounds of a huge cemetery with its extensive accessories: flower shops, stone sculptors, and cafés with large back rooms to cater for funeral wakes. Next to the cemetery, there is a 'Magician's Shop', which appears by some miracle to have slept through the 'Harry Potter fever'. Even the shop window looks dusty, gloomy and forgotten, not to mention the joke paraphernalia on display: plastic rats alongside seedy, semi-pornographic toilet rolls and fake dog excrement. Right next door, a gloomy rundown junk shop fittingly completes the ramshackle picture.

The other side of the street is somewhat livelier: next to a mobile phone shop and a shop where you can get your TV set repaired, is a hardware shop with stacks of colourful plastic crates, clothes hangers and toilet brushes for sale outside. Next door, a Turkish jewellery shop shows off its treasures enticingly— in the entrance stands a gold-plated female torso, where, at nipple-level, the plaster is beginning to show through.

The side-streets to the left and right of this busy high street give an impression that is 'typically Berlin'—narrow streets with high, turn of the century tenement houses, cobbled pavements, high stone curbs, and a double row of trees, delicately displaying a generous assortment of dog excrement. There is a mix of various shops down these side-streets, including social project offices, and several physiotherapy practices as well as red-light establishments displaying 'Private' signs or adverts for sex films. What stands out is the constant switch between traditional German corner pubs, and Turkish men's cafés with cold bright lights giving out a Mediterranean feel. Women, in the public spaces around the catchment area of the school, seem to gravitate towards the supermarkets and the cemetery café, where at midday, commercial travellers can be seen eating egg and chips, and the cakes in the window rotate endlessly. The women also go to the park café or sit on the benches of the various children's playgrounds. There are quite a few playgrounds in this area that otherwise offers very little for children. Besides the school playground, there are another three locations with covered areas for play apparatus that appear to be kept in good condition. These playgrounds are usually not directly visible from the street, and they all have a fenced-in area for ball games.

There is a visible mix of cultures and generations amongst the people on the street. Besides the school children, there are mothers and girls with or without veils, but also many German and non-German teenage girls, who like to walk around showing their belly buttons in the summer and wear the same baggy trousers as their many German and non-German male counterparts, who flaunt their masculinity with hair gel, muscles, tattoos, gold chains, and a particular way of walking. Amongst this age group, young people clearly feel a strong urge to mimetically resemble one another as well as the pop stars they see on music videos, and to keep in line with various youth cultures that are also a performative product of the city—and its ghettos.

The School Building

The first most noticeable thing is that at first sight the school does not really look like a school. The three-story building, built of solid brick, does not stand out from the other buildings in the street of tenement blocks and the somewhat gloomy estates of the housing cooperatives from which many of the school's pupils are recruited. It is simply part of the row of houses. The school which, despite its somewhat larger windows, is almost hidden, is located at the end of a street which is cut off by a stone balustrade that looks over on to a park. This could almost be part of the gardens of Schönbrunn Palace in Vienna and has more of a Viennese than a Berlin feel to it.

It does not take long to realise that the area of the school in fact reaches beyond its entrance door. When asked what the time is, a woman standing outside with an infant, at first signals that she does not understand, but then she draws an approximate time on the stone balustrade, a gesture which relates to the clock in the school entrance which has hands showing the times of lessons.

Walking into the school, one is struck by the fact that there is space for the 'children's art' to be displayed here and that it has a very special quality. In the red tiles of the entrance hall, areas have been left untiled which are now covered in 'class work' exhibits, children's tile designs using hand prints, animal images and initials. The children's works are 'decorative', and fit in well with the general picture. They seem more professional displayed in this way, including those of the youngest classes. There are two stairways which make the building as a whole seem very organic—children, on their way from one room to another, circulate up and down the stairs. It is here, in these channels, that school life fully buzzes and pulsates, like a living organism. The general atmosphere in the building is bright, warm and lively, and surprisingly quiet.

The school corridor, which is connected to the entrance hall, is decorated with certificates for outstanding achievements and staff photos, and there are illuminated cabinets documenting school activities. These range from traditional-looking photos of the annual school play (*Emil and the Detectives*) and exhibits from the handicraft lesson (*From thread to picture*), to rebellious, political actions through which the school attempts to influence its environment: these are displayed through exhibits of the *Attack on Dog Excrement* and of the winning of a prize for designing a child-friendly traffic system. Something else that catches the eye here is something very special: an enormous shoe belonging to a basketball celebrity from the Alba Berlin team, who appears to have acquired the role of patron.

The classrooms, which go off from the corridor, seem very bright and cheerful. On the lower floor they are multifunctional—there is a space for cooking, and, besides the usual classroom furniture, there are a lot of plants. A recent acquisition is a computer room with internet access. The staff room is in the middle of the corridor, with windows looking out onto the whole of the playground.

Artistic effort has gone into designing the school playground; its snail-like shapes and colours are reminiscent of the social architecture of Hundertwasser.

The school playground, with its trees and plants, is shared with another primary school opposite. As we go out we see that the children are playing in groups which are formed according to age and sex: the girls are playing elastic band skipping, bouncy ball, or catch, whilst a group of boys has gathered on the school steps and the landing in front of the door to play *Pokémon*, and are therefore separate, but not only physically. Through the rituals of swapping, hand-slapping and card-throwing, they have created their own particular 'adult'-like atmosphere, something like a foreign culture of their own.

Finally, in describing this particular school environment, we must note that in between the playground and the *Pokémon* stairs, there seems to be a kind of frontier zone, a narrow bridge at knee-level, separating the flowerbed area and the wall. It seems to have taken on something of the function of a 'wailing wall' or 'confessional box', a place where children who somehow do not feel well, or want to be close to the supervising adult, seem to take refuge in order to express their complaints or to stay away and be protected from the surging masses of playing children in the playground.

City life environment, in its current form, does not generally provide children with much space. Indeed, research has shown that a child's world of experience is strongly reduced in the city. The Berlin inner-city district that this ritual project focuses on, allows especially little space for childhood city explorations and discoveries such the ones described by Martha Muchow (1978), in which child and environment effect each other reciprocally—and ecologically—and in which children perceive their city environment in a very different way. Indeed, it seems hard to imagine, at first sight at least, how children nowadays could possibly still have the kind of experience that Walter Benjamin recounts of his childhood, in *Berliner Kindheit um Neunzehnhundert*,[6] whereby he could wander the streets as if collecting specimens, not only creating things through his own gaze, but also being captivated himself by the returning gaze of things. This would seem impossible for today's children in Berlin. All children have today are 'child worlds' created for them by adults. There are no longer any empty places or free spaces that they could create and design for themselves. And yet children today still do appear to have their own 'secret places' (Bilstein, 1999) into which they can retreat: virtual reality, the world of new computer games such as *Pokémon*, and also the world of *Harry Potter*, which one enters through a gap in the normal reality of King's Cross Station, Platform 9¾. The preceding studies have attempted to show that in families, classrooms, in the media and in games, there are still many ways and means for children, through their own rituals, to create other performative worlds.

6   Berlin Childhood around 1900

Bibliography

Alexander, B. K., Anderson, G. L. and Gallegos, B. P. (eds.) (2004) *Performance theories in education: Power, pedagogy, and the politics of identity*, London: Lawrence Erlbaum Associates.

Austin, J. L. (1962) *How to do things with words*, Oxford: Clarendon Press.

Bakhtin, M. (1968) *Rabelais and his world*, trans. H. Iswolsky, Cambridge: MIT Press.

Baltzer, P. (1999) 'Wenn die Autobahn kommt, dann gibt's da auch keine Armut mehr.' Die Wederstraße — Ethnographie eines Abrisses, in Knecht, M. (ed.), *Die andere Seite der Stadt. Armut und Ausgrenzung in Berlin*, Cologne, Weimar and Vienna: Böhlau.

Bateson, G. (1972) *Steps to an ecology of mind*, Chicago: University of Chicago Press 2000.

Beach, D. (1993) Making sense of the problems of change. An ethnographic study of a teacher education reform, *Göteborg Studies in Educational Research* 100.

Bell, C. (1992) *Ritual theory, ritual practice*, New York: Oxford University Press.

Bell, C. (1997) *Ritual: Perspectives and dimensions*, New York: Oxford University Press.

Benjamin, W. (1980) Berliner Kindheit um Neunzehnhundert, in Benjamin, W. *Gesammelte Schriften, Bd. IV.1*, 235-304, Frankfurt/M.: Suhrkamp: published in English as *Berlin Childhood around 1900*, trans. Eiland, H., Belknap, Harvard, 2006

Berg, E. and Fuchs, M. (eds.) (1993) *Kultur, soziale Praxis, Text. Die Krise der ethnographischen Repräsentation*, Frankfurt/M.: Suhrkamp.

Berger, J. (1980) *About looking*, London: Writers and Readers.

Bilstein, J. (1999) Geheime Stellen im Leben der Kinder, in Liebau, E., Miller-Kipp, G. and Wulf, Ch. (eds.) *Metamorphosen des Raums. Erziehungswissenschaftliche Forschungen zur Chronotopologie*, Weinheim: Deutscher Studien-Verlag.

Böhme, G. (1998) *Anmutungen. Über das Athmosphärische*, Ostfildern: Ed. Tertium.

Bohnsack, R. (1997) Dokumentarische Methoden, in Hitzler, R. and Honer, A. (eds.) *Sozialwissenschaftliche Hermeneutik*, Opladen: Leske und Budrich.

Bohnsack, R. (1999) *Rekonstruktive Sozialforschung. Einführung in Methodologie und Praxis qualitativer Forschung*, Opladen: Leske und Budrich.

Bohnsack, R. (2009) *Qualitative Bild- und Videointerpretation*, Opladen and Farmington Hillls: Barbara Budrich.

Borneman, J. and Hammoudi, A. (eds.) (2009) *Being There. The Fieldwork Encounter and the Making of Truth.* Berkeley: University of California Press.

Bourdieu, P. (1977) *Outline of a theory of practice*, trans. R. Nice, Cambridge: Cambridge University Press.

Bourdieu, P. (1984) *Distinction: A social critique of the judgement of taste*, trans. R. Nice, London: Routledge and Kegan Paul.

Bouveresse, J. (1993) Was ist eine Regel?, in Gebauer, G. and Wulf, Ch. (eds.) *Praxis und Ästhetik. Neue Perspektiven im Denken Pierre Bourdieus*, Frankfurt/M.: Suhrkamp.

Burgess, E. W. (1926) The family as a unity of interacting personalities, *The Family*, 7: 3-9.

Butler, J. (1993) *Bodies that matter*, New York: Routledge.

Butler, J. (1997) *Excitable speech. A politics of the performative*, New York: Routledge.

Collier, J. and Collier, M. (1986) *Visual anthropology. Photography as a research method*, Albuquerque: University of New Mexico Press.

Czikszentmihalyi, M. (1974) *Flow: Studies of enjoyment*, University of Chicago: PHS Grant Report.

Delors, J. (1996) *Learning. The treasure within*, Paris: UNESCO.

Délory-Momberger, Ch. (2000) *Les histoires de vie. De l'invention de soi au projet de formation*, Paris: anthropos.

Denzin, N. K. (2000) Reading film—Filme und Videos, in Flick, U., von Kardorff, E. and Steinke, I. (eds.) *Qualitative Forschung: Ein Handbuch*, Reinbek: Rowohlt.

Dieckmann, B., Wulf, Ch. and Wimmer, M. (eds.) (1997) *Violence. Nationalism, Racism, Xenophobia*, Münster and New York: Waxmann.

Douglas, M. (1966) *Purity and danger. An analysis of concepts of pollution and taboo*, London: Routledge and Kegan Paul.

Douglas, M. (1986) *How institutions think*, Syracuse: Syracuse University Press.

Durkheim, E. (1995) *The elementary forms of religious life*, New York: Free Press.

Eberle, T. (1997) Ethnomethodologische Konversationsanalyse, in Hitzler, R. and Honer, A. (eds.) *Sozialwissenschaftliche Hermeneutik*, Opladen: Leske und Budrich.

Eickhoff, H. (1997) Sitzen, in Wulf, Ch. (ed.) *Vom Menschen. Handbuch Historische Anthropologie*, Weinheim: Beltz.

Erdheim, M. (1988) Die Repräsentanz des Fremden, in Erdheim, M., *Psychoanalyse und Unbewußtheit in der Kultur*, Frankfurt/M.: Suhrkamp.

Flick, U. (1995) Triangulation in der qualitativen Forschung, in Flick, U., von Kardorff, E. and Steinke, I. (eds.) *Qualitative Forschung: Ein Handbuch*, Reinbek: Rowohlt.

Flick, U. (2000) Konstruktion und Rekonstruktion. Methodologische Überlegungen zur Fallrekonstruktion, in Kraimer, K. (ed.) *Die Fallrekonstruktion*, Frankfurt/M.: Suhrkamp.

Flick, Uwe (2006) *Qualitative Evaluationsforschung. Konzepte, Methoden, Umsetzungen*, Reinbek: Rowohlt.

Fischer-Lichte, E. and Wulf, Ch. (eds.) (2001) Theorien des Performativen, *Paragrana. Zeitschrift für Historische Anthropologie* 10 (1).

Fischer-Lichte, E. and Wulf, Ch. (eds.) (2004) Praktiken des Performativen, *Paragrana. Zeitschrift für Historische Anthropologie* 13 (1).

Foucault, M. (1978) *The history of sexuality* vol. 1, trans. R. Hurley, New York: Random House.

Garfinkel, H. (1982) Bedingungen für den Erfolg von Degradierungszeremonien, in Lüderssen, K. and Sack, F. (eds.) *Seminar: Abweichendes Verhalten III. Die gesellschaftliche Reaktion auf Kriminalität*. Band II: Strafprozess und Strafvollzug, Frankfurt/M.: Suhrkamp.

Gebauer, G. (1998) Sport—die dargestellte Gesellschaft, *Paragrana. Internationale Zeitschrift für Historische Anthropologie* 7 (1): 223-239.

Gebauer, G. and Wulf, Ch. (1995) *Mimesis. Culture—art—society*, Berkeley: University of California Press.

Gebauer, G. and Wulf, Ch. (1998) *Spiel—Ritual—Geste. Mimetisches Handeln in der sozialen Welt*, Reinbek: Rowohlt.

Gebauer, G. and Wulf, Ch. (2003) *Mimetische Weltzugänge. Soziales Handeln, Rituale und Spiele, ästhetische Produktionen*, Stuttgart: Kohlhammer.

Geertz, C. (1973) *The interpretation of cultures. Selected essays*. New York: Basic Books.

van Gennep, A. (1960) *The rites of passage*, London: Routledge and Kegan Paul.

Girard, R. (1989) *The scapegoat*, trans. Y. Freccero, Baltimore: Johns Hopkins University Press.

Glaser, B. G. and Strauss, A. (1969) *The discovery of grounded theory*, Chicago: Chicago University Press.

Goffman, E. (1971) *Relations in public: Microstudies of the public order*, New York: Basic Books.

Goffman, E. (1974) *Frame analysis. An essay on the organization of experience*, New York: Harper and Row.

Göhlich, M. (2001) Performative Äußerungen. Austins Begriff als Instrument erziehungsw issenschaftlicher Forschung, in Wulf, Ch., Göhlich, M. and Zirfas, J. *Grundlagen des Performativen. Einführung in die Zusammenhänge von Sprache, Macht und Handeln*, Weinheim: Juventa.

Goodman, N. (1978) *Ways of world making*, Hassocks: Harvester Press.

Grimes, R. (1995) *Beginnings in ritual studies*, Columbia: University of South Carolina Press.

Gumperz, J. J. (1992) Contextualization revisited, in Auer, P. and DiLuzio, A. (eds.) *The contextualization of language*, Amsterdam: Benjamins.

Helsper, W. (2000) Soziale Welten von Schülerinnen und Schülern, *Zeitschrift für Pädagogik*, 5: 663-666.

Hermès, 'Rituels', n 42, Paris: CNRS Éditions 2005, Boetch, G. and Wulf, Ch. (eds.).

Hitzler, R. and Honer, A. (eds.) (1997) *Sozialwissenschaftliche Hermeneutik*, Opladen: Leske und Budrich.

Huppauf, B. and Wulf, Ch. (eds.) (2009) *Dynamics and performativity of imagination. The image between the visible and the invisible*, New York: Routledge.

Jackson, P. (1968) *Life in classrooms*, New York: Holt, Rineheart and Winston.

Jennings, T. W. Jr. (1998) Rituelles Wissen, in Belliger, A. and Krieger, D. J. (eds.) *Ritualtheorien*, Opladen: Westdeutscher Verlag.

Jeudy, H.-P. (1998) *Stadterfahrungen — Tokio, Rio, Berlin, New York, Lissabon*, Berlin: Merve.

Kade, J. (1999) Irritationen — zur Pädagogik der Talkshow, in Gogolin, I. and Lenzen, D. (eds.) *Medien-Generation*. Beiträge zum 16. Kongreß der Deutschen Gesellschaft für Erziehungswissenschaft, Opladen: Leske und Budrich.

Kamper, D. and Wulf, Ch. (eds.) (1997) *Das Heilige. Seine Spur in der Moderne*, Frankfurt/M.: Syndikat.

Keppler, A. (1995) *Tischgespräche. Über Formen kommunikativer Vergemeinschaftung am Beispiel der Konversation in Familien*, Frankfurt/M.: Suhrkamp.

Knoblauch, H., Schnettler, B., Raab, J., and Soeffner, H.-G. (eds.) (2006) *Video analysis. Methodology and methods. Qualitative data analysis in sociology*, Frankfurt/M.: Peter Lang.

Kraimer, K. (ed.) (2000) *Die Fallrekonstruktion. Sinnverstehen in der sozialwissenschaftlichen Forschung*, Frankfurt/M.: Suhrkamp.

Kreinath, J., Snoek, J. and Stausberg, M. (eds.) (2006) *Theorizing rituals. Issues, topics, approaches, concepts*, Leiden, Boston: Brill.

Krüger, H.-H. (2000) Stichwort. Qualitative Forschung in der Erziehungswissenschaft, *Zeitschrift für Erziehungswissenschaft* 3: 323-342.

Krüger, H.-H. and Marotzki, W. (eds.) (1998) *Handbuch erziehungswissenschaftliche Biographieforschung*, Opladen: Leske und Budrich.

Levine, R. (1998) *Eine Landkarte der Zeit. Wie Kulturen mit Zeit umgehen*, Munich: Piper.

Liebau, E., Schumacher-Chilla, D. and Wulf, Ch. (eds.) (2001) *Anthropologie pädagogischer Institutionen*, Weinheim: Deutscher Studienverlag.

Löw, M. (1999) Vom Raum zum Spacing—Neuformationen und deren Konsequenzen für Bildungsräume, in Liebau, E., Miller-Kipp, G. and Wulf, Ch. (eds.) *Metamorphosen des Raums. Erziehungswissenschaftliche Forschungen zur Chronotopologie*, Weinheim: Deutscher Studien-Verlag.

Mannheim, K. (1964) Beiträge zur Theorie der Weltanschauungsinterpretation, in Mannheim, K. *Wissenssoziologie*, Neuwied: Luchterhand.

Mannheim, K. (1982) *Structures of thinking*, London: Routledge and Kegan Paul.

Mattenklott, G. (1984) Geschmackssachen. Über den Zusammenhang von sinnlicher und geistiger Ernährung, in Kamper, D. and Wulf, Ch. (eds.) *Das Schwinden der Sinne*, Frankfurt/M.: Suhrkamp.

Mauss, M. (1990) *The gift*, London: Routledge.

McLaren, P. (1993) *Schooling as a ritual performance. Towards a political economy of educational symbols and gestures*, London and New York: Routledge.

Mikos, L. (1998) Die Inszenierung von Privatheit. Selbstdarstellungen und Diskurspraxis in Daily Talks, in Willems, H. and Jurga, M. (eds.) *Inszenierungsgesellschaft*, Opladen: Westdeutscher Verlag.

Mikos, L. (2000) Intertextualität und Populärkultur. Fernsehen als Medium alltäglicher Erfahrung, in Flach, S. and Grisko, M. (eds.) *Fernsehperspektiven. Aspekte zeitgenössischer Fernsehkultur*, Munich: KoPäd.

Mollenhauer, K. and Wulf, Ch. (eds.) (1996) *Aisthesis, Ästhetik. Zwischen Wahrnehmung und Bewußtsein*, Weinheim: Deutscher Studien Verlag.

Muchow, M. and Muchow, H.-H. (1978) *Der Lebensraum des Großstadtkindes*, Bensheim: Päd.-Extra (orig. 1935).

Oevermann, U. (2000) Die Methode der Fallrekonstruktion in der Grundlagenforschung sowie der klinischen und pädagogischen Praxis, in Kraimer, K. (ed.) *Die Fallrekonstruktion*, 95-123, Frankfurt/M.: Suhrkamp.

Otto, R. (1979) *Das Heilige. Über das Irrationale in der Idee des Göttlichen und sein Verhältnis zum Rationalen*, Munich: Beck.

Piaget, J. (1968) *The moral judgment of the child*, trans. M. Gabain, London: Routledge and Kegan Paul.

Pink, S. (2007) Doing visual ethnography, Thousand Oaks: Sage

Plake, K. (1999) *Talkshows. Zur Industrialisierung der Kommunikation*, Darmstadt: Primus.

Ricoeur, P. (1984) *Time and narrative*, vol. 1, Chicago: University of Chicago Press.

Rittelmeyer, Ch. (1999) Anthropologie des Schulraums. Aspekte einer imaginativen Phänomenologie, in Liebau, E., Miller-Kipp, G. and Wulf, Ch. (eds.) *Metamorphosen des Raums. Erziehungswissenschaftliche Forschungen zur Chronotopologie*, Weinheim: Deutscher Studien-Verlag.

Sacks, H., Schegloff, E. A. and Jefferson, G. (1978) A simple systematics for the organization of turn taking for conversation, in Schenkein, J. (ed.) *Studies in the organization of conversational interaction*, New York: Academic Press.

Sassen, S. (1991) *The global city: New York, London, Tokyo*, Princeton, NJ: Princeton University Press.

Schäfer, G. and Wulf, Ch. (eds.) (1999) *Bild—Bilder—Bildung*, Weinheim: Deutscher Studien-Verlag.

Schechner, R. (1977) *Essays on Performance Theory* 1970-1976, New York: Drama Book Specialists.

Schell, F., Stolzenburg, E. and Theunert, H. (eds.) (1999) *Medienkompetenz. Grundlagen und pädagogisches Handeln*, Munich: KoPäd.

Schiffauer, W. (1997) *Fremde in der Stadt*, Frankfurt/M.: Suhrkamp.

Schmerl, Ch. (1983) *Frauenfeindliche Werbung. Sexismus als heimlicher Lehrplan*, Reinbek: Rowohlt.

Schmitt, J.-C. (1990) *La raison des gestes dans l'Occident médiéval*, Paris: Gallimard.

Schütze, F. (1983) Biographieforschung und narratives Interview, *Neue Praxis*, 3: 283-293.

SEE, S*ociété Européenne d'Ethnographie de l'Éducation*: Revue annuelle, vols 1-5, 2004-2008.

Sennett, R. (1976) *The fall of public man*, New York: Knopf.

Sennett, R. (1990) *The conscience of the eye: the design and social life of cities*, New York: Random House.

Sennett, R. (1994) *Flesh and stone: the body and the city in Western civilization*, New York: Norton.

Siebel, W. (1999) Die Stadt und die Fremden, in Bollmann, S. (ed.) *Kursbuch Stadt— Stadtleben und Stadtkultur an der Jahrtausendwende*, Stuttgart: Deutsche Verlags Anstalt.

Simmel, G. (1995) Soziologie des Raumes, in Simmel, G. *Aufsätze und Abhandlungen* vol. 1: 1901-1908, Frankfurt/M.: Suhrkamp.

Singer, M. (1959) *Traditional India. Structure and change*. Philadelphia: American Folklore Society.

Soeffner, H.-G. (1992) *Die Auslegung des Alltags*, Teil 2: Die Ordnung der Rituale, Frankfurt/M.: Suhrkamp.

Spindler, G. D. and Spindler, L. (1987) *Interpretive ethnography of education at home and abroad*, Hillsdale, New Jersey: Erlbaum.

Strauss, A, and Corbin, J. (1990) *Basics of qualitative research*, London: Sage.

Strauss, A. and Corbin, J. (1994) Grounded theory: An overview. In: Denzin and Lincoln (eds.), *Handbook of Qualitative Research*, Thousand Oaks: Sage.

Sutton-Smith, B. (1971) Boundaries, in Herron, R. E. and Sutton-Smith, B. *Child's Play*, New York: Wiley.

Tambiah, S. (1979) A performative approach to ritual, *Proceedings of the British Academy*, 65: 113-163.

Tholen, G. Ch. (2000) Selbstbekenntnisse im Fernsehen. Eine neue Variante im panoptischen Diskurs der Kontrollgesellschaft, in Flach, S. and Grisko, M. (eds.) *Fernsehperspektiven. Aspekte zeitgenössischer Fernsehkultur*, Munich: KoPäd.

Thomas, G. (1998) *Medien, Ritual, Religion*, Frankfurt/M.: Suhrkamp.

Troman, G., Jeffrey, B., and Beach, D. (2006): *Researching education policy: Ethnographic experiences*. London: Tufnell.

Turner, V. (1969) *The ritual process. Structure and anti-structure*, Chicago: Aldine.

Turner, V. (1982) *From ritual to theatre. The human seriousness of play*, New York: PAJ Publications.

Vogelgesang, W. (1999) Kompetentes und selbstbestimmtes Medienhandeln in Jugendszenen, in Schell, F., Stolzenburg, E. and Theunert, H. (eds.) *Medienkompetenz. Grundlagen und pädagogisches Handeln*, Munich: KoPäd.

Vollbrecht, R. (1997) Jugendkulturelle Selbstinszenierungen, *medienunderziehung*, 41: 7-14.

Wagner-Willi, M. (2001) Liminalität und soziales Drama—Zur Ritualtheorie Turners, in Wulf, Ch., Göhlich, M. and Zirfas, J. (eds.) *Grundlagen des Performativen. Einführung in die Zusammenhänge von Sprache, Macht, Handeln*, Weinheim: Juventa.

Walford, G. (ed.) (2008) *How to do educational ethnography*, London: Tufnell.

Weigand, G. and Hess, R. (eds.) (2007) *Teilnehmende Beobachtung in interkulturellen Situationen*, Frankfurt/M. Campus.

Wexler, P. (1994) Schichtenspezifisches Selbst und soziale Interaktion in der Schule, in Sünker, H., Timmemann, D. and Kolbe, F.-U. (eds.) *Bildung, Gesellschaft, soziale Ungleichheit*, Frankfurt/M.: Suhrkamp.

Willis, P. (1999) Labour power, culture and the cultural commodity, in Castlls, M., Flecha, R., Freire, P., Giroux, H., Macedo, D. and Willis, P. (eds.) *Critical education in the New Information Age*, Oxford: Rowman and Littlefield.

Wimmer, M. (2006) *Dekonstruktion und Erziehung: Studien zum Paradoxieproblem in der Pädagogik*, Bielefeld: transcript.

Wolf, N. (1991) *The beauty myth*, New York: Morrow.

Woods, P. (1986): *Inside the school. Ethnography in educational research*, London Routledge.

Woods, P. (1996): *Researching the art of teaching. Ethnography for educational use*, London: Routledge.

Woods, P., Jeffrey, B., Troman, G. and Boyle, M. (1997): *Restructuring schools. Reconstructing teachers*, Buckingham: Open University Press.

Wulf, Ch. (ed.) (1997) *Vom Menschen. Handbuch Historische Anthropologie*, Weinheim and Basel: Beltz (second edition 2010).

Wulf, Ch. (1999) Raumerfahrungen im Umbruch—Körper, Bewegung, Globalisierung, in Liebau, E., Miller-Kipp, G., and Wulf, Ch. (eds.) *Metamorphosen des Raums. Erziehungswissenschaftliche Forschungen zur Chronotopologie*, Weinheim: Deutscher Studien-Verlag.

Wulf, Ch. (2001) *Einführung in die Anthropologie der Erziehung*, Weinheim: Beltz.

Wulf, Ch. (2002) *Anthropology of education*, Münster and New York: Lit.

Wulf, Ch. (2003) *Educational science. Hermeneutics, empirical research, critical theory*, Münster and New York 2003.

Wulf, Ch. (2005) *Zur Genese des Sozialen: Mimesis, Performativität, Ritual*, Bielefeld: transcript.

Wulf, Ch. (2006a) *Anthropologie kultureller Vielfalt. Interkulturelle Bildung in Zeiten der Globalisierung*, Bielefeld: transcript.

Wulf, C. (2006b) Praxis, in Kreinath, J., Snoek, J. and Stausberg, M. (eds.) *Theorizing rituals. Issues, topics, approaches, concepts*, Leiden and Boston: Brill.

Wulf, Ch. (2008) Le défi de la diversité culturelle: mondialisation et européisation différenciées. Un cadre conceptuel pour une ethnographie interculturelle, in Société Européenne d'Ethnographie de l'Éducation: Revista anual 5. *Diversité culturelle et dialogue intercultural*, 13-33

Wulf, Ch. (2009) *Anthropologie. Geschichte, Kultur, Philosophie*, Köln: Anaconda.

Wulf, Ch., Göhlich, M. and Zirfas, J. (eds.) (2001) *Grundlagen des Performativen. Eine Einführung in die Zusammenhänge von Sprache, Macht und Handeln*, Weinheim and Munich: Juventa.

Wulf, Ch. and Zirfas, J. (2001) Die performative Bildung von Gemeinschaften. Zur Hervorbringung des Sozialen in Ritualen und Ritualisierungen, *Paragrana. Internationale Zeitschrift für Historische Anthropologie*, 10 (1): 93-116.

Wulf, Ch. and Zirfas, J. (eds.) (2004) *Die Kultur des Rituals*, Munich: Wilhelm Fink.

Wulf, Ch. and Zirfas, J. (eds.) (2005) *Ikonologie des Performativen*, Munich: Wilhelm Fink.

Wulf, Ch. and Zirfas, J. (eds.) (2007) *Die Pädagogik des Performativen*, Weinheim and Basel: Beltz.

Wulf, Ch. et al. (2001) *Das Soziale als Ritual. Zur performativen Bildung von Gemeinschaften*, Opladen: Leske und Budrich.

Wulf, Ch. et al. (2004) *Bildung im Ritual. Schule, Familie, Jugend, Medien*, Wiesbaden: VS.

Wulf, Ch. et al., (2007) *Lernkulturen im Umbruch*, Wiesbaden: VS.

Wulf, Ch. et al. (2010) *Gesten in Erziehung, Bildung und Sozialisation*, Wiesbaden

Zinnecker, J. (2000) Pädagogische Ethnographie,

Zeitschrift für Erziehungswissenschaft, 3: 381-400.

The Berlin Study on Rituals

The Berlin Study on Rituals took place in the years between 1999 und 2010 at the Freie Universität, and was led by Prof. Dr. Christoph Wulf. This was part of the Centre for Collaborative Research (SFB), *Cultures of the Performative*, which ran under the auspices of the German Research Foundation (DFG). Using ethnographic methods we studied rituals and gesture in the fields of childrearing, education and socialisation, focussing on the family, school, peer culture and the media. At the centre of this wide-ranging study was a primary school with 300 children from 20 different ethnic backgrounds and the area around it in an inner city district of Berlin. As one of UNESCO's model schools this school was inspired by the traditions of Progressive Education, in particular by the theories of Peter Petersen. Twenty research scientists have contributed to the many studies that have been written up into four comprehensive volumes as well as inspiring numerous essays and several individual books. The results of this research have been translated into several languages. The following bibliography offers a selection of the most important publications.

The Berlin Study on Rituals (Selection)

Audehm, K. (2007) *Erziehung bei Tisch. Zur sozialen Magie eines Familienrituals*, Bielefeld.

Bausch, C. (2006) *Verkörperte Medien. Die soziale Macht televisueller Inszenierungen*, Bielefeld.

Bohnsack, R. (2007) Performativität, Performanz und Dokumentarische Methode, in Wulf, Ch. and Zirfas, J. (ed.) *Pädagogik des Performativen. Theorien, Methoden, Perspektiven*, Weinheim and Basel.

Boëtsch, G. and Wulf, C. (eds.) (2005) *Hermès* No. 43 Rituels. Paris.

Fischer-Lichte, E. and Wulf, Ch. (eds.) (2001) Theorien des Performativen, *Paragrana. Internationale Zeitschrift für Historische Anthropologie*, 10 (1).

Fischer-Lichte, E. and Wulf, Ch. (eds.) (2004) Praktiken des Performativen, *Paragrana. Internationale Zeitschrift für Historische Anthropologie*, 13 (1).

Gebauer, G. and Wulf, Ch. (1995) *Mimesis. Culture, art, society*, Berkeley and Los Angeles.

Gebauer, G. and Wulf, Ch. (1998) *Spiel—Ritual—Geste. Mimetisches Handeln in der sozialen Welt*, Reinbek.

Gebauer, G. and Wulf, Ch. (2003) *Mimetische Weltzugänge*, Stuttgart.

Göhlich, M., Wulf, Ch. and Zirfas, J. (eds.) (2007) *Pädagogische Theorien des Lernens*, Weinheim and Basel.

Göhlich, M. and Zirfas, J. (eds.) (2007) *Lernen. Ein pädagogischer Grundbegriff*, Stuttgart.

Göhlich, M. and Zirfas, J. (eds.) (2009) *Der Mensch als Maß der Erziehung*, Weinheim and Basel.

Huppauf, B. and Wulf, Ch. (eds.) (2009) *Dynamics and performativity of imagination. The image between the visible and the invisible*, New York.

Imai, Y. and Wulf, Ch. (eds.) (2007) *Concepts of aesthetic education*, Münster and New York.

Jörissen, B. (2007) *Beobachtungen der Realität. Die Frage nach der Wirklichkeit im Zeitalter der Neuen Medien*, Bielefeld.

Kellermann, I. (2008) *Vom Kind zum Schulkind. Die rituelle Gestaltung des Schulanfangs in einer jahrgangsgemischten Lerngruppe. Eine ethnographische Studie*, Opladen and Farmington Hills.

Schäfer, A. and Wulf, Ch. (eds.) (1999) *Bild, Bilder, Bildung*, Weinheim.

Suzuki, S. and Wulf, Ch. (eds.) (2007) *Mimesis, poiesis, performativity in education*, Münster and New York.

Tervooren, A. (2006) *Im Spielraum von Geschlecht und Begehren. Ethnographie der ausgehenden Kindheit*, Weinheim and Munich.

Wagner-Willi, M. (2004) Videointerpretation als mehrdimensionale Mikroanalyse am Beispiel schulischer Alltagsszenen, *Zeitschrift für qualitative Bildungs-, Beratungs- und Sozialforschung*, 5 (1): 49-66.

Wagner-Willi, M. (2005) *Kinder-Rituale zwischen Vorder- und Hinterbühne. Der Übergang von der Pause zum Unterricht*, Wiesbaden.

Werler, T. and Wulf, Ch. (eds.) (2006) *Hidden dimensions of education. Rhetoric, rituals and anthropology*, Münster and New York.

Wimmer, M. (2006) *Dekonstruktion und Erziehung: Studien zum Paradoxieproblem in der Pädagogik*, Bielefeld.

Wulf, Ch. (1995): *Education in Europe. An intercultural task*, Münster and New York.

Wulf, Ch. (ed.) (1997) *Vom Menschen. Handbuch Historische Anthropologie*, Weinheim and Basel (French and Italian ed. 2002; Japanese ed. 2008; Chinese ed. forthcoming).

Wulf, Ch. (2002) *Anthropology of education*, Münster and New York.

Wulf, Ch. (2003) *Educational science. Hermeneutics, empirical research, critical theory*, Münster and New York.

Wulf, Ch. (ed.) (2005) *Zur Genese des Sozialen. Mimesis, Performativität, Ritual*, Bielefeld.

Wulf, Ch. (2005) Rituels. Performativité et dynamique des pratiques sociales, in Boëtsch, G. and Wulf, Ch. (eds.) *Hermès* No. 43 Rituels, Paris, 9-20.

Wulf, Ch. (2006) Praxis, in Kreinath, J., Snoek, J. and Stausberg, M. (eds.) *Theorizing rituals: Issues, topics, approaches, concepts*, Leiden.

Wulf, C. (2006) *Anthropologie kultureller Vielfalt. Interkulturelles Lernen in Zeiten der Globalisierung*, Bielefeld.

Wulf, Ch. (2008) *Une anthropologie historique et culturelle. Rituels, mimésis sociale, performativité*, Paris.

Wulf, Ch. (2008) Rituale im Grundschulalter. Ritual, Mimesis, Performativität, *Zeitschrift für Erziehungswissenschaft*, Wiesbaden.

Wulf, Ch. (2009) *Anthropologie. Geschichte, Kultur, Philosophie*, Köln.

Wulf, Ch. (forthcoming): *Anthropology. History. Culture, Philosophy.*

Wulf, Ch., Althans, B., Audehm, K., Bausch, C., Göhlich, M., Sting, S., Tervooren, A., Wagner-Willi, M. and Zirfas, J. (2001) *Das Soziale als Ritual. Zur performativen Bedeutung von Gemeinschaft*, Opladen.

Wulf, Ch., Althans, B., Audehm, K., Bausch, C., Jörissen, B., Göhlich, M., Mattig, R., Tervooren, A., Wagner-Willi, M. and Zirfas, J. (2004) *Bildung im Ritual. Schule, Familie, Jugend, Medien*, Wiesbaden.

Wulf, Ch., Althans, B., Blaschke, G., Ferrin, N., Göhlich, M., Jörissen, B., Mattig, R., Nentwig-Gesemann, I., Schinkel, S., Tervooren, A., Wagner-Willi, M. and Zirfas, J. (2007) *Lernkulturen im Umbruch. Rituelle Praktiken in Schule, Medien, Familie und Jugend*, Wiesbaden.

Wulf, Ch., Althans, B., Blaschke, G., Ferrin, N., Kellermann, I., Mattig, R. and Schinkel, S. (2010) *Gesten in Erziehung, Bildung und Sozialisation*, Wiesbaden.

Wulf, Ch., Göhlich, M. and Zirfas, J. (eds.) (2001) *Grundlagen des Performativen. Eine Einführung in die Zusammenhänge von Sprache, Macht und Handeln*, Weinheim and Munich.

Wulf, Ch. and Zirfas, J. (eds.) (2003) Rituelle Welten, *Paragrana. Internationale Zeitschrift für Historische Anthropologie*, 12 (1 and 2).

Wulf, Ch. and Zirfas, J. (eds.) (2004) *Die Kultur des Rituals*, Munich.

Wulf, Ch. and Zirfas, J. (eds.) (2005) *Ikonologie des Performativen*, Munich.

Wulf, Ch. and Zirfas, J. (eds.) (2007) *Die Pädagogik des Performativen. Theorien, Methoden, Perspektiven*, Weinheim and Basel.

Zirfas, J. and Jörissen, B. (2007) *Phänomene der Identität. Human-, sozial- und kulturwissenschaftliche Analysen*, Wiesbaden.

The Research Team of the Berlin Study on Rituals at the Freie Universität Berlin

Birgit Althans
    The city as a performative space

Kathrin Audehm
    A space for rituals: the family as a performative unit

Constanze Bausch
    The creation of peer group identity through TV adverts and popular shows

Michael Göhlich
    Rituals in daily school life

Stephan Sting
    The creation of peer group identity through TV adverts and popular shows

Anja Tervooren
    GoGo performance in the playground

Monika Wagner-Willi
    Rituals in daily school life

Christoph Wulf (head of the project)
    Introduction
    The role that mimesis plays in rituals

    The creation of social cohesion in rituals. Some results of the Berlin Study on rituals

Jörg Zirfas
    A space for rituals: the family as a performative unit
    The creation of social cohesion in rituals. Some results of the Berlin Study on Rituals

Notes on the members of the project team

Dr. Birgit Althans, at present Professor of Education at Trier University. Recent publications include: (2000) (Der Klatsch, die Frauen und das Sprechen bei der Arbeit, Frankfurt/M.; (2007) Das maskierte Begehren, Frankfurt/M.; (with Ch. Wulf et al., 2008) Geburt in Familien, Klinik und Medien. Eine qualitative Fallstudie, Opladen and Farmington Hills.

Dr. Kathrin Audehm, at present Assistant Professor of Education at the Freie Universität, Berlin; she is Research Fellow in the Collaborate Research Centre 'Cultures of the

Performative'; the focus of her work includes: educational ethnography, philosophy of education, post-structuralism, qualitative social research and rituals. Recent publications include: (2007) Erziehung bei Tisch. Zur sozialen Magie eines Familienrituals, Bielefeld; (mit K. Velten, eds., 2007) Transgression—Hybridisierung—Differenzierung, Freiburg.

Dr. Constanze Bausch, Research Fellow in the Collaborate Research Centre 'Cultures of the Performative' at the Freie Universität, Berlin; after two years' work with street children in the Parisian suburbs she studied Educational Science at the Technical University in Berlin and is currently teaching in British Columbia (Canada). Recent publications include: (2006) Verkörperte Medien: Die soziale Macht televisueller Inszenierungen, Bielefeld.

Dr. Michael Göhlich, at present Professor of Education at the University of Erlangen-Nürnberg. Recent publications include: (1988) Reggiopädagogik—Innovative Pädagogik heute, Frankfurt/M., 7th ed. 1997; (1993) Die pädagogische Umgebung: Die Geschichte des Schulraums seit dem Mittelalter, Weinheim and Basel; (2001) System, Handeln, Lernen unterstützen. Eine Theorie pädagogischer Institutionen, Weinheim; (with Zirfas, J., 2007) Lernen. Ein pädagogischer Grundbegriff, Stuttgart.

Dr. Stephan Sting, at present Professor of Education at the University of Klagenfurt. Focus of research: ethnograpy, educational theory, media research, health and social work, intercultural education. Recent publications include: (1998) Schrift, Bildung and Selbst. Eine pädagogische Geschichte der Schriftlichkeit, Weinheim; (with Zurhorst, G., eds., 2000) Gesundheit und soziale Arbeit, Munich and Weinheim; (with Schröer, W., eds., 2003) Gespaltene Migration, Opladen; (with Hompfeldt, H.G., 2006) Soziale Arbeit und Gesundheit: eine Einführung, Munich; (with Schweppe, C., eds., 2006) Sozialpädagogik im Übergang: neue Herausforderungen für Disziplin, Profession und Ausbildung.

Dr. Anja Tervooren, at present Assistant Professor of Education, University of Hamburg. Focus of research: gender research, ethnographic childhood research, studies on the body and handicap, poststructuralism in educational science. Recent publications include: (with Fritzsche, B., Hartmann, J., Schmidt, A., 2001) Dekonstruktive Pädagogik. Erzi ehungswissenschaftliche Debatten unter poststrukturalistischen Perspektiven, Munich; (2006) Im Spielraum von Geschlecht und Begehren: Ethnographie der ausgehenden Kindheit, Munich.

Dr. Monika Wagner-Willi, at present Assistant Professor of Education, University of Zurich. Focus of research: reconstructive social research, video analysis, school socialisation, rituals, inclusion research; (2005) Kinder-Rituale zwischen Vorder- und Hinterbühne. Der Übergang von der Pause zum Unterricht, Wiesbaden.

Dr. Christoph Wulf, Professor of General and Comparative Educational Science; member of the Collaborate Research Centre 'Cultures of the Performative', the centre of excellence 'Languages of Emotion', the Interdisciplinary Centre for Historical Anthropology and the international InterArts graduate school at the Freie Universität Berlin. Research periods, invited stays and visiting professorships at the universities of Stanford, Beijing, Tokyo, Kyoto, Mysore, Paris, Modena, Amsterdam, Stockholm, London and St. Petersburg. His books have been translated into 15 languages. Recent publications in English include: (with Gebauer, G., 1995) Mimesis. Culture—art—society, Berkeley; (2002) Anthropology of education, Münster and New York; (2003) Educational science. Hermeneutics, empirical research, critical theory, Münster and New York; (with Werler, Th., eds., 2006) Hidden dimensions of education, Münster and New York; (with Imai, Y., eds., 2007) Concepts of aesthetic education, Münster and New York; (with Suzuki, S., eds., 2007) Mimesis, poiesis, performativity in education, Münster and New York; Co-editor of 'Zeitschrift für Erziehungswissenschaft', and the series 'Historische Anthropologie' (1988ff.), 'European Studies in Education' (1995ff.) and 'Pädagogische Anthropologie' (1996 ff.); editor in chief of Paragrana. International Journal for Historical Anthropology (1992ff.), Vice-president of the German Commission for UNESCO.

Dr. Jörg Zirfas, at present Professor of Education at the University of Erlangen/ Nürnberg; focus of research: educational ethnography, historical educational anthropology; philosophy of education; educational ethics; qualitative social research. Recent publications include: (1993) Präsenz und Ewigkeit; (with Wulf, Ch., eds., 1994) Theorien und Konzepte der pädagogischen Anthropologie, Donauwörth; (with Dieckmann, B. and Sting, S., eds., 1998) Gedächtnis und Bildung, Weinheim; (1999) Die Lehre der Ethik, Weinheim; (with Wulf, Ch., eds., 2004) Die Kultur des Rituals, München; (with Göhlich, M., and Wulf, Ch., eds., 2007) Pädagogische Theorien des Lernens, Weinheim and Basel 2007.

www.ingramcontent.com/pod-product-compliance
Lightning Source LLC
Chambersburg PA
CBHW070913270326
41927CB00011B/2550